TALES OF
THE HORSE-BONDED

Companion Stories to The Horses Know Trilogy

LYNN MANN

Coxstone Press

ISBN 978-1-7398314-4-8
Published by Coxstone Press 2022

For my Readers, without whom
the Horse-Bonded would exist only in my head

Contents

Jonus

I was exhausted. Worse, Mettle was too. I leant back against my horse as he lay flat out on his side, snoring. His eyelids were flickering. Usually, his feet would have been twitching as he ran free in his dreams; free of me, free of my problems, free of humans – free to be the wild, majestic, powerful horse he was born to be. But his feet weren't twitching. He was too tired to even manage that.

I looked around and breathed in my surroundings, as Mettle always advised me to do when I was feeling overwhelmed. I breathed in the cool, spring air and savoured its sharpness as it chilled my airways. I breathed in the movement of the water I could see sparkling in the distance as it plunged down from the hills and hurtled onward. I breathed in the sight of the grassland that stretched all the way from the river, across the flat land and up into the hills amongst which Mettle and I had come to a stop, too tired to make it all the way to the river that had drawn us in this direction.

It was a peaceful place. A perfect place. I wondered to myself why none of us who had left the cities of The Old had been drawn here. It would be a productive place to live, sheltered as it was by the hills behind me and to the left, from which the river emerged. It would never be short of water due to the proximity of the river, and it was on a slight slope so that even with heavy rainfall, the river would take any excess water with it on its way, ensuring the grassland didn't flood.

I sensed my horse's amusement. *Mettle, go back to sleep, you haven't rested for nearly long enough.*

And you have not rested at all.

Knowing you're sleeping is the only rest I need. Sleep.

Mettle heaved himself up onto his elbows and stretched around to rest his chin gently on my shoulder.

I sighed. *You're stubborn, you know that? What woke you, anyway? And what is it that amuses you now?*

You wonder why no one has been drawn to begin a community here while failing to notice that there are two who have been.

I frowned. *But we're just here for the water. I'm completely out and it's been way too long since you had a decent drink from anything more than a puddle.*

Mettle's amusement increased. *We have been bonded for as long as we have and that is all you sensed from me? That I smelt water? Why were we close enough to this location for me to scent it?*

I thought back to the previous few days and the events that had led up to them, and frowned.

In the five years that Mettle and I had been bonded, we had travelled to one newly formed, struggling community of The New after another. We stayed in each just long enough to help the villagers remember abilities with which they were born – but like all humans over the millennia, had been caused to forget – and which they would need in order to make a success of their fledgling communities, and then moved straight on to the next.

On leaving the second-to-last village, we – or at least I – had been triumphant. We had made our way around them all. The members of each and every village of The New now had the knowledge and ability they needed to survive. The villagers would be able to pass their knowledge down to their children, and as humanity survived and increased its numbers, new villages would spring up with the ability to survive already inherent. Mettle and I had done our job. Humanity had the potential to flourish.

At my request, we had made our way back to the community of which I'd originally been a part before Mettle tugged me. When we had last been there, the first stone cottage had been almost finished. When we arrived this time, I was flattered to see that a large sign of metal twisted not only into the sign itself but into its constituent letters, announced to visitors that they were welcome in Jonustown.

I was staggered by the cottages of stone that lined the central road of cobbles, with windows of glass and front gardens filled with crops. I was impressed by the smokehouses, which, judging by the smell, were being used to prepare fish for the coming winter, and by the clean, brightly-coloured clothes worn by those who rushed to greet Mettle and me, all radiating health and shouting excitedly. But I was saddened by the pushing and shoving that ensued, followed shortly afterward by raised voices continuing, from what I could make out, long-standing and abundant disputes. It seemed that plentiful food, health, companionship and freedom weren't enough for my friends to be happy.

Two neighbours were arguing over exactly where the fence between their cottages should be. One man shouted to another that disturbing the village Herbalist while she had been preparing a poultice for him, with demands that she immediately break off from her task in order to put together a preparation for an acute headache, was justifiable grounds for them to no longer be friends and that all requests for what he, as a Glass-Singer, could produce, should cease immediately.

As I scowled around me, Mettle broke into my thoughts. *Do not join them in their discontent. Focus upon the knowledge that there is nothing that cannot be resolved once it is viewed from a different perspective.*

A different perspective from the one that comes to mind, that they're a load of ungrateful, petty idiots?

View them as those who do not know any better because they have never been in a position where it was necessary. Does that change your opinion of them?

From my place on Mettle's back, I looked down at the pushing, arguing crowd in front of us. Like me, these people had been born and raised in a harsh, vile regime of discipline and control that took away much of their ability to think for themselves. Like me, they had rebelled against it, risked everything to escape it, and fought hard to survive. Judging by the flourishing settlement that had once been a pitiful collection of tumbledown shelters, they had taken on board everything Mettle had told them and worked hard to create a new life for themselves.

Unlike me, they didn't have a horse to advise them every step of the way, to bring them up short when they acted in ways that were reminiscent of the regime they had left behind, to explain how to view situations differently. They now knew how to survive physically, but they had no clue how to survive mentally and emotionally. Left to themselves, they would soon revert back to the very way of living that they had been so desperate to leave behind.

I sighed. *Okay, point taken. What do I do? How do I help?*

Question the pair arguing over the boundary as to why it matters.

'Wymon and Shilo, why does it matter where your fence is?' I called to the two men closest to me.

Wymon scowled at me, his thick, black brows almost obscuring his eyes. 'He moved it during the night when all normal, respectful people were asleep, so ask him.'

Shilo stuck out his chest and pointed his finger in Wymon's face. 'Because you put it in the wrong place to start with, and wouldn't see why it should be moved exactly halfway between our two plots.'

Wymon drew himself up taller and clenched his fist.

'WHO CARES WHERE IT IS, WHEN YOU'LL BE SHARING THE FOOD YOU GROW IN THOSE PLOTS ANYWAY?' I shouted. Immediately, all of the villagers fell silent and looked up at me with wide eyes. 'When we came together to form this community, we agreed that any food we found, hunted, grew, whatever, would be shared equally between us all. Please tell me that's still the case?'

There was nodding all around, some resigned, some reluctant, some vigorous.

'So then, where is your problem?' I asked Wymon and Shilo. Shilo dropped his arm and Wymon relaxed his shoulders and unclenched his fist. They glanced at one another and shrugged.

Request that those arguing over the attention paid to them by the Healer consider how she is affected by their dispute, Mettle advised.

I glared at the two arguing about their visits to the village Herbalist. 'Did either of you stop to think how your demands to be attended to first by Priss may have affected her?' I looked around. 'You all used to value all of the hard work Priss put in to be the best Healer she could be for this village, to the point that you agreed she should have the first cottage to be built. If I know her, she'll be working herself into the ground to have you all feeling as well as possible. Has anyone thought to ask if there's anything she needs, or are you all as busy fighting for your own interests as these two?'

Two women and one of the men who had been arguing about it, broke away from the crowd and hurried towards the cottage that had been first to be built in the village, where presumably Priss was still hard at work and one of the few who hadn't left her duties to come and welcome Mettle and me.

Suggest to the one who complains that her new furniture is late that she offers her assistance with the baby who keeps the Carpenter from her work.

'And you, Sweenie, should know better. How many children do you have? Four or five by now, I should think, and yet it never occurred to you to offer Marina help with her firstborn, so that she could get on with the new table you're so desperate to have?'

By the time I had berated everyone who had been shouting, and sent them off to sort themselves out, there were only three people left standing where before there had been a crowd; Tomlin and Trix – the world's first modern-day Rock-Singers – and their son, Ben. My favourite three people in the whole village. Tomlin had his arm around Trix's shoulders and a hand on Ben's shoulder. When I grinned at them all, Ben hurried over.

I jumped to the ground and slapped the young man on his back as he put his forehead to Mettle's and rubbed my horse's neck. 'He's pleased to see you too, Ben,' I told him. I held my arms out to Trix and Tomlin, who hugged me and then held out their hands for Mettle to sniff, before stroking his face.

'He said you two would come back some day,' Tomlin said, nodding his head towards his son.

'He comes to this spot every day on his way home for lunch,

he's been convinced you would arrive at this exact spot, at this time of day, and you did,' Trix whispered, shaking her head slowly as she looked from Ben – who was murmuring to Mettle – to me. 'How did he know?'

He is sensitive. His time is almost upon him, Mettle informed me.

Time for what? He's already become a man.

I could feel that Mettle had no intention of expanding on his statement, so I said, 'Mettle says he knew because he's sensitive.'

Trix nodded slowly. 'He is that. He came racing to tell us you were nearly here but when we all got here, you were shouting, so we weren't sure you'd be happy to see us.'

I grinned. 'Of course I'm happy to see you, you're a blessed relief after that lot. When Mettle and I left here, everyone was happy and excited about the lives you were all building for yourselves. When did that change?'

Trix and Tomlin looked at one another and shrugged.

'It changed after a couple of years, as soon as everyone got comfortable,' Ben said, finally turning to me. When I'd last seen him, he had stood to my shoulder in height and he was lanky, as teenage boys often are just before they become men. Now, he was my height and his shoulders were wide and muscular. His eyes were fierce in his freckled face. 'They've been like this for three years. THREE YEARS! Where have you been? We needed you both. I watched them going back to how they used to be before you and Mettle helped us, and I didn't know what to do. I knew you'd come back, I just didn't think it would take this long.'

Mettle shifted so that his dappled head hung over Ben's shoulder. He pulled back with his chin so that Ben moved back against his wide, muscular chest, and held the lad there. Ben reached a hand up to stroke my horse's cheek. Mettle nuzzled his chest, then his shoulder, then his ear.

'We're here now, Ben,' I said.

He breathed out deeply and slowly. Then he looked at me and nodded.

Mettle and I stayed in Jonustown for several weeks. I lodged with Tomlin, Trix and Ben. When I was within their home, I could relax and almost believe that Mettle and I had achieved all that we had set out to in helping the people of The New to adjust to living a different way of life from that in which we had all been raised; my hosts told me how the village had a full complement of people who could perform the Skills as a result of the precise wording Mettle had passed on to them, through me, when last we were here.

Not only did they have a Herbalist in Priss, but a Bone-Singer who had been called upon regularly to sing broken bones back to health when the Farmers were learning to use the tools made for them by the Metal-Singers, and two Tissue-Singers who were nearly as busy. The village's three Tree-Singers were doing an admirable job of singing crops full of health and vitality, and trees from saplings to fully grown trees in mere months, so that the trees cut down for furniture, tools and fuel were quickly replaced.

The lone Weather-Singer assisted the Tree-Singers whenever he was called upon, the Glass-Singers sang storage and drinking vessels, ornaments and windows to order, and the Earth-Singers worked alongside the Farmers as they gradually cleared more land so that more crops could be grown and stored.

Those who hadn't been stimulated to remember how to perform the Skills weren't idle. Potters were improving the quality of the mugs, bowls and plates they had learnt to produce, Carpenters were producing very respectable items of furniture judging by the table we all tended to sit around while we chatted, and Weavers and Tailors were learning together which crops could be made into clothing. The achievements of these villagers in the five years since I was last there was nothing short of miraculous.

It was when I left the cottage to go to Mettle, who grazed the areas yet to be cleared for planting, that my heart would sink. Each time, I was plagued by the villagers, all shouting, pushing and shoving as they fought to get closest to me with their demands for advice on everything from family disputes to those between neighbours and occasionally whole households. As the days went by, I answered their questions according to the advice Mettle gave me, as patiently as I could, which according to Mettle, was with very little patience at all.

You have altered since you were last here. They have not. With patience and support they will, he advised me as I made my way to him one morning, gritting my teeth to stop myself shouting at the two men who followed me, each demanding that I take their side in a disagreement that had originated when the child of one had punched the child of the other.

I don't know how much patience I can find, I replied.

Remember once more how little freedom they all had to think for themselves. Now that they have it they express everything they think in every moment. They must learn to consider. To feel instead of merely to react. Their survival depends not only on being able to satisfy their physical needs but on being able to function as an emotional whole instead of as a collection of constituent parts all working against one another.

I sighed. *How is that ever going to happen?*

We are here. We will help them. The time has come to remind them of how they came to live here together in the first place.

By the time I reached my horse, a large proportion of the village tailed me, all fighting for their place in the line, all arguing and a few also crying. Mettle lifted his head, his white forelock and mane in stark contrast to the dapples of his face and his large, almost black eyes. He whickered and instantly my shoulders relaxed and my breathing rate slowed. In that moment, I felt for those who only seconds before had exasperated me. Without Mettle, I would be exactly like my peers. They didn't have the refuge of his calm, measured thoughts, his consistent view that everything was always, and would always be, okay, to keep them on track like I did. They were like leaves blowing around in the wind of their emotions – soft and able to settle when there was nothing to fuel them, sharp and volatile as soon as anything moved them. They needed a way to ground themselves as Mettle grounded me.

I put a hand to my horse's withers, bent my knees and vaulted onto his bare back. Mettle turned to face the crowd, drew himself up and whinnied. The villagers gasped and then were silent.

'Do you remember when we all arrived here within days of one another?' I called out. 'Do you remember how tired we were, how hungry, but how ecstatic we were to find one another, all having come from different cities that were nevertheless the same? How relieved we were to have left behind the threats, the control, the uniformity, and to have arrived somewhere that birds sang and leaves rustled in the wind, somewhere we could think for ourselves, feed ourselves, sleep when we wanted, rise when we wanted, talk about what we wanted and with whoever we wanted?'

There were nods all around.

'And do you remember WHY we came here and HOW we got here?'

'We came because it didn't feel right where we were. We found our way here because we kept walking the way that did feel right, until we felt we should stop,' someone called out.

'Exactly,' I said. 'You FELT. We all did. We didn't know each other, we came from different directions, different cities, but we came together because we felt our way here – it felt right, where everything in the cities felt wrong. So, my question is this. The way you're all living together now, the way you speak to one another, the way you behave to one another – does it FEEL right?'

'That's irrelevant, his son hit my…' began one of the men in front of me.

'How can it be irrelevant when it's the whole reason we're all here?' I interrupted. 'Remember back to how it felt to be following the sense deep inside that there was a better way to live than the way we were. Remember how it felt to reject the safety and comfort we were all told was so important, and to follow the feeling that living, actually living instead of just breathing, is about not knowing what will happen from day to day and being brave enough to embrace that. Remember when you all left your old lives behind because you trusted the sense you had that it would all be okay, over all the thoughts that told you it wouldn't. You were right to trust it. Look at what you've all created here. This all came from trusting how you felt inside. So, I'm asking you again. Does how you're behaving towards one another now FEEL right?'

Some of the villagers began to shake their heads. Others looked down at the ground. The two men in front of me glanced at one another, then at Mettle, then back at each other. One of them sighed. 'I guess not.'

I looked around them all. 'Mettle and I will be here for another couple of days. If anyone has any problems that they can't resolve by feeling their way, then come and see us, but I urge you to try to resolve your grievances yourselves.'

'What happened to you, Jonus?' Someone called out. 'You were always one of the first to argue, to lose your temper.'

I grinned. 'Mettle happened to me. I'm sorry I've been short-tempered with you all since I got back. I forget sometimes that it's being with him that makes things obvious to me that wouldn't otherwise be. If it wasn't for him, I'd still be every bit as objectionable as I was.'

There was chuckling all around and the mood lifted. 'Mettle needs to stretch his legs properly, so we'll be gone for a few hours. I'll be at Tomlin's if you need me after that,' I told them all.

Mettle turned away from the crowd and moved into a trot and then a fast canter. *I can fulfil my requirement for exercise at any time. You need not come along.*

You know very well I need to get away for a bit. I'm less objectionable than I was, but I'm still human.

When we left the village a few days later, I should have been feeling rested and fresh; Mettle and I had experienced two relatively quiet days with only the odd visitor needing Mettle's counsel, and Tomlin, Trix and Ben had all been busy in their roles as the village Rock-Singers, building more cottages ready for those with expanding families and those old enough to leave their families and start homes of their own. Instead, exhaustion had begun to set in as for the first time, I fully comprehended the task still ahead of me.

It had taken five years to travel between the fledgling communities of The New the first time around, and judging by how the villagers in Jonustown had been behaving, I would now need to visit them all again to keep them on the path on which Mettle set them the first time around. And what would I find when, in five or so years' time, we arrived back here? I didn't for one moment believe that Mettle and I wouldn't be needed again. It felt as if my horse and I had a monumental, never-ending task ahead of us.

I turned to grin and lift a hand at the cheering, waving villagers of Jonustown behind us. When Ben appeared by my knee, his eyes full of worry, and pleaded with us not to leave, or at the very least, to allow him to leave with us, it was tempting to ask Mettle to turn around and go back with him. Tempting, easier than what lay ahead of us – but not right.

'Mettle told me it's nearly your time. He won't say what he means, but I think it means that soon, you won't be as frustrated as you are now,' I told him.

Ben stepped backward, away from us, shaking his head and looking miserable. 'If that's what he says, I suppose I have to go with it, don't I? I have to live with that crazy lot and trust it'll be different?'

I nodded. 'He's never wrong, Ben, you know that. I'll see you around.'

Mettle continued on his way, I assumed to the next village to which he was drawn as needing our help. When he picked up speed, I felt his urgency and sighed, wondering what catastrophe he had sensed, and what we would need to do about it. When he kept up a punishing pace for several days, barely stopping to allow himself or me time to eat or rest, I questioned him as to the urgency, and to our whereabouts, which grew increasingly unfamiliar – and yet felt right, as if I had been that way before, but couldn't quite place it.

We go where we are needed, was all he would offer by way of a response. I grew too tired, both in body and mind, to insist on more of an explanation, so, as always, trusted him to take us where we needed to go.

Now, as I considered his question as to how we came to be close enough to the river for him to scent it, I remembered the feeling of rightness about our headlong journey here. It reminded me of when I had left the city in which I grew up, with only the clothes I was wearing and as much food as I could carry, with no idea where to go or what to expect. I had started walking in the direction that felt right, and kept going no matter what lay in my path, until I reached what was now Jonustown.

We are here because this is where we need to be, but why? I asked my horse. *There's no village here, no people needing our help.*

There soon will be. Then your mind will be busier than ever yet you will find yourself able to rest.

Who's coming all the way out here?

See for yourself. Mettle heaved himself to his feet, stretched to his full height and whinnied down to the grassland. I got to my feet too, and followed his gaze. I couldn't see anything… but wait, there, in the far distance by the river, something was moving. Two somethings.

I will carry you to them. I felt Mettle's anticipation, no, excitement, over-riding the exhaustion that had, only moments before, consumed us both. I'd never before, in all the time we had been bonded, felt that from him. I vaulted onto his back and just about got myself into position before he leapt into a canter and flew down the hillside, causing me to gasp, not only as I fought to catch the air hurtling past my face, but at the energy my horse was somehow managing to find.

When we reached level ground, he tore across it, whinnying. This time, he was answered. I blinked away the tears that kept my eyes from drying out as we blasted our way through the cold, spring air, and made out a large shape moving at speed towards us. I just about managed to stay in place on Mettle's back as he slowed to a trot and then skidded to a halt. I wiped my eyes to see a brown horse standing twenty paces in front of us, ears pricked, sides heaving, eyes bright. I dismounted and stepped away from Mettle.

I felt his delight at being near another horse for the first time in more than five years, and his sense of kinship – no it was more than that – his sense of… oneness with this other horse. I felt the other horse become part of Mettle, while knowing somehow that it wasn't possible because they had never been apart. In that instant, I knew that the horse was a stallion, this was his sixth spring and he was to someone else what Mettle was to me – he was bonded!

'Jonus, thank goodness, I've never been so relieved to see anyone as when you and Mettle just came belting down that hillside. How the hell are you? Can you believe this? Can you believe I'm Horse-Bonded too? It all happened just like you said it happened to you – one minute, I was arguing with Mum over what colour to dye the new cloth she managed to weave, the next, it was like my mind was being pulled somewhere else, and I just had to follow it.'

I turned from where Mettle and the brown stallion were now trotting towards one another in two identical yet opposing semi-circles, to where a slim, brown-haired young woman was striding towards me. I frowned. I recognised her, but could remember neither her name nor in which village I had met her.

'It's Julie, remember? You came to Longwood years ago. I was only nineteen, I guess I've changed a bit. I always hoped I would be chosen by a horse like Mettle chose you, and here I am. That's Pioneer, isn't he stunning? It took me five days to find him, and then two weeks to get here. It's a good job you taught us all to fish and hunt, or I'd have starved to death. I had no idea I wouldn't be going home once I'd found him, I thought it would be like when you found Mettle and then you and he went to your home village so you could help your friends, but Pioneer was adamant that we come here. Now it makes sense, because you're

here and I have so many things to ask you. Where will we go
next? Jonus, are you alright?'

I found myself on my knees with Julie crouching in front of
me, peering into my eyes, her own brown ones full of concern. It
was just as those who had helped me when Mettle and I first
bonded, told me; I was the first Horse-Bonded, others would
follow, and Mettle and I would need to help them as we were
helped, so that they could help us to keep humanity on the path
they had begun to travel. It was no longer all down to me and
Mettle.

I smiled wearily. 'I'm fine. I'm just tired, thirsty and…
relieved you're here.'

We set up camp by the river to the sound of Mettle and Pioneer
squealing and stamping as they postured to one another, before
tearing around and then spinning to face one another, ready to
begin posturing all over again. Eventually, they trotted, snorting,
to the river, drank their fill and dropped their heads to the sweet,
spring grass to graze side by side. It gave me a warm feeling to
see Mettle in the company of one of his own, but I felt guilty as I
realised how much he had given up to come and find me, to help
me – to help all of us.

'We're the luckiest people alive, aren't we?' Julie said,
dumping a load of sticks by the small fire I was feeding with dry
grass and twigs of heather.

I looked up at her and grinned. 'That we are. Whether you'll
still think that after your first riding lesson this afternoon remains
to be seen.'

'Riding lesson? This afternoon?'

'Yep, that's why Pioneer has brought you to me. I need to

teach you to ride, to care for him, and what your responsibilities are now that you're Horse-Bonded. There's so much to do and so far, only you and me to do it, so we need to begin as soon as possible.'

Julie sat down across the fire from me, scraped her long hair away from her face with both hands and tucked it firmly behind her ears. She looked directly into my eyes. 'So, let's start now. Tell me what I need to know.'

I held her gaze and gave a brief nod. Her horse had chosen well.

'Three lessons in and you're barely bouncing at all – you're doing great. Let's move it up to a canter, shall we?' I called out to Julie. She was a natural. I envied the ease and grace with which she absorbed Pioneer's extravagant movement, and wished it had come that effortlessly to me when I was learning to ride.

Another approaches. Mettle's warning was accompanied by a sense of who it was that would shortly be upon us.

I held a hand up to Julie. 'Cancel that, I'd jump down if I were you, and quickly.'

'What? Why?'

'Because as good a rider as you will be, you don't yet have the reflexes or muscle memory to cope with what's probably about to happen. You can argue, or you can trust me.'

Julie cocked her head slightly as she always did when Pioneer communicated with her. Then her eyes widened and she stopped following her horse's movement. Pioneer halted beneath her and she dismounted hurriedly as a whinny sounded from around the bend in the river. Pioneer and Mettle both stiffened and whinnied back.

Julie and I put our hands to our brows and squinted into the morning sunshine as two figures appeared in the distance. The larger of the two appeared to be prancing between four feet but did not leave the side of the other. As they got closer, they resolved into a leggy, dun horse with a black mane, tail and forelock, and a short man of middle years. When they were almost upon us, the horse left her Bond-Partner's side and trotted towards Mettle and Pioneer.

The man watched the three horses squeal, stamp, rear and tear around the grassland, before switching his attention to Julie and me. He grinned and hurried over, his hand outstretched. 'Forgive me, everything she does is a wonder to me, I can't seem to keep my attention on anything other than listening to what she tells me and trying to make sense of it, and watching her to see what she'll do next. I'm Thane.'

Julie and I both smiled as we shook his hand. 'I'm the same,' Julie said. 'It's hard to concentrate on life as we used to know it, isn't it?'

Thane nodded and looked at me. 'When you came to Springbank and helped us, and told us all that others would be chosen by horses as you had been, I had no idea I would be one of those chosen, or that it would be like this.'

I nodded. 'It's not something that's easy to describe. What's your mare's name?'

He flushed and looked down at the ground. 'Um, you'll think it's silly, but it's Home.'

Julie and I were quiet while we remembered how our horses had invited us to choose their names.

'I understand,' I said. Thane's eyes shot up to meet mine, his eyebrows raised.

'I get it too. Home is a lovely name,' Julie said.

Thane shook his head and looked at us both with a slight crease to his brow. 'Seriously?'

I chuckled. 'Seriously. We get it. We're Horse-Bonded too, remember?'

A wide grin spread across Thane's face, causing the lines at the corners of his eyes to become more defined. 'I'm Horse-Bonded,' he said to himself.

'You are, but I wouldn't smile too widely, you don't know what a taskmaster Jonus is. He's had me in tears twice already,' Julie said.

'Untrue,' I replied. 'You managed it the first time all by yourself because you wouldn't let me help you to mount and then found you couldn't get on by yourself. The second time was because you had the wind in your face.'

'Both times, it was as a result of you insisting that I ride that very second, when I would have preferred a few minutes to prepare myself,' Julie retorted.

'Then don't ride. I have Thane to teach now, so you can do what you like,' I said, winking at Thane, whose grin widened.

Julie narrowed her eyes and cocked her head to one side. 'You need me and Pioneer to go out to the villages and stop the bickering and disputes we're going to find there, so you don't have to do it all yourself, you told me. You wouldn't stop teaching me.'

'Watch me. Come on, Thane, let's get your gear stacked with ours and get some food down you, then when Home is ready, we'll get you on board.'

Julie's sigh was belied by a hint of a smile. 'Fine, I give in, I'll let you carry on teaching me.'

'If you cry again, we're over, you and me,' I said.

Julie laughed. 'You'll cry before I do, I guarantee it.'

I opened my mouth to reply, then closed it as Mettle, Pioneer and Home all suddenly spun in the direction of the hills from which Mettle and I had descended when we first arrived, and watched two figures making their way down to us. I looked at Julie and Thane, my eyes wide. 'Another pair? How am I going to teach all of you?'

'I said you'd cry first,' Julie said with a grin. 'Don't worry, I'll work even harder with my riding so I can help you. I know Pioneer will be up for it, he's desperate for us to be able to go faster. Then I'll be further ahead of Thane and whoever this is, so I can show them what you mean while you teach them. We can all help each other. Like you said, we're all Horse-Bonded. We're in this together.'

I nodded and took a deep breath. 'Okay.'

Six bonded pairs arrived during the week that followed. I spent all of my time teaching them, Julie and Thane to ride, increasingly with Julie's help as her ability improved at an ever increasing rate. By the time another four arrived, we found ourselves in something of a routine; Julie rode Pioneer while I pointed out to the others exactly what she was doing with her body in order to both communicate with her horse, and to follow his movement so she didn't restrict him in any way. Then between us, we taught from the ground for a while, then mounted and rode alongside our students, so that we could demonstrate while we talked. Before long, the vast grassland between the river and the hills was dotted with horses and riders practising what they had been taught.

In the evenings, we crowded around the campfire and I related my experiences of being Horse-Bonded, and answered questions from those still coming to terms with their new situation. Without exception, my fellow Horse-Bonded were ecstatic to have been chosen by their horses, and grateful beyond any of their abilities to describe. They didn't have to, the rest of us assured them as the topic of conversation came up time after time. We knew.

By the time four weeks had passed, we numbered twenty bonded pairs and I began to realise the need for a greater level of organisation. While Julie and Thane would soon be ready to leave with their horses to begin visiting villages, they would need to return at regular intervals so that they and their horses could rest from what I knew would be challenging trips. Moreover, Mettle assured me that there were more newly bonded pairs on their way. However many left, more would be returning or arriving for the first time.

We were fortunate that we numbered several Farmers, an Earth-Singer, two Weather-Singers, three Metal-Singers, a Tree-Singer and two very proficient Healers – one a Herbalist and one a Bone-Singer – among us, as well as three who were very capable hunters. While my days continued to be spent teaching, I put Thane in charge of setting them all to their Skills and Trades and organising the others to help them where necessary. Soon, there were plots of land with newly-sown crops beginning to spring up, and designated areas for the Herbalist and Bone-Singer to treat those needing help.

'And there was me thinking I would be the first. This is quite a gathering you have here, Jonus,' a familiar voice said from behind me as I stood watching a group of four newly arrived Horse-Bonded attempting to ride their horses for the first time.

I turned around. 'Ben! What on earth… ahhh.'

'How could you not have known that when Mettle said it was nearly my time, he meant I would soon be one of the Horse-

Bonded?' Ben laughed and put a hand up to rub the face of the sturdily-built, brown and white horse standing calmly by his side, seemingly oblivious to all of the horses calling to her from where they were either carrying their Bond-Partners or grazing. 'This is Impact. Isn't she amazing?'

I clapped him on the shoulder and held a hand out for Impact to sniff, which she did politely before nuzzling my wrist. 'She is. I'm so pleased for you, mate. I'm sorry I didn't hear you both arrive. When the first few came, it was a huge event for all of us and I couldn't miss them, but now, as you say we have something of a gathering here. You and Impact bring us up to twenty-eight bonded pairs.'

Ben whistled. 'And what, we all live here together? In our own community?'

I took a step back. 'I hadn't thought of it that way, but yes, I suppose we do.'

Ben looked around, his eyes wide. 'You're just camping? What about buildings? I mean, it's okay living outside now, but it's almost summer, and then it'll be autumn and we all know how rubbish it is not having proper shelter when it's cold and wet.' The fear that suddenly appeared in his eyes caused me to remember the conditions we had both endured before Mettle chose me as his Bond-Partner and changed everything.

I nodded. 'Again, I hadn't thought of it that way, but you're right. Take a breath though, okay? None of us will have to live the way we did in the beginning. We have a beautiful spot here, we have those among us with Skills and Trades to offer, yourself included, and we have our horses to guide us. It'll be okay.'

Ben sighed, then grinned. 'Sorry, yes, I know it will. Are there any other Rock-Singers here, or is it just me?'

'It's just you for now. I hardly think that will be a problem, knowing how strong you are; you're your parents' son. The hillside up there is littered with boulders, so no doubt there'll be a whole load more buried in the ground, and we have an Earth-Singer who can lift the soil for you. That can all wait, though. You and Impact rest and eat, then when you're ready, we'll begin your riding lessons.'

It's been too long. I should leave Julie and Thane here teaching while you and I get back out to the villages, I told Mettle as I sat cross-legged around the fire in the twilight, stripping bark from a twig for want of something to do with my hands. I could just about make him out as he grazed nearby alongside a dark shape who I guessed was Pioneer; the two were inseparable when left to their own devices.

Those who are newly bonded will settle and take instruction more easily from one they already know and trust. You alone have been to all of the communities. You alone are known to all of those who will come.

But Julie and Thane are already teaching a lot of them.

Overseen by you. You all do well here but your memories of feeling under-equipped for life ahead are yet fresh within you all. You witnessed how rapidly fear arose in our newest arrival at the thought of returning to that which he viewed as hardship. His horse advises him well but their bond is new. It will take time for her to be the refuge to whom he turns when fear would infect his thoughts. You alone had help from those who know what it is to be Horse-Bonded. It must be you who passes that assistance on to those who gather here seeking it.

In that case, I'm going to have to ask Julie, Thane and Gillie to leave in the next day or so. Goodness only knows what's going on in the villages if Jonustown was anything to go by when we were there. I sighed at the memory. Our new community was mere weeks old but already had a higher level of co-operation than the villages of people who had known one another for years. Such was the influence of the horses. I loved watching newly bonded pairs becoming ever closer, and witnessing my fellow Horse-Bonded becoming more measured and beginning to relate to one another differently as each took their horse's advice.

When we had a steady supply of Bond-Partners out visiting the communities of The New, so that the influence of the horses was almost as much a constant for the villagers as it was for us, I would be able to relax. No, I corrected myself. When we had enough buildings here to provide shelter for all of the Horse-Bonded and their horses gathered here at any one time, when we were functioning as an efficient community, then I would be able to relax.

Or you could choose to relax now and remain so. You will then be better placed to achieve both aims, Mettle observed.

I grinned and felt the tension leave my neck, shoulders and back. *I'm the same as those you said I need to be here to help, aren't I? You and I have been bonded for more than five years, and I still don't always remember to see things your way, even though I know I'll feel better when I do.*

You are aware of the fact. That is why it must be you who remains here to influence the newly bonded. Trust those you have trained to remember what you have taught them. Their Bond-Partners will do the rest. It is indeed time for those who arrived here first to leave.

I nodded. *I'll let them know.*

～

During the four years that followed, our Horse-Bonded community thrived in the spot in which the first few of us had gathered, and grew beyond recognition. But even when the first buildings had been sung into existence and were in use, none of us viewed the place as a settlement as such, for none who resided there, with the exception of myself, ever settled for long before venturing out to visit the villages; it therefore, somewhere along the way, became known as The Gathering.

I was proud that we had a Saddler who had taught himself not only to work leather but to make saddles in response to his horse's request – and subsequently those of the rest of our horses – for one. I was proud of those who farmed the land for us all, those who co-operated to make The Gathering a great place to live, and those who continued to sing the surrounding rocks into place to create field shelters, workshops, a dining hall and the ground floors of two other buildings. I hoped that one of the new structures would eventually be the main accommodation block, and the other an overflow block with the Healers' treatment rooms readily accessible on the ground floor.

Mettle assured me that both blocks would need to be three or four floors higher to accommodate those who would follow as our human population flourished and more Horse-Bonded were required in order to reach all of the villages regularly; none who visited the villages were in any doubt that the horses' ongoing counsel was, and would for some time be, very necessary.

Those who left to visit the villages were always happy, buoyant and full of enthusiasm for their planned trips. When they returned, they and their horses were tired and in much need of a break from the rigours of travel and the demands of the villagers they visited. They were frustrated and worn down by having to repeat the same advice over and over to those arguing about petty things, to remember themselves and how they got to where they were, what they had achieved and the potential for humanity now that we had stepped away from living in a regime of fear and desperation.

It was exhausting, wearing and seemingly never-ending, but when those who returned from their travels sat down with the rest of us and vented their frustration, our discussions always ended up at the same place, for our horses were as unwavering in their advice to us as they were in their counsel to the villagers.

They reminded us, over and over, that change was like a massive boulder that had been in position for millennia. It would have weathered and sunk into place and would resist attempts to be moved. But if those attempts to move it were ongoing, the boulder would begin to shift slightly. Eventually the ground around it would become compressed and then would flatten more and more, until there was nothing holding the boulder there. If it kept being rocked with enough strength and intention, eventually it would move. Once it was moving, keeping it in motion would get easier and when it reached the brow of the hill on which it had remained for all that time, it would roll down of its own accord. We just had to keep trying to move it.

It was another year before, finally, the buildings of The Gathering were finished, thanks to Ben and his crew of Rock-Singers, who worked as long as it was light whenever they were in residence. Each of them had a strength of voice and intention far beyond that which I gathered was present in any of the villages – indeed, where the largest cottages in the villages were only ever two storeys tall, our largest buildings reached five.

Ben told me that it was Impact's belief in him that strengthened his intention to lift rocks as high as he did, and I imagined the same was true for those who combined their voices with his until their chosen rock began to tremble, and then lent him the strength of their intentions to combine with his own as he guided the rock into the air and into place.

Now that The Gathering was complete, running smoothly, and always with at least a few Horse-Bonded in residence who were every bit as experienced as I had been when I began to teach the first of those to join me, finally, Mettle acceded to my request that we leave for a trip of our own around some of the villages. After five years, I was interested and excited to see the effect the Horse-Bonded had exerted on the communities of The New. I had planned to leave alone, but just as Mettle and I reached the top of the first hills, a thundering of hooves preceded the arrival of Ben and Impact at our side.

'If I know you, you're going to Jonustown first,' Ben announced breathlessly. 'It's been ages since I've seen my parents, so I thought I'd join you, if you don't mind?'

'You were there last month,' I said. 'Why do you really want to come? Mettle and I may not have left since we first arrived, but we've kept ourselves fit, you don't need to worry about us.'

Ben chuckled. 'Do I look worried? Like I said, I just thought I'd tag along.'

Mettle, why is he being weird? I asked my horse.

Restricting our discussions to subjects of consequence is a more constructive use of our bond, was all the response my horse would give me.

I shrugged. 'Fine, whatever. I hope you had a decent breakfast, though, because you're going to need it.'

Mettle picked up on my intention and burst forward into a canter, then a flat-out gallop. We were off on our own again – well almost – with no demands on us, at least until we reached Jonustown. I couldn't say which of us was more delighted.

'You don't get to leave us behind that easily,' called Ben from behind us. Then, his voice fainter, he added, 'Okay then, maybe you do.'

I grinned.

I was immensely pleased to find Jonustown a far more harmonious place than when I had last been there. I enjoyed my stay immensely, lodging as I was with Priss, the village Herbalist and someone with whom I'd always had a lot to chat about. Mettle was content grazing in Priss's paddock when he wasn't giving counsel to those villagers requesting it, so when after a few days, I was ready to move on but Ben dragged his feet as a result – I assumed – of wanting to stay longer with his parents, I didn't make too much of a fuss.

When Ben also delayed us in the next village we visited, however, with a never-ending stream of reasons why "just another few days" were repeatedly necessary, I began to get irritated. When he repeated his behaviour at all of the following villages, I was furious. I was all too happy to do my share of visiting villages to dispense my horse's counsel, but, as those who had travelled to them before me had all found, it was draining and exhausting. I was desperate to be making my way back to The Gathering for a break, and Ben seemed intent on thwarting me at every stage.

When we finally left the last village, nearly two months after leaving The Gathering, we were barely speaking, despite our horse's assurances that our behaviour towards one another was barely better than those to whom we had been passing on their advice.

We made the journey back to The Gathering in silence. I took to asking Mettle to take the lead ahead of Ben and Impact so that I didn't have to repeatedly see Ben looking sideways, grinning, at me. I counted him as a friend, yet he was, and for weeks had been, behaving like an idiot.

I couldn't have been more relieved when we passed between the steep-sided hills immediately behind The Gathering, and came to the track that lead down to the buildings. But then I stiffened and Mettle halted beneath me. Why was everyone clustered in the middle of the square around which the buildings were arranged? And why were some of them sitting on something at the centre of it – something huge? What was it? What had happened?

'Something's wrong,' I muttered over my shoulder to Ben.

'If you say so,' he said with a chuckle.

I scowled at him and asked Mettle to hurry down to the square. As we got closer, I realised that the voices I could hear sounded excited rather than worried or afraid. Strange. As Mettle walked past the accommodation block and into the square, cheering erupted and then everyone began to chant, 'Mettle, Jonus, Mettle, Jonus, Mettle, Jonus.'

The crowd parted in front of us to reveal an enormous, metal statue of a man standing with a horse – but not just any horse. It was Mettle. I knew every dapple that had been sung into his coat, every strand of mane that rested in waves against his neck. I gasped as I recognised my own face on the man who stood beside my horse's likeness.

'Like it?' Ben said with a grin as Impact sidled into place beside Mettle. 'The Metal-Singers assured me they could do it, but they didn't know how long it would take. I was under strict instructions to keep you away as long as possible. Looks like they only just got it finished in time. I'm not really as irritating as you've decided I am, you know.'

I shook my head slowly. 'But why?' I whispered to him. 'Why did they… did you, all of you, why did you do this?'

'Because without you and Mettle, there would be no Horse-

Bonded, no Gathering – probably no people at all, by now,' Ben said. 'It's our way of saying thanks. You should stop gawking and go and thank the Metal-Singers, they look as if they're about to drop.'

I blinked. 'Yes of course. It's just so unexpected. I can't believe it and I'm not sure I understand it but – thanks, Ben.' He winked and nodded for me to dismount.

I rubbed my horse's neck and then slid down to the ground by his side. *What do you think, Mettle? Did you know you were that beautiful? Isn't it an amazing statue?* I knew immediately that he had no opinion – of course he didn't. Statues had meaning to us humans alone.

I couldn't stop looking at the stunning depiction of my horse as I thanked and shook the hands of those who had worked so hard to produce it. I would have preferred it to have stood alone, without my likeness beside it, both because it was down to Mettle that everything Ben had described had been achieved, and because I felt embarrassed at seeing myself replicated in such an unmissable fashion. I realised, however, that in the years to come, those who resided here would have no idea who the statue of the man and horse was meant to be, but they would identify with it and hopefully, they would know what I and every other human currently at The Gathering knew; that when a horse chose you as a Bond-Partner, you became one of the most privileged people ever to have lived.

Mason

I was always a big lad. Nothing I could do about it, so my ma would tell me. She and my pa were both "built to be robust", as she put it, and I was the same. But where they put their tall, muscular physiques to good use working long days in the fields as Farmers, I put mine to being awkward and clumsy at school. It was as if my body were growing too quickly for my brain to be able to keep up with how to control it, and not a day went by without me knocking something off someone's desk as I lumbered past, or banging my head or stubbing my toes.

I was always the last to be picked for sports teams and playground games. While no one was unkind to me, I always felt like the younger kids were scared of me and those my age were worried I'd want them as my friends, so I learnt to keep myself to myself.

When my voice started breaking, I stopped putting my hand up in class, or even answering the teachers when they singled me out, it was just too embarrassing. My voice didn't just break, see, it exploded. One minute, I'd be saying something normally, the next, my voice would boom around the classroom, making everyone jump and then laugh. It didn't matter what I said, whether my answer was right or wrong, because no one could hear me anyway, they were all laughing too much.

No one apart from me ever knew whether I showed aptitude for the Skills when I tested, because I never spoke up during testing, nor afterwards, neither. As it happened, I could feel exactly which tone of voice would have resonated with the sapling placed in front of me by the tree-singing Tester, but I had no intention of putting myself through the humiliation of any type of singing apprenticeship.

Try as they might, my parents tried to get me to tell them what had happened at testing, but I kept my mouth tightly shut. I felt guilty, sure I did; as a Tree-Singer, I could have worked alongside my parents, singing their crops into bigger, better versions of themselves. But I just wanted to leave school as soon as possible and do something simple, something that a great lummox like me couldn't stuff up or get laughed at for.

I thought about farming alongside Ma and Pa, but I knew how varied their work was, how much there was to learn, and I had no confidence that I would be able to take it all on board. So, when I left school at fifteen, I apprenticed to Abe, the village Leathersmith.

'You're a big, strong lad, Mason,' Pa said when I took my apprenticeship papers home for him and Ma to sign. 'Are you really going to be happy sittin' hunched over a workbench all day? Look at those hands of yours, they're big lumps of beef, just like mine. Are you goin' to be able to even hold a needle, let alone sew with it?'

'Abe thinks so,' I said, heat rising in my cheeks.

'Some of his work is pretty intricate though,' Ma said, 'and subtlety has never been your strong point, has it, son? Why don't you come and work the fields with us? I know you feel awkward around people, but everyone working out there will value that strong back of yours and you'll soon feel differently, just wait and see.'

I shook my head stubbornly, but kept my mouth closed. I never could argue with Ma.

She sighed and signed her name, then passed the apprenticeship papers to Pa and glared at him until he signed his name below hers.

Stubborn as I was with them, their doubts found their way inside me and lodged there, so that by the time I started my apprenticeship, they had become mine.

I was relieved when Abe started me off by giving me a knife and getting me to cut pieces of leather for him, first for belts, then, when he was satisfied I could read his writing and cut accurately, for bags, then shoes and boots, and eventually, gloves. I loved the smell of the leather, the feel of the knife slicing through it, and the look of the finished articles once Abe had taken a needle to the shapes I piled on his workbench.

'Slow down, there, Mason,' he said to me one lunchtime. 'My old fingers can't keep up with that brawn of yours. I've never seen anyone slice through leather like you do. It's time for you to…'

'I can't take up a needle. Not yet,' I interrupted.

He pulled his head further back on his neck and frowned. 'I was going to say, it's time for you to learn to use the burnisher to good effect, but what's the problem with the needle?'

I panicked and picked up a wooden implement. 'This is the burnisher, isn't it? I use it to smooth out the strips I cut for belts? I've seen you do it. I'll just take this pile back to my bench, shall I, and get goin'?'

Abe grinned an almost toothless grin and nodded. 'You're a keen one. Do one belt and then come and show me so I can check your work. Work on a hand's length – mine, not yours – at a time, and don't forget to wet the edge of the leather first.'

I nodded and hurried back to my bench with the pile of newly cut belts.

My heart was in my mouth again when Abe congratulated me on my work with the burnisher and pronounced me ready to move on to another tool. The blood was pounding so hard and fast around my head, I almost didn't hear him mention the skiver he wanted me to learn how to use, so that I could taper the edges of some of the pieces of leather before he stitched them to others.

Within months, I could use all of the various knives, the skiver, the burnisher and an edger to Abe's satisfaction, and again, the finished pieces of leather were piling up on his workbench ready for him to stitch together. I realised my mistake too late.

'You're going to have to learn to stitch, boy, I can't keep up with you,' Abe informed me before I left for home one evening.

I cursed myself for the idiot I had always known myself to be. My face burned as I shook my head violently and said, 'Sorry, I've probably gone too fast to be as thorough as I should have been. I'll work through everythin' in the pile tomorrow and check it's all as it should be.'

Abe narrowed his eyes at me. 'You think I haven't noticed you changing the subject every time I've mentioned you taking up a needle and thread? I think it's about time you told me what's bothering you. Come on, out with it.'

'I'm too big and clumsy to even hold a needle, let alone use it,' I mumbled, going even redder.

'How many needles have you tried to hold?' Abe said. 'Leathersmith's needles, I mean?'

'None, but I've seen you using them. They may be bigger than Tailor's needles, but look at my fingers, they're already twice the size of yours. When I'm a grown man, they'll be even bigger. I'm just good for doing all the cuttin' and edgin', I know that. I'll leave the stitchin' to you.'

Abe stood up from his stool with surprising speed and put his hands on his hips. He leant towards me and said, 'You'll do no such thing. Look at my eyes, they're as cloudy as the autumn sky out there, and I'm stitching by feel as much as by sight, now. Why do you think I took on an Apprentice? Eh? Because before long, I'm going to need you to take over from me, or this village will find itself without a Leathersmith.'

'I'm sorry,' I mumbled. 'I'm a disappointment, I know it. I suppose you'll be wantin' to let me go and take on someone who can do the whole job.'

'DON'T YOU TELL ME WHAT I'LL BE WANTING TO DO,' Abe roared.

I flinched and raised a hand to protect myself.

Abe sat back down on his stool and stared at me. 'What I want, boy,' he said more kindly, 'is for you to come into work tomorrow, pick up a needle and thread and copy me as I stitch a buckle on a belt. You signed up to be my Apprentice, and a hard-working, obedient Apprentice you will be. Is that clear?'

Ashamed of myself, I nodded. 'Very.'

I didn't sleep that night. I was never one to talk much first thing in the morning, so, thankfully, when I sat down to breakfast with my parents, they didn't try to draw me into their conversation about whether Lendel, the Master Earth-Singer, would finally pronounce his two more than able Apprentices qualified so that they could work the harvest alongside the Farmers unsupervised. When I stood up to take my cereal bowl to the sink, however, Ma frowned at me.

'You haven't slept properly,' she said. 'Were you reading into the small hours again? You know you have to give Abe your best every single day, not just when you haven't got a book on the go.'

'I wasn't readin', I just have a bit on my mind.' As soon as I spoke, I regretted it. Why had I not just nodded and kept quiet?

Sure enough, Ma was on me like a cat on a mouse. Her chair scraped back and her face appeared directly in front of mine. 'What can a fifteen-year-old boy with an apprenticeship he loves possibly have to worry about?'

'Nothin'. It's nothin'. I just want to be good at my job.'

Ma took both of my arms and held me further away from her, as if it were me crowding her. 'I know you, you're worrying about a detail no one else would notice, aren't you? What is it, did you sew a few stitches too many into something? Or one too few?' Her voice was soft, sympathetic, and I felt like I was going to cry. If only she knew I still hadn't picked up a needle. I felt even more ashamed of myself than on the previous day.

I pulled myself out of her clutches, practically threw my breakfast bowl into the sink and managed to turn and smile at her and Pa, who was watching me from his place at the table. 'I told you, it's nothin'. I'll see you later.' I practically ran for the door.

'Don't forget your lunch,' Pa said.

I stopped and turned around to see him holding a hand up towards Ma, his fingers waving up and down, asking her not to question me further.

She held a paper bag out to me. 'Here you go, son. We love you and we're proud of you. Just remember that, okay?'

I tried to smile as I took the bag from her. She opened her mouth to say something, but stopped when Pa cleared his throat.

'Whatever it is that's botherin' him, he's nearly a man now and he needs to work it out by himself,' I heard him say once I'd shut the kitchen door behind me.

'Everyone thinks he's tough because he's big, but he isn't, you know that,' Ma said, 'and Abe can be sharp. I just hope he's not being too hard on him, the light knows, Mason's hard enough on himself without anyone else joining in.'

'Which is why we need to step back and let him toughen up a bit…' Pa's voice faded to a murmur as I walked down the grey stone hallway to the front door.

He was right, I needed to toughen up. I needed to get to work, pick up a needle and just copy whatever Abe showed me. I swallowed down the worry that I would fail, that I would prove all over again what everyone including me had known along – I was just a big, useless lump – and hurried out of the door.

I muttered greetings to everyone I passed while walking the cobbled streets of the village to Abe's workshop, making the ten minute walk in only eight. Even though I was a few minutes early, Abe sat at my workbench, waiting for me. I had barely put my lunch on the end of the bench and lifted my apron over my head when a long, thick needle already threaded with a heavy, black thread was placed in my hand.

Abe tapped a buckle around which he had already wrapped the buckle fold of a belt that I had cut and shaped the day before. 'There's yours.' He lifted up another. 'Here's mine. We'll stitch them together.'

I tried to pick up the needle from the palm of my other hand, but couldn't.

Abe grasped my fingers. 'Stop trembling, boy, you have nothing to fear from me. There's no rush, just find a way to pick up the needle and then take as long as you need to work out how best to hold it. Then we'll stitch these buckles in place, one stitch at a time. I've set aside the whole morning for us to do one belt each.'

'You can't do that, look at the pile on your bench,' I protested.

'I know exactly how much is there, I cut and edged it all for you yesterday.'

'Staring at my workbench won't get these belts finished any quicker, will it?' Abe said. 'As Leathersmiths, we'll always have a pile of work waiting for us. Panicking about it isn't going to make the pile go down; good, steady, accurate work is what will do that, and that's our focus for this morning. One stitch at a time, boy. Got it?'

I nodded.

'Pick up your needle.'

It took me three hours to stitch the buckle in place; three hours of continually dropping the needle, searching for it and having to rethread it, of trying to see past my sausage-like fingers so that I could push the point of the needle into the leather in the right place, and of fumbling to pull it through from the other side, barely able to feel it between my sweating thumb and forefinger.

Three whole hours of my life were spent toiling over the end of a flaming belt, only for me to find that when the buckle was firmly in place, my stitches were much longer and far more crooked than Abe's.

I was mortified. My humiliation quickly turned to anger. I had told Abe I wouldn't be able to do it but he had made me, and now the belt was ruined. I flung it to the floor and glared at him, daring him to berate me.

'Pick it up and hang it on the back of the door,' Abe said, his voice so soft that it shocked me into immediately doing as he had said.

I pulled the workshop door – which was always wide open before I arrived in the mornings and until after I had left for home each evening – away from where it was jammed against the wall, and lifted my embarrassment of an effort onto the hook I expected to find there. Another belt was already in place.

'Lift mine down and put it next to yours,' Abe said. 'Go on, compare them. You won't mix them up, I'd know my work anywhere. What do you see?'

I frowned as I followed his instruction. 'I've seen enough of your work to know this isn't yours, Abe. Nothin' like it. It's even worse than mine.' I nodded slowly. 'I get it, this is the work of the worst Apprentice you've ever had, and made some time ago, goin' by the look of this leather. Is it supposed to make me feel better, that I'm your second worst Apprentice? Because it doesn't.'

'Have you finished feeling sorry for yourself?' Abe said. 'I don't need an answer, even my eyes can see that you haven't. That belt was the first piece of stitching I ever did when I was an Apprentice. I don't keep it hanging in my workshop to make my Apprentices feel better about their first efforts, I keep it because I'm proud of it.'

I looked back down at it. The stitches were longer, looser and even more crooked than mine. How could Abe possibly be proud of it?

'I'm proud of it because stitching that belt meant that all of those that followed were better,' Abe said, then laughed as my mouth dropped open. 'I didn't read your mind, I didn't have to, your face said it all. Hang my belt back on the door, and hang yours next to it. When you're a qualified Leathersmith, you'll keep that effort of yours with you always, for the same reason I've kept mine. We're perfectionists, Mason, you and I. It's good to want to do your best, but if you're scared of making a mistake, you'll never do anything at all. That belt will remind you that you had the guts to risk getting something wrong, and by the way, it's a flaming good effort, as you can see by comparing it with mine.'

I stared at him, waiting for him to laugh at his joke, but he stared right back at me. 'You're serious? This is really yours?' I said finally.

Abe chuckled. 'I'm a Leathersmith, not a prankster, boy. Hang the belts on the door and we'll get on, shall we?'

I stitched buckles onto two belts that afternoon, both of which Abe put into trays with orders pinned to the outside of them.

'Nooooooooo!' I said, rushing to the trays with my hands outstretched to remove the belts before those who had ordered them arrived to collect them.

Abe, who stood only as tall as my shoulder and was half my weight at that, moved to stand in front of me. His glare more than made up for his lack of stature. 'Yes,' he said calmly. 'You've watched me stitching these past months and you know what you're aiming for. That's a good thing. But those who've ordered belts – BELTS, Mason – want strong, functional straps to hold up their trousers. That's what you've made.'

I opened my mouth to argue, but he held up his hand to stop me.

'Your stitching will be straighter, smaller, tighter and more accurate in time. It's straight enough, small enough, tight enough and well placed enough now that your belts appear professionally made, and will be comfortable and do their job. Or d'you think you know better than I do?'

'Can't I make two more to go in their place? Better ones?' I said, looking at the ground. 'I'll stay behind and make them now.'

'You'll go home to your parents and tell them you've taken up a needle for the first time, and you'll leave this old man in peace, that's what you'll do,' Abe said. He reached up and clapped a hand on my shoulder. 'You've done well today. Tell your ma and pa I said so.'

I couldn't. I refused to utter words that I was convinced were just a Leathersmith being kind to his Apprentice. I'd done a terrible job, and I knew it. I was horrified at the idea of people I knew wearing my substandard belts, and then peeved at myself for hoping that the orders they had fulfilled had come from out of town.

I had another sleepless night. Where the previous night, I had dreaded proving to myself what I thought I already knew, I now tossed and turned as I churned over how to more precisely place the stitching, and how to even out the tension of the stitches without my excess brawn pulling them too tight or my fear at snapping the thread causing me to leave them too loose.

I was up early in the morning, breakfasted while my parents were still in bed, then rushed to Abe's workshop, arriving just as he was opening the door.

He shook his head slowly as he looked me up and down. 'You're not fit for work today, boy. Go home, sleep, eat and calm the hell down. I'll see you normal time tomorrow. Go on.' He flicked his gnarled fingers at me.

'But I want to work.'

Abe clenched his fist. His forefinger sprung out of it, pointing at me. 'You want to drive yourself into the ground until your stitching matches mine, that's what you want to do. You've been awake all night, thinking about it. Tell me I'm wrong and you can come in.'

I was so surprised, I couldn't answer him.

He nodded. 'Like I said, go home. And if you look like that

tomorrow morning, I'll send you away again. Understand? Working leather requires nimble fingers, whatever their size, and nimble fingers are the result of a relaxed, focused mind. You're uptight and exhausted and even if you don't ruin my leather, you'll ruin your fingers. Go.' He pointed back to my house.

I shook my head. 'I'll get worse if I go home. You said I'm like you, so you know I'll be even worse by tomorrow if you don't let me work today.'

Abe lowered his arm and squinted at me thoughtfully. 'Fine,' he said eventually. 'You can clean out the workshop.' He stood aside and beckoned me in, then swept his pointed finger around the large, airy workshop. 'I want everything taken out of each and every shelving unit, then you can pull the units away from the walls and sweep behind them, put them back into position and sort all the tools, offcuts, threads, samples and leather rolls, before storing them in an orderly fashion. Then I want all three benches cleared and swept – I'll move from one to the next to give you the space – and I want all of the order trays cleaned out and their contents checked. Then, and only then, you can go home.'

I nodded and set about the list of tasks.

Abe knew exactly what he was doing; I was exhausted by the time I made it home. I ate my dinner in silence while Ma repeatedly shot worried glances in my direction and Pa nodded at me with approval whenever he caught my eye. I was asleep as soon as my head touched my pillow, and woke the following morning feeling rested, refreshed and keen.

Abe looked me up and down when I entered the workshop, nodded and said, 'Good lad. There's a pile of belts with your name on it over there.'

～

I progressed quickly. By the end of the week, even I was hard pressed to find fault with my stitching. Relief didn't come close to covering how I felt.

I practically skipped to work the first morning of the following week, only for my happiness to evaporate the second I sat down at my workbench and found not belts, but the component pieces of bags which I had cut some time back.

I shook my head. 'I can't do these, they aren't belts that people will barely look at, they're bags that people will look at and admire all the time.'

Abe nodded. 'Well observed.'

I leafed through the orders. 'I don't know how to do any of these stitches, any of these patterns.'

'Someone should organise the Masters of the Trades to teach Apprentices everything they know so that their knowledge lives on. Hold fire – they did,' Abe said with a chuckle. 'We'll make a start, shall we?'

I went to pieces. My hands shook, my fingers sweated and couldn't grip the needle, and my vision kept blurring so I couldn't place the needle with any degree of confidence. It was as if my previous week's achievement had never been.

I shook my head miserably when Abe finally held up the bag I had stitched next to the one he had made whilst demonstrating its stitching and construction for me to copy.

He raised his eyebrows. 'Are we going to have the same performance whenever I ask you to progress to something new? Look at it, boy.' He shook the bag I had made. 'It's good enough to mark against the order. Are you going to acknowledge you did well, calm down and get on with the rest of them, or are you going to sit and fret, lose sleep tonight, then waste another day tomorrow clearing out the workshop? The full order is due before the week is out.'

'But I can easily see which one is yours and which is mine,' I mumbled.

'Because you know what you're looking for. It doesn't have to be perfect, it needs to be good enough,' Abe said. 'My question still stands. Which is it to be?'

'I suppose I'll get on with the rest of the bags.'

By the end of the week, I was smiling again, my bags once again having reached the standard of Abe's even though it took me three times as long as it did him to produce each one.

The following week saw me distraught all over again when Abe had me learning to stitch the easiest sections of shoes together. It was two weeks before I considered my work up to standard in quality if not in quantity. The week after that, Abe wanted my shoe-making to progress, and I was a mess all over again. So proceeded my apprenticeship, with all of the weeks that began with my having to learn something new following the exact same pattern.

By the time six months had passed, I was as exhausted as Abe was proud and confident in me. He reduced the pressure of constantly pushing me to learn to make new things, instead allowing me to gain experience in organising my time between cutting, shaping, edging and stitching, so that I could complete a steady flow of orders by myself, if still at a much slower speed than did he.

He would regularly come over to my bench to inspect my work, always nodding his approval and very occasionally making a suggestion as to how to improve my skills or work rate. If ever he looked back to his own bench while standing by mine – a sign that I recognised as him considering which of the contents of his orders he would teach me to create next – I would immediately distract him with a question about my current creation, orders that had just come in, material orders I needed to make, or anything else that would keep him talking long enough that he would forget to take me away from the products I was confident I could produce to a high standard.

Every now and then, Abe would manage to take me by surprise and I would have the upset of having to try something new, but somehow, I always managed to avoid making gloves. I knew their creation involved thin leather, tiny, intricate stitching, and delicate thread; they were my worst nightmare.

Four and a half years into my apprenticeship, I arrived at the workshop one morning to find Abe sorting through a pile of items on my workbench, and checking them off a list. I picked up a few of the items. They were my work – whilst no one else would now be able to tell the difference between my work and Abe's, the two of us could tell from a mile away – and had all been created to fulfil orders, some as far back as months ago.

I frowned. 'Have these been returned? What did I do wrong?'

Abe shook his head as he continued to tick items off his list. 'Only you would come to that assumption first. These items are all of the highest quality, which is why I put them to one side for your portfolio.'

'My what?'

'Your portfolio. In order to qualify you as a Leathersmith, I need to check that you've completed all the items on my list, from the preparation of component parts to the production of completed objects.' He raised his eyes up to meet mine while keeping his face pointing downwards, so that he peered over the glasses he had just begun wearing. 'And that's what I'm doing.'

'Without tellin' me? If I'd known, I'd have worked extra hard,

I'd have made sure all the pieces on the list were perfect, I'd have...'

'Had a nervous breakdown, I know,' Abe said, dropping his eyes back down to the list. 'You have everything here except gloves. I've put them on your order list several times now, but somehow, you've managed to avoid making them.' He narrowed his eyes as understanding dawned. 'You've been adding the orders for them back to my pile. Still worried about new projects, huh? I thought we were past all that?'

'We are. I am. We've just been so busy and we get through the orders quicker when we're workin' to our strengths.'

He wasn't fooled, but I wasn't the meek young lad I had been, and he had learnt that broaching a touchy subject head on only brought out my stubborn streak.

'Right you are, but your portfolio is a priority now, so I'll fetch some samples for you to work from. If you get going on the gloves this morning, you'll be qualified by this evening.'

I turned away from him and strode to where my apron hung from a hook. 'Not today, Abe, you know how much there is to do. I won't waste hours and hours on two items when my time can be better spent working on many.'

'You think there's anything more important than getting your qualification?'

'I know there is. You've been trustin' me with more and more of the runnin' of this workshop, so I know how many boot repairs we have now that winter's on its way, not to mention orders for new ones. We'll be the least popular men in this village if people aren't properly booted before it gets really nasty out there. I'll get around to the gloves once it quietens down.' I held his stare as he waited for me to look away, and was proud of myself for not blinking even though my heart was hammering in my chest at the thought of trying to stitch such delicate items.

Finally, Abe straightened his back, lowered his pen to the workbench and nodded. 'Right then, we'll do it your way for the time being. But as soon as things quieten down, I want a child's glove, a lady's glove and a man's glove from you so I can qualify you and these old, painful hands of mine can finally have a rest.'

I chuckled. 'Guilt? You're actually going to try and guilt me into finishin' my portfolio when you have no intention of ever retirin'? You know me well, Abe, granted, but I know you too. You'll be in here every day, mitherin' about one thing or another and insistin' that I can't manage on my own and you'll be needin' to help. You'll moan about it, like you're doin' me a favour, when in fact, there's nowhere you'd rather be. Nice try, but I need to get on, you've held me up enough for one day.'

Abe's face spilt into a broad, toothy grin. 'You're a cheeky beggar. Get along with you now and mend some boots, before I flaming well sack you for idleness.'

'Get yourself away from my bench, and I'll do just that,' I said, grinning back at him. 'And take the "portfolio" with you.' My fingers flickered either side of my head as I mocked the pieces of work Abe had squirreled away with the aim of qualifying me without my knowledge. 'Some of us have a pile of work to do that won't wait.'

He grinned, swiped the leather items into a sack from which, presumably, he had taken them, and dragged it to one side. 'You're funny, lad, I'll give you that, but don't forget whose workshop this is.'

'Mine,' I retorted as I grabbed the first boot from the pile under my bench. 'You're retirin' at the first opportunity, remember?'

It took a further year of Abe hinting, coaxing and finally shouting at me, before I finally got myself together and stitched the gloves. The pattern was easy, the leather supple and easy to work with, and the stitches straightforward. Nevertheless, I panicked over how tiny and accurate the stitching needed to be, and how embarrassed I would be if I had to waste leather and make a second attempt. When sweat began to drip from my brow, I worried it would land on and ruin the leather, and I stabbed myself countless times with my needle due to trembling fingers.

When I had finished, Abe took the items from me and made a big show of peering down at them through his glasses, then taking them closer to the window as if there were details he needed to check more thoroughly, even rummaging around in a drawer of his workbench for a magnifying glass so he could inspect each glove in even more detail. It was all for show, I knew it; he was making me pay for all the trouble I'd given him during the past year of avoidance and denial until I had finally run out of excuses to not make the gloves.

When he turned back to me with a stern face, my heart dropped. The gloves were good, weren't they? Even I hadn't been able to find fault with them, despite the agony of making them.

'You've been my best Apprentice and my worst,' he said sternly. 'Your work ethic is outstanding. Your attention to detail surpasses mine, and that's saying something. There's nothing a Leathersmith will ever be asked to make that you can't make better than I can. But your perfectionism combined with your stubbornness has made you a proper pain in this bony old backside of mine. I don't know whether I'm pleased, relieved or just plain old exhausted to tell you that, at the age of twenty-one and at least two years later than when I should have been saying this, Mason, I pronounce you a qualified Leathersmith.'

I sat back and grinned at him, relief taking away my ability to speak.

'I'll draw your papers up. You've spent most of your waking hours here since you began your apprenticeship, but now you can take on an Apprentice of your own and have a bit more time to yourself, maybe pay a little attention to one of the young ladies who've begun trailing you to work?'

Heat rose quickly in my cheeks and I was glad of the beard I had recently begun to grow. 'Who says I'm stayin' on workin' here? Once I have my papers, I can work anywhere.' I chuckled as his eyes widened. 'Keep that lone hair of yours on, Abe, I'll stay workin' here. I can't have another Apprentice havin' to suffer your temper on their own, now can I?'

He shook his head as he hurried, chuckling, over to the sink and grabbed a couple of mugs, into which he poured a large measure of the whiskey he thought he'd hidden behind some buckets stacked in a corner. He handed one to me and clinked his against it. 'To my friend and newly qualified Leathersmith, Mason Linch.'

We both took a sip. I coughed as the alcohol burnt my throat. When I'd recovered and Abe had stopped laughing, I clinked my mug against his again. 'To you, Abe. Thanks for trainin' me, cursin' me, teasin' me, shoutin' at me, coaxin' me, and never givin' up on me so that I eventually made it to this point. You're a good man and a great friend. Sincerely, thank you.'

He nodded and took another sip as I did the same. This time, it was he who choked. I pretended not to see him wipe a tear from his eye.

We had always worked well together, Abe and I, and that continued once I was no longer his Apprentice. Since the village was slowly growing in size and population, however, I did as he had suggested and took on an Apprentice of my own to help us.

Vedora was similar to me in many ways; she worked hard and methodically, and had the eye for detail that was imperative in our Trade. She was very different from me in other ways though; she was petite, with delicate, nimble fingers, and her workbench was as neat as mine was untidy. She also had a total lack of concern that she might mess up, and as a result, progressed far more quickly than I had. She was eager to try new threads, stitches and cutting techniques, and as soon as she had mastered something, she pestered me until I taught her something new. She progressed further in a year than I had in four, which, as it turned out, was fortunate.

I knew my job inside out and was good at it. I still lived with my parents, but had recently begun courting a newly qualified Baker who was two years my junior. Deirdre was as confident and outgoing as I was shy and introverted, but we got along well, so much so that Ma had invited Deirdre's parents over for dinner. Finally, I had reached a point in my life where I no longer felt like a blundering idiot, so I was shocked when I began to feel a little disorientated as I walked to work one spring morning. I wasn't worried about anything, was I? I hadn't worried about anything for a while now, so why were my feet slowing? Why did I want to turn around and run back home? Not home, I realised suddenly. Towards home, and then past it, out of the far end of the village.

I stopped in my tracks. Was it because Deirdre had mentioned how excited her parents were to have been invited to dinner with mine, the previous evening? Was I panicking because things were moving too quickly? No, I didn't think so. The urge to turn around increased, so turn around I did. Why did I have an impulsion to run and keep running until... my mouth dropped open as realisation dawned. I wanted to run and keep running until I found the horse who was tugging at my mind; the horse who had chosen me as a Bond-Partner.

This couldn't be. I had fully grown into my frame and I was a big man – I couldn't ride a horse. And I still constantly tripped over my own feet both literally and figuratively. I couldn't be one of the Horse-Bonded, visiting villages and dispensing a horse's advice, who would take me seriously? And then there was Deirdre...

My feet began to move seemingly by themselves as the pull on my mind increased.

'Mason?' Vedora's voice followed me. 'Where are you going? Are you okay?'

I stopped and turned around. The pulling on my mind increased and I began to sweat. 'I don't know.'

'You don't know where you're going, or you don't know if you're okay?' She walked towards me, her eyes full of concern.

'Both. I'm bein' tugged. By a horse. I think. I know.'

Her face lit up. 'Mason, that's wonderful, congratulations!' She ran up to me and hugged me while I stood there like an idiot. She pulled back and looked up at me. 'What's wrong? You've been chosen by a horse, that's the greatest honour there is.'

The tugging on my mind increased further, and I only just about managed to remain standing still. 'But what about you? You're my Apprentice, I can't just up and leave you. And there's Abe, he's wantin' to retire soon. And I'll be upsettin' Deirdre and her parents, and my parents.'

Vedora took hold of my arms and shook me. 'None of that matters. This village wouldn't even exist if it hadn't been for the horses and the Horse-Bonded, we all know that. You have to go to the horse who's tugging you, Mason, you have to be one of the

Horse-Bonded so you can help us all. Abe can teach me, and when I qualify, I'll take an Apprentice and Abe can retire if he wants to, but he won't, you know he won't. Deirdre, her parents, your parents – they'll all get over it, but if you don't go to your horse, you won't, not now you know there's one out there who's chosen you. Go home and get ready to leave, Mason. I'll tell Abe and we'll see you at your Quest Ceremony. Go on, go.'

I nodded slowly and felt a smile beginning to lift the corners of my mouth. I was being tugged! By a horse!

Vedora smiled too. 'That's more like it. But you're still here?'

I grinned at her. 'You're a bossy one, that's for sure. Poor Abe, I almost feel sorry for him.'

She laughed and pushed me to get me moving. As soon as I began walking for home, my feet quickened to a jog and then to a run. I had never run voluntarily in my life! But I wasn't now, not really, I suddenly realised. I couldn't find it in me to mind.

I burst through the front door, slamming it into Pa, who was just behind it, putting on his boots. 'Pa, I'm bein' tugged! Can you believe it?'

He rubbed his forehead as he stood up. 'You're bein' what?'

'He's being tugged by a horse!' Ma cried as she raced down the stairs, two at a time. Then she stopped and put her hand to my forehead as she had when I was a child. 'You're sure? You're not coming down with something?'

'Only a desperate need to run that way.' I pointed at a grey stone in the wall of the hallway. 'My horse is that way. I'm sorry, Ma, Pa, and I'm sorry for Deirdre, but I'll have to go.'

Ma hugged me, Pa slapped me on the back and then hugged us both, and then all three of us looked at one another and laughed for no reason other than the delightful ridiculousness of it all.

Ma was the first to stop laughing. 'You need to go and see Deirdre before she hears it from someone else. The second I start gathering everything you're going to need for your quest to find your horse, word will spread around the village that one of our own is going to be Horse-Bonded, and there'll be excitement like there hasn't been in years.'

I nodded. 'I'll go now. I'm not lookin' forward to it.'

'She'll be upset, but she'll understand. She's a sensible lass is Deirdre, I'd never have stood for you courting her otherwise.'

Pa rolled his eyes at her and then looked at me sympathetically. 'Go on, son. Your ma and I will get busy collectin' everything for your Quest Ceremony. You'll be wantin' to leave today?'

I nodded. 'The tuggin's gettin' stronger. I'll never be able to stay here the night.'

I left the village after lunch. Deidre had been – as my mother had surmised – upset but understanding, as had Abe. Both came to my Quest Ceremony.

I walked along the corridor of cheering people that stretched from the front door of my parents' cottage almost to the end of the village, and when I reached Abe, I was unable to speak. I hugged my friend and mentor tightly until he pushed at me, gasping, 'You're crushing my old bones. Let me go, or I'll never get to train my newest and best Apprentice.' I stood back from him and he grinned up at me. 'I'm proud to know you, to have trained you, and to call you my friend,' he said. 'Now be off with you, and don't you dare look back.'

Still not trusting myself to speak, I moved on but I couldn't stop myself defying Abe and looking back. When I saw him sobbing into Vedora's embrace, I had to turn away again before I joined in.

Deirdre reached out to me from her place in one of the opposing lines of villagers, and squeezed my hand. 'He'll be alright, Mason. I'll check on him later, but I bet I'll find him barking orders at Vedora while she ignores him and carries on with what she wants to do.'

I pulled her closer and whispered, 'And you? Will you be alright? You're bein' amazin', but how can you forgive me?'

'Because I'd do the same in your place,' she whispered back. 'We all would, and anyone who says otherwise is lying. When I have children, I'll tell them I was once courted by one of the Horse-Bonded. You've given me that, so how can I possibly complain?' She pulled away from me and smiled even as a tear rolled down her cheek.

I wiped it away with my thumb. 'You make sure you find someone who deserves you. You hear me?'

She nodded and then tilted her head towards the remaining people waiting to send me on my way. 'Go and find your horse.'

I nearly broke, but I bit down hard on my lip and did as she said, shaking hands held out in front of me, and accepting good wishes and the tiny horseshoe ornaments that most of my well-wishers hung in my hair, on my clothes and on my back-sack.

When I reached the end of the corridor of people, I turned to wave at them all, only to see Ma and Pa rushing towards me from where they had presented me with my back-sack full of food, clothes and cooking gear at the beginning of the ceremony. After a final hug with both of them, I was on my way.

I had rarely left the village and had no idea where I was going – yet I did. The pull on my mind was as certain as it was relentless. I was going to find my horse.

～

I had always thought that you were born, you went to school, you grew up, you apprenticed in one of the Skills or Trades and worked hard so you could contribute to your community once you qualified. How was it possible that I had never considered there might be more to life than that? I wondered as I followed my mind – and increasingly my heart, the more I thought of the horse awaiting me – through woodland that was alive with plants and animals as if it were one big animal itself, across grassland littered with flowers of every colour just coming into bloom, and even up into mountains briefly at one point.

I had seen some of the Horse-Bonded with their horses when they visited our village, yet it had never occurred to me to wonder where they came from, what their journey had been like, where they had slept, what they had seen or who they might have met on the way. How had I been so blinkered? How had I never even considered what might be beyond the village I had believed contained my life – was my life?

As I walked the countryside whilst taking in its raw beauty, or sat, leaning against a tree whilst eating the food Ma had packed for me, or woke from sleep that was deeper than I had ever experienced before, I thanked the horse I had yet to meet. Already, I was changing, opening my eyes to a world bigger than I had ever believed possible.

My quest to find my horse took twelve eye-opening days. I knew I would love her before I even saw her, but as soon as I clapped eyes on the tall, sturdy, iron grey mare grazing before me, my heart swelled so much, it almost hurt. When she lifted her head and looked at me with soft, brown eyes that seemed to overflow with kindness, I couldn't stop myself smiling, even as I missed the sudden loss of her mind pulling on mine.

You need not mourn my loss for I am here where I will always be. Her thought was suddenly my thought, as if we had thought it together. It was full of the kindness I had seen in her eyes and I immediately felt like nothing I could ever do would be disapproved of, nothing I could ever do would be wrong as far as she was concerned.

All of the self-deprecation I had ever felt just fell away. I didn't want to move; I didn't want to break the spell she had put me under, so I just stood there, staring at her, drinking in the sight of her solid beauty and the feel of her warmth in my mind.

Eventually, she wandered over to me. She sniffed my forehead and then down my face, neck and body to my feet. Then she snatched at the grass, the warmth of her body now seeping through me as surely as that of her mind. Still, I didn't move, afraid that if I did, she and everything that came with her would disappear.

You will learn to trust. Her thought was gentle with no hint of accusation.

I trust you already, how could I not? I flinched as soon as I had thought it, terrified that I had broken the spell.

It was not your trust in me to which I referred.

So then my trust in...who?

She lifted her head and gazed at me while she chewed her mouthful. *In yourself. You will learn to trust yourself.*

I could feel her honesty, not in the sense that she had decided to tell the truth, but because the truth was who she was. The world began to spin around me, faster and faster until the hilly grassland became a blur, as her truth settled within me. I didn't trust myself.

I felt weak and exposed, as if the slightest breeze could blow me over. My stomach began to churn and I thought I would vomit.

The mare's warmth increased in my mind until it was all I could feel. *We will find the way forward together. Allow me to take your weight while I show you who I am. Who you are in truth.*

Find a word for who we are and use it as my name. It will remind you of yourself when you forget.

How will you take my weight? I can't...

I never got to tell her I couldn't ride. She exploded into the warmth with which she had infused my mind, and I almost toppled over. I put a hand out to save myself, and found a strong body that was more than capable of holding me up.

She was everywhere at once; there was no place in my mind that wasn't her – no, I realised, it was as she had told me, there was no place that wasn't us. We were utterly content, as if there was never anything we would want or need, as if we had already achieved everything there was to achieve just by existing – as if our purpose in life was merely to experience every possibility it contained, regardless of the outcome.

I frowned. That couldn't be right, that wasn't me at all. I had to achieve perfection in everything I did.

It was as if the idea of who we were fractured, splitting us into two different entities where before we were one. Where I was careful in everything I did so I wouldn't have to bear the agony of feeling like a failure, she was careful in everything she did so that she could be sure to experience it to its fullest.

You're diligence itself. I'm just afraid, I admitted.

You are intelligent and perceptive. You merely need trust yourself. Once you do you will recognise the name you have chosen for me as belonging to both of us.

Diligence?

She didn't respond in thought, but I could feel her satisfaction.

So how do I learn to trust myself?

Her amusement was as warm as the rest of her, and not in the least mocking. *You have already begun.*

Slowly, I came back to myself. I rubbed the dark grey fur that covered her shoulder as she continued to graze at my feet like nothing unusual had just happened. *So, what happens now?*

We will travel to the home of others like you and me. We can learn from them as much as from one another.

The Gatherin'. The home of the Horse-Bonded. I nodded slowly. It made sense.

A pang of fear shot through me. What if I couldn't learn what they had to teach me? What if I couldn't ride, a great bear of a man like me? What if I made a fool of myself?

Remember who we are.

You're Diligence. I'm just terrified of failure, remember?

Are you fearful of travelling there?

No, I can walk fine.

Then let us walk. She took a step with one of her front legs and then sniffed the grasses and herbs that surrounded her newly placed foot. I experienced with her the pleasure of their scents and the wonder at how different a few of them were from those she had been grazing merely a stride away.

I stepped beside her. She took another step with her other front leg and repeated the procedure, drawing me with her so that I was with her in her senses as she lifted her head and looked across at me. We saw me as a large, kindly man with patience and love in his eyes – just like I saw Diligence.

We are the same, she confirmed. *Come. Enjoy the walk and everything it reveals.*

I did. If I had found my journey to find my horse enjoyable, it was nothing compared to walking at her side. All thoughts of our destination dissolved as we revelled in everything that surrounded us and flowed between us. When we stopped for my horse to graze, and later to rest for the night, I was as content as when we were walking.

There was always something to experience, whether it be the

swirling breeze that blew first from one side and soon after from behind, or the steady rhythm of Diligence munching on grass, or the feel of the spring sunshine warming my skin, or the sudden chill as the sun disappeared behind the clouds, or the raucous squawking of a crow overhead, or the wailing of fox cubs to their mother, or the swishing of Diligence's tail at the first few biters to wake up from their winter slumber, or the landscape that invited us to discover more of its secrets.

There was never any hurry to move on, to change focus from one experience to the next, to wake up, or to sleep; we just did those things when we were ready. We experienced everything and missed nothing.When we arrived at The Gathering four days later, I was a different man. Or so I thought.

When I caught sight of paddocks in the distance, stretching away towards what looked like huge, grey stone buildings at the base of some hills, I was consumed by all of the sounds that accompanied the river that tore along by our side, and with mimicking Diligence's slow, careful footsteps as she picked her way between the rocks and boulders that littered the hillside we were descending. It fascinated me that where, had I been alone, I would have picked up my pace having spotted my destination, I felt no need to hurry, no need to do anything other than mooch along at my mare's pace.

When we turned away from the river and up a path between the paddocks, many people working in them – sowing seed, tending to sheep, collecting horse dung, brushing horses, even riding in one of them – paused to wave and call out greetings to us.

My heart fluttered with nerves at the sight of those atop their horses, one of whom rode over to the paddock fence to meet us.

He was a slim man with greying hair and piercing eyes that warned against any attempts to deceive him, but his smile appeared genuine. 'Greetings, I'm Mistral, the Master of Riding here, and this is Prudence.' He leant forward and stroked the neck of the bright white mare beneath him. 'You are?'

'Mason. And this is Diligence.'

The man smiled and narrowed his eyes slightly. 'Is she now. A warm welcome to both of you. How long since you bonded?'

'Um, er, oh. Bonded? Yes, I suppose we did. Um. When was it? Three days ago? No, four. I think.' I flushed and was glad that my beard covered most of my face, although I made an instant decision to allow it to grow thicker. 'Sorry, it's hard to think of when we bonded because I'm already findin' it hard to remember when we weren't, and I haven't really been payin' attention to the days and nights.'

Mistral's face softened as he chuckled. 'Don't worry about a thing, the early days and weeks following bonding are always a confusing time. Many newly bonded find they've forgotten their own names by the time they arrive here, so you're doing pretty well.'

I nodded, feeling a little less stupid. Dili snorted at my side, causing Prudence to squeal, jump up and down on her front feet and then take a few steps backward.

Mistral didn't appear to notice, sitting his horse as if nothing had happened. He pointed towards the buildings in the distance. 'Carry on that way until you reach the paddock closest to the buildings, which is currently empty. There's plenty of grass and the water barrel is full, so Diligence will be comfortable there, and within easy reach of the buildings if you feel a sudden need to be with her; it's perfectly normal to feel that way when you're newly bonded. Leave her there and carry on to the buildings, someone in the square will point you to the accommodation block and tell you what to do. I'd show you around myself, but I'm due to be teaching in a few minutes.'

'No problem, I'll find my way. Thanks for the directions.'

Mistral nodded. 'Be sure to visit the Saddler today. New saddles are given priority over other items, so she'll no doubt have one made for Diligence within a few days, and then you can begin your riding lessons with me. I'll be seeing you.'

Prudence whirled around and galloped off, leaving me standing alone with Diligence, my head spinning. Diligence nudged me gently and then took a step along the path, waiting for me to fall in beside her.

Nothing has changed, she informed me when I remained where I was.

Everythin's changed. I have to learn to ride, and I'll be rubbish at it. Look at me, have you ever seen anyone less suited to sittin' on a horse? And there's a Saddler here. She'll have trained as a Leathersmith like me, and now she's here, she's makin' saddles. She'll be wantin' me to help her, but I can't do that, Dili, I've seen saddles before, when the Horse-Bonded visited our village with their horses. They're complicated and they have to be well-fittin' and stitched to perfection. Any mistakes in their construction and a horse or person could get hurt.

You and I enjoyed every footstep that composed our journey here regardless of our destination. We will enjoy every footstep I take with you on my back irrespective of the reason for doing it. We will enjoy creating every stitch while composing the saddle you will make for me without thought of the final product. It is all the same.

I can't make you a saddle, Dili.

I will not tolerate one made by another. I would be a part of its creation just as I would be part of everything else you do. It is all the same. You and I are the same.

I couldn't doubt it. I wanted to, but I couldn't; her conviction wouldn't allow it. I took a step beside her, and then another.

Dili and I settled at The Gathering more quickly than I could have believed possible. I came to realise that Dili would have immediately settled anywhere, because anywhere and everywhere, anything and everything were fine by her. She enjoyed every second of every minute of every day with a warm sense of contentment that sat in the back of my mind, soothing me whenever I wanted to fret.

I took a room on the top floor of the accommodation block – a huge, grey stone building with four floors of bedrooms and bathrooms – which I soon regretted and about which I grumbled to myself until I noticed Dili's delight in every step it took me to climb the three flights of stairs. Her happiness at the exercise that stimulated my legs, heart and circulation became my own and I began to take them faster and faster, all the time revelling in my increased heart rate and the burn in my legs, and curious to see how fast I could go before I ran out of breath.

When I was given a share of the chores that kept The Gathering running, I took to my daily log-splitting shift with the same enthusiasm I applied to the accommodation block's stairs. When I wasn't chopping wood or clearing dung from Dili's paddock, topping up her water or taking lessons in caring for her, I worked in the Saddler's workshop.

Sumer was delighted to have a fellow Leathersmith joining her and was all for putting me to work on the huge pile of boot, shoe and bag repairs and orders while she made Dili's saddle, but when

I explained that Dili was keen for me to make her saddle, she was more than happy to show me how, stitch by painful stitch.

I trembled, sweated and repeatedly pricked myself with the needle, just like when I'd been an Apprentice. I could sense Sumer's frowns and eye rolls, and knew she must be wondering who in their right mind had pronounced me a qualified Leathersmith. But, as I was beginning to trust would always be the case, Dili wove her fascination with my work, her appreciation of my concentration, and her enjoyment of my creativity, into every stitch, until I began to focus on each and every one of them in isolation instead of fretting about whether they would be good enough to contribute to the finished product. As I began to relax, the stitches came more easily. I forgot Sumer was watching over me until I had finished each step of the saddle's construction and looked up to her ready to be shown what to do next.

The saddle took me four days to make instead of the two it would have taken Sumer, a fact that delighted my Bond-Partner.

I'm proud of myself for makin' it, Dili, I am, I told her as I brushed her down one evening. *But I'm not proud of takin' up so much of Sumer's time, and I'm definitely not proud of the fact that the number of outstandin' orders and repairs in the workshop has increased, rather than decreased, since there were two of us workin' leather.*

Dili let out a long, peaceful sigh. *Before you took on a physical body you could be anywhere and everywhere at once. When you leave your body you will have the same capability. You are operating at a much slower vibration whilst part of the physical experience because it is exactly that. An opportunity to experience. Rush to reach whatever goal you have decided is important and you will miss much along the way.*

So I have to do everythin' at half speed?

The speed is not important. Operate quickly or slowly but do not rush.

I'm not sure I'm followin' you.

That is a good thing for I would have you at my side.

You're just playin' with me. You know what I mean, I can feel it.

Play is to be encouraged. As is joy for the sake of being happy rather than as a result of achievement. Take a long break when you are at your busiest. Stand and look up at the sky when you have an urgent need to be somewhere. Allow yourself to be diverted from a mundane task to that which craves your attention. Whenever you feel the need to rush ensure that you slow yourself down until your focus comes from a place of relaxation and enjoyment. It is in that place that you are at your most creative. It is in that place that you are at your most powerful.

I took her advice. Whenever I wanted to rush to be somewhere or hurry at my task, or set myself goals that would encourage me to work at a certain rate, I remembered Dili's counsel and did my best to slow my feet, my mind, my fingers – whichever part of me it was that was intent on reaching a goal or destination. It was excruciatingly uncomfortable, but all I had to do was dive into the part of my mind occupied by Dili, and feel her warmth and contentment, for it to be easy.

Far from being a burden to Sumer, my work rate soon surpassed hers. I was at the workshop for marginally less time than she was, yet my output was greater and with no decline in the quality of my work – in fact to my eye, my stitching actually improved. I enjoyed whichever chores I was allocated in any given week, whether it be chopping logs, preparing food in the kitchens or working in the fields, and I learnt not to feel guilty at occasionally arriving later than everyone else, since again, I never failed to perform all of my tasks efficiently and well, often finishing before everyone else and taking on some of their share of the job.

The only area of my life where I couldn't seem to apply Dili's counsel was our riding lessons with Mistral. Every time I sat on my horse's wide back in the saddle I had made for her, I felt like a useless lump. I couldn't seem to co-ordinate any parts of my body with any others, so when I focused on following one instruction, I forgot to do everything else at the same time.

When I squeezed with my ankles to ask Dili to move forward, I forgot to sit up straight, slumping in the saddle, and getting left behind when she began to walk. When I sat up straight, I forgot to keep my heels down, and kept losing my stirrups and my balance. When I remembered to turn my body to ask Dili to change direction, I forgot to move my head, and vice versa.

I thought Mistral had gone mad when he told us we were doing well and instructed me to ask Dili to trot. My point was proven correct when I failed to rise and sit to the two-time trot rhythm, and found myself bouncing around on her back like a sack of onions on a cart, until she slowed herself to a walk to spare me the indignity of falling off.

I was mortified. *I'm sorry, Dili. You should have chosen someone else as your Bond-Partner, someone lighter and more co-ordinated. I can't do this, I'm a rubbish rider.*

You are merely focused on that which you believe to be the endpoint of our lessons instead of enjoying the time it takes to reach it. You enjoyed creating each and every stitch it took to create the saddle in which you now sit. This is the same.

It isn't though, is it? I'm unbalancin' you, hurtin' you even, when I bounce around on your back. I can't enjoy that, Dili.

Enjoy the feeling of your body moving with mine during each step I take and everything else will come in time.

'Well done, Mason, that was a great first effort at trot,' Mistral said as he reached Dili's shoulder. 'As I've told you before, you have a natural seat and balance, and your posture isn't bad either, it'll improve as you gain more experience and muscle tone. You just tightened up a bit when Dili went into trot, so you got a little behind her movement. Relax through the transition next time, and you'll be fine.'

I shook my head in disbelief. 'I was all over the place.'

Mistral smiled. 'It just felt that way because you weren't quite in the position you needed to be. When you've been riding a little while and have built up muscle memory, maintaining your balance and position will come easily to you, but for now you have to work at them. When you lose them, work to get them back. If you bounce a bit while you're doing it, well so what? We've all been there. Dili knows you're trying and improving, she'll bear with you.'

'She shouldn't have to,' I mumbled.

'What's that?'

'I feel like I'm lettin' her down.'

'Does Dili feel like you're letting her down?'

'No. She's told me to enjoy learnin' to ride, but I'm strugglin' with it.'

I continued to struggle with it. Even when, years after our arrival at The Gathering, Mistral pronounced me a sensitive and proficient rider, I couldn't bring myself to agree. As far as I was concerned, not a ride went by when I didn't get something wrong and subsequently compromise Dili's movement and balance, even if in such a small way that not even Mistral noticed.

When he shook my hand and told me that while he would always be available if Dili and I needed his help at any time, I had no need for further regular lessons, I was both relieved and disappointed; relieved that I wouldn't have to subject Dili to my inadequacy on a regular basis, but disappointed that I had never managed to take her counsel on board to enough of a degree to enjoy my way to being a decent rider.

In the months and years that followed, I didn't ride unless I had to. Dili and I took on our share of travelling to villages so that I could pass on my horse's counsel to any who asked for it, and when the mood took us to want to move at greater speed, or if I was tired and Dili wasn't, I rode her. Every time, I tried to do as she had told me when I had been learning to ride her, and immersed myself in the movement of her body as she took each step. Every time, I was distracted by my own inadequacy when I restricted her movement momentarily by not quite following her body with mine; when I upset her balance slightly by losing mine; when I confused her body by asking her slightly different things with different parts of mine before I managed to get them completely synchronised.

Dili's attitude and approach to life never wavered regardless of whether I managed to adhere to it, regardless of whether I questioned it, and regardless of whether or not I rode her. As with everything else, she applied herself completely and absolutely to enjoying every moment of her life and seeing where it took us both. Whenever I apologised about not riding either better or more, she refused to be drawn into discussing it as an issue, always leaving me with a sense that, like everything else, there was no endpoint to it on which to focus, but merely an enjoyment of the process of life.

As years turned into decades, I rode less and less. Dili never questioned me, preferring, as always, to completely engage with whatever she or I – or both – were doing, whether it be going for a stroll by the river, pulling upright the huge, heavy poles that supported the canopies covering the riding paddocks in winter, stitching leather, counselling villagers on our travels, even helping some of the other Horse-Bonded from time to time.

I was forty-one and Dili twenty-four when Amarilla Nixon arrived at The Gathering with her Bond-Partner, the beautiful and wonderful Infinity. A gentler, sweeter partnership I had never come across, yet there was something about the two of them that gave me pause.

It wasn't just that Amarilla seemed to walk into one confrontation after another without trying, and it wasn't that Infinity, small as she was, had such an enormous presence that no one could doubt she was about something far greater than whatever issues her Bond-Partner might need to work through. It was how Dili felt about the two of them that really made me pay attention to what they were about; she expanded her warmth to include them so that I almost felt they were part of our bond, and part of her attention was always with them, as if whatever they were doing together was of the utmost importance.

When Amarilla expressed her misgivings about having riding lessons with Feryl – the Master Of Riding since Mistral's death some years previously – I encouraged her to listen to Infinity and experiment by themselves, regardless of the tongue-lashing I knew Feryl would, and subsequently did, give me. When Infinity asked for a bridle to lean on while her young, inexperienced rider was trying to both find her own balance and help Infinity to improve her own, I agreed to make one for them, again knowing I'd be in hot water with Feryl. Little did I know I'd be up all night making it, since Dili considered it one of those things to which I needed to allow my attention – which would have been on having a decent meal after a hard day's work, before retiring to bed – to be diverted. And when some Woeful attacked The Gathering and one of them almost killed Infinity, both Dili and I made sure to be in attendance to both Amarilla and Infinity until they had fully recovered from their ordeal.

It was while Infinity was still unconscious that I began to have a glimmer for myself of exactly how important she and Amarilla were to Dili and me. Where Dili had included the two of them in her warmth and our bond since their arrival, she went a step further and began communicating with Amarilla in her mind. Never before in the history of the Horse-Bonded had any human been able to converse mind to mind with any horse other than their Bond-Partner, but Amarilla heard my Dili. It fitted with everything I knew about Dili that it was she who threw that convention to the wind to dissipate where it would; she saw a way for us all to draw the most out of our shared experience and drew us all along with her.

Ever since Amarilla and Infinity had rebelled against the way Feryl taught his students to ride – the same way we had all been taught – Amarilla had been trying to help Infinity to balance better, and she had made good progress; anyone who had watched them together before the Woeful attack had seen that. But as I understood it, their progress was slow because Amarilla was trying to learn to ride while trying to help Infinity rearrange herself in a way that wasn't easy for an experienced rider to manage, let alone a beginner. When Infinity was incapacitated, Dili's idea was that Amarilla should ride her so that Amarilla could find her own balance, and then once she was stronger and a little more balanced, Amarilla could begin to help Dili to improve her own balance in the way she had already helped Infinity to achieve.

To begin with, I was excited by the notion; finally, Dili would have a lightweight, fit, athletic rider who was young and learnt quickly, and would be a help to her rather than the burden I had always felt myself to be.

As time went on and I watched Amarilla ride my Diligence in session after session, I began to feel ashamed of myself. Amarilla had little natural balance, and despite her slim frame and young age, was no fitter than I had been when I was learning to ride, and had far less muscle to help her out. But she didn't let that stop her. Every single time she sat on my horse, she gave everything of herself to the experience. She concentrated on everything Dili did and everything her own body did – or wanted to do – in response, and she listened to advice from Dili, me, her friends, anyone who could help her, and then adjusted, changed... and improved. All the while she was working so hard to improve her own riding, she applied herself to helping Dili to balance better too. This young slip of a girl was doing for my horse what I should have done for her years ago. What I should have been doing for her now.

I began to rise before dawn and run laps around the riding paddocks, buoyed along both by Dili's enthusiasm for my endeavour and by the young girl who I had thought needed me, but had turned out to be the inspiration I had needed for so long. By the time Infinity had recovered enough from her injuries that Amarilla could return – her strength and balance every bit as improved as she had helped my Dili to achieve – to riding her own horse, I was ready to try to take over helping Dili to improve her balance further.

Amarilla, Dili and I agreed that Amarilla would ride Dili first and help her to achieve the level of balance they had reached together, then she would help me to maintain it once I was on board.

It was both easy and difficult. Dili had never felt so fluid, so supple, so lifted in front of me, so light on her front legs, and I could feel how much it meant to her to be using her body in such an improved way. I didn't have to work nearly as hard as Amarilla did, to sit in balance and use my body to help Dili to continue to improve the way she used hers, but I got frustrated with myself. A lot. Just because my body was capable of doing everything I needed it to do, it didn't mean I always timed my signals to Dili well, or jumped in quickly enough to support her when she faltered.

All of my old feelings of guilt returned every time I felt I was letting her down. Then, I would glance across at Amarilla walking and running next to Infinity as the mare regained her strength, completely focused on her horse and what Infinity needed from her in every given second, and I would feel guilty for wasting time beating myself up when I should be everything to Dili that Amarilla was to Infinity.

She is diligent not because it is easy but because she chooses to be, Dili observed on one occasion. I nodded and continued with fresh determination.

I immersed myself in Dili's enjoyment of our partnership, our strength and our balance, and in her delight at every step she took, at every movement in every part of her body… and my timing began to improve; I was able to help my beloved Dili to stay in balance for longer and longer before not quite being quick enough to step in when she needed me to help her adjust herself.

If I stayed with her warmth and enjoyment of the process, I was able to react to my mistake and support her with my body while between us, we got her balance back. If I allowed myself to even consider what a lummox I was for getting it wrong for a split second, we would lose our balance altogether, grind to a halt and then have to reorganise ourselves all over again.

It was when Amarilla began to ride Infinity again that the two of them pulled me far beyond the point I could ever look back. A group of us were all riding our horses in one of the riding paddocks, when all of a sudden, Infinity threw Amarilla to the ground and took off, careering around like a mad thing. Amarilla was badly hurt but before I knew it, she was on her feet and making her way over to where Infinity was throwing herself around. The girl blazed with love for her horse, and with determination to do whatever she had to for Infinity to be alright. She was frightened when she sat down on Infinity's back, I could see it in her eyes, but then her love and determination returned.

I had never seen anything like that which happened next; Amarilla became one with her horse, I could see it and I could feel it. She rode Infinity to such perfect balance that she took the mare away from what was frightening her so much, and back to the love – the perfection – they shared. To all they were.

I cried, I couldn't help it. It was like I absorbed everything I saw them become and it became part of me. The need to be perfect fell away from me as if it had never existed; I didn't need to achieve perfection, I just needed to give all of myself to every single moment with my horse, and we would be all that we were, just like Dili had always told me.

The next time I rode Dili, I cried again. There I was, a big lump sitting on his horse, crying. Why? Because there was and is nothing more beautiful or more humbling than sharing the ridden experience with a horse.

Dili's warmth swept along our bond with her thought. *He Who Is Diligence, you have remembered who you are.*

Feryl

I wanted to cry, but I couldn't let myself. My three older brothers would only have laughed at me and told me I was as much of a baby as my youngest brother – who at six months old was actually a baby. I, on the other hand, was ten, and had just completed my first day at secondary school, not that anyone was the slightest bit interested.

When Lance, my eldest brother, had returned from his first day at "big" school, none of the rest of us were allowed to make a sound while my parents sat spellbound, listening to Lance's blow by blow account of everything that happened on his first day out of juniors. I was only four, but I remember being furious that my mother's attention was taken up solely by her firstborn son.

When it was Fratten's turn two years later, my second eldest brother managed to hold everyone's attention as he related his first day of being a "big boy" despite my parents' decreased interest, because he was loud and shouted over us all until he was heard.

Another two years after that, Jules came home from his first day and had everyone in hysterics as he told how he'd – as was usual – acted the clown, bursting into secondary school literally by tripping into his classroom and landing at his teacher's feet. I laughed along with everyone else, and couldn't wait for it to be my turn to mark the passage from child to young man by leaving the little kids behind. But it didn't work out for me, like nothing ever seemed to.

By the time it was my turn, my loud, attention-seeking baby brother, Pelan, had already spent six months ensuring that he was the centre of attention. My mother barely waved me goodbye when I left in the morning, and when I returned home and took my place at the kitchen table for dinner, she was busy feeding Pelan whilst laughing at Fratten's tale about how he had tried to impress a girl with his early attempts at Tree-Singing. Apparently, he had attempted to make a wild flower grow taller in front of her so that he could pick it and present it to her, but had succeeded only in making the grasses around it grow so that it disappeared from sight altogether.

When he finally stopped talking, I tried to speak, but then Lance started relating how he had identified the uses of not one but two new herbs for his herbalism apprenticeship that day, and Jules started telling a whole stream of jokes he'd picked up from the older boys with whom he had started hanging around. As always, any attempts I made to speak were drowned out.

It was always the same; I wasn't interesting, I wasn't clever, I wasn't loud, I wasn't funny, everything I did had already been done by one or more of my brothers, and I was no longer the baby of the family once Pelan arrived, so I didn't even get that share of my parents' attention anymore. I was just me. Plain, boring Feryl. And I hated that fact. Just for once, I wanted them all to listen to me, to be interested in me.

I considered shouting and stamping my feet, but Lance would only have sneered at me, Fratten would have carried on talking over me until everyone looked away from me and at him, Jules would have teased me so that everyone laughed at me, and Pelan would have screamed or gurgled until he got what he wanted. So, like always, I kept quiet, swallowed my tears and anger and remained invisible.

I ate my dinner, trying to keep my lips from trembling every time I opened my mouth for another spoonful of stew, and chewing the meat and vegetables to a pulp before swallowing, otherwise I'd never have got them down without choking. When I'd finished, I raised my hand as I'd been taught, until my father, stern as ever, nodded to me, giving me permission to leave the table. Then I managed to walk – and not run – out of the kitchen, devastated that no one apart from my father even noticed my departure.

Once clear of the kitchen, I ran down the stone-walled hallway to the back door, my family's laughter following in my wake and spurring me on ever faster. I wrenched the door open and slammed it behind me, glad of the wind that buffeted me as soon as I stepped into the paddock, which I could use as an excuse for my noisy exit if questioned. Who was I kidding? I asked myself. I wouldn't be questioned, none of them would have even heard the door bang, any more than they ever heard me.

I stood in the wind, clenching and unclenching my fists, still holding back my tears. I spied a branch that had fallen from the beech tree under which our goats were sheltering. I ran to it, picked it up and hit the tree with it, over and over. I screamed and yelled, my voice taken by the wind as soon as it left me. Even out here, I was rendered silent.

When the stick, previously as long as my legs, had been reduced to a stub that barely protruded from my hands, I flung it to the floor and screamed again. Then I noticed I was alone. I looked for the goats and saw that they were huddled against the hedge, now sheltering from me as well as from the wind.

Remorse flooded me. I began to run towards the goats, but slowed to a walk when their eyes widened even further and they began looking frantically around themselves, deciding which way to run.

'I'm sorry.' My words were taken by the wind so that not even I heard them, yet the goats seemed to have done. Either that, or they felt them, just like I felt my brothers' words when they teased me and made me feel stupid. All twelve goats relaxed and seemed to see me as their friend again – as the boy who fed and looked after them, not because I was asked to but because I loved to.

With the goats, I could talk without being shouted over. I could show them I cared, and they enjoyed my attention. They loved it when I spoke to them, when I scratched them in the places that I knew each one enjoyed, when I fed and watered them, when I sat amongst them while they grazed around me.

I wandered over to them and sat down in their midst. One of them sniffed my face and then lay down beside me. The others stayed where they were, sheltering from the wind alongside me in companionable silence. I told them all about my first day at school – how I had loved walking past the junior playground towards the building of the secondary school, because it made me feel grown up; how I had been seated next to my best friend in our new classroom, and how happy we both were; how, in my last lesson of the day, I had plucked up the courage to put up my hand and answer a question correctly, and how I had felt when my teacher praised me. I wanted more of that. It had made me decide to work hard so that even though I was invisible at home, I would be someone at school.

The goats listened as I spoke, their ears flicking back to their grazing when I paused for breath, then back to me when I began talking again. Gradually, my anger left me.

I stroked the goat lying by my side, whom I had named Mabel. She was the oldest of our herd, nearly as old as I was. She was mother to most of the others, and always had an air about her that she cared. I would never have said that out loud; I would only have been laughed at and my proclamation would have been immortalised into a family joke by Jules, but that was how I felt. I loved being around her and her family – far more so than my own. She listened to my plans to excel at school as she always listened to everything else, and I began to feel excited at the thought.

Lance was halfway through his herbalism apprenticeship, Fratten would no doubt be every bit as good at tree-singing as Lance was at herbalism, and when Jules was tested for the Skills in a few years' time, I had no doubt he would show aptitude for at least one of them and be every bit as brilliant at it as were our older two brothers – but none of them had excelled at school. There, I would make my mark. There, I would show my parents that I was someone of whom it was worth taking notice. Even if they never listened to me, they would listen to my teachers, to my school reports.

I kissed Mabel on the top of her head and thanked her for listening to me, for being my friend. Then I skipped back inside and up to the bedroom I shared with Jules, to begin my homework.

I tried my best. Day in, day out, week after week, month after month, I tried to work my way to the top of my class. I was the only one in my year who never missed a day of school, who was never late, who never handed homework in after it was due, who never got told off for talking. I listened, I made notes, I did extra reading and writing practice, I put my hand up whenever I knew the answers – and I suffered for it. My classmates called me names and teased me for asking to sit at the front where I couldn't be distracted from their whispering and gossiping when our teacher's back was turned. They told me I was a "suck-up" for always putting my hand up when Mrs Hansom asked for a volunteer, whatever the job was. My best friend soon became someone else's. I sat alone at breaktimes and at lunchtime, not that it bothered me since I was always reading or doing my homework.

I tried and tried to be clever, to be noteworthy, but however hard I worked, I was still just... average. There was never any reason for any of my teachers to comment about my success when they met my parents in the street. There was usually a brief note about the amount of effort I put in to my studies in my school report, which only made it all the more humiliating when my grades were, without exception, middling. And still, I never gave up. The thought of my family being silent, even just for once, while they listened to me relate how I had achieved the top spot at something, no matter what it was, drove me on to keep trying to achieve it.

Every now and then, I would get despondent. I would go and tell Mabel and the other goats all about it – how hard I was trying, how unpopular I was and all to no avail. They would look up at me as they always did, as if I were worth something, as if they saw me for who I really was, and I would believe in myself again and throw myself back into my studies.

I gave up talking at mealtimes because there was never any point. When I was twelve and Lance turned eighteen, all talk was of him leaving for a neighbouring village where he would have the chance to, in time, be the Master Herbalist, as well as of Fratten's genius as a Tree-Singer, and Jules's having just shown aptitude for metal-singing. When I was thirteen, Lance became engaged and there was great excitement about his upcoming nuptials and the cottage that his fiancée, a talented Rock-Singer would be building for them both with help from her sister who was every bit as talented.

Mabel heard all about my feeling swamped by our family joining with one that I was sure would be full of people every bit as loud, attention-seeking and self-centred as my own. As usual, her calm gaze and belief that I would feed and take care of her, that I was someone noteworthy, gave me peace, and I returned to my studies and let my family get on with everything that was so much more exciting, so much more important than I was.

By the time I was fourteen, I was pinning all my hopes of finally being a visible, valued member of my family, on showing aptitude for one of the Skills at testing. Both of my parents were Weather-Singers and as such were in high demand from pretty much every person in the village at one time or another. Lance was on course to be the Master Herbalist of his village, Fratten was in as much demand from the farmers as were my parents, due to his ability to sing crops to give more than twice the yields they would have alone. And at just sixteen, Jules was coming to the end of his metal-singing apprenticeship. Happy-go-lucky as ever, he barely had to try to sing the most enormous pieces of metal into gates, ploughs, doors, whatever was required, in one go, without needing to create them in smaller parts and then sing them together as did many Metal-Singers. I had to show aptitude for one of the Skills, I just had to.

I didn't. Tester after Tester smiled sympathetically and bade me leave for the next one, assuring me that I would find the one I was meant to do, but if I didn't then that was fine too as the Trades were every bit as important as the Skills. Yeah, right – in any other family, maybe. In mine, there was no chance that being the only son to not stand out in one of the Skills would help my cause to finally be seen as worthy of notice. By the time I reached the final Tester, I was chewing down on my bottom lip to stop it trembling. I knew I would fail the test for bone-singing even before I proved it to myself.

My feet dragged as I wandered home. The birds sang at the tops of their voices, welcoming in the spring as surely as the brightly-coloured flowers waving in the gardens I passed, but neither did anything to lift my spirits. I kept tripping on the cobbles even though they had been expertly laid and worn almost flat over the years since Freshtown came into existence. It seemed that my toes found every single undulation in the street, however tiny. I grimaced. Finally, I had found something I was good at, and it was something as pathetic, as insignificant as being sensitive to unevenness. Like that was of any good to anyone. At least my failure at testing would, like everything else, go unnoticed when I got home.

I opened the gate to the front pathway of my family home and wandered up to the front door. It was flung open by none other than Lance.

'What are you doing here?' I said.

'That's a charming way to greet your long-lost brother, hello to you too, Feryl. I'm here, as is Rayette, to announce that we are having a baby. Isn't that great?'

'Marvellous,' I said dully. 'Congratulations, I bet Mum's stoked.'

'She is, I mean obviously, with her first grandchild being on the way. Come in, come in, don't just stand out there, come and join in the celebrations.'

I was ushered in and then herded past the stairs and living room to the kitchen, from where I could hear talking and laughter.

'Go on in, go and see Rayette,' Lance said.

I couldn't think of anything I'd rather do less, but I didn't have the strength to argue. I entered the kitchen to see Rayette sitting at the head of the kitchen table, her chair pulled well away from the table so that everyone could see her slightly protruding belly. She was surrounded by both my and her parents while Fratten and Jules hung back looking bored.

'Okay, I've seen her,' I said to Lance. 'I'm going upstairs, I don't feel well.'

'You always look a bit sickly, how is today any worse?' Lance said. 'Just tell Rayette how happy you are for us both first, this is a very important day for our two families.'

'Everything is very important when it's to do with you, isn't it? And nothing is important when it's to do with me. Get over yourself, Lance, and get out of my way, I'm going upstairs.'

My mother saw me and came hurrying over. She kissed me on the forehead and said, 'Are you okay, dear? You look a bit pale.'

I wanted to tell her. I wanted to tell her that I had tried as hard as I could to be as talented and as important to her as all of my brothers, but that I had failed. I wanted her to hug me, to tell me that it didn't matter, that whatever I did, whatever I said, whoever I was, I was a valued member of the family, but I knew she wouldn't. She only ever listened to whomever shouted loudest, whomever was funniest or most interesting, and that was never going to be me, a fact that I had proven to myself for the final time during testing that day.

'I'm okay, Mum. I had my testing today…'

A loud wailing made her look from me to an almost four-year-old Pelan, whom Fratten had just thrown to be caught by Jules. Jules had caught him awkwardly and was attempting to put him down as my mother rushed over to see if he had suffered any damage. By the time he was on his feet and laughing along with my two older brothers, she had forgotten all about me, and rushed to the oven to check on whatever celebratory feast she was preparing. Lance rushed to Rayette's side to help her as she tried – with far too much fuss, I thought – to get to her feet. I stood in the doorway while my family went about their business, leaving me feeling as invisible as ever. I turned to go.

'Feryl, hold on there, son,' my father called out.

My heart leapt at the thought that he might have remembered it was my testing today, then sank at the thought of having to tell him how it went.

He came and stood before me, holding a glass of ale. 'You're still a little young, but under the happy circumstances, you can have a sip of my ale.' He held the glass out to me. 'How did testing go, by the way?'

'By the way?' I said weakly. I looked around at everyone chattering happily as pain prodded at me, deep down in my belly. 'By the way?' I said more strongly. 'That's all I am to you, isn't it, a "by the way".'

My father frowned. 'I'm not following you.'

'You never do. You never have. Go back to the party and leave me alone, Dad.' I turned to go, but my father caught hold of my arm and spun me around.

'How dare you turn your back on me. Explain yourself, young man.'

'I have decided to train in one of the Trades, as a Farmer. That way, I can be outside with animals – who, by the way, are the only ones who actually notice I exist – and away from all of you. I don't feel well and I'm going upstairs.'

'But what about the Skills? Which ones did you show aptitude for?'

'None of them. None at all. There you go, Dad, I've given you all yet another reason to look down on me, ignore me and make me the butt of family jokes. Enjoy yourselves, on me.' I wrenched my arm away from him and stomped out into the hallway and then up the stairs.

It wasn't until I was falling asleep that night that my mother whispered, 'Feryl?' from the doorway of my bedroom. I barely heard it over Jules's snoring but when she said, 'Feryl, are you awake, love?' I knew I hadn't imagined it. She had come to see me as she often did when Pelan was finally asleep and she had time to herself. Sometimes, I turned to face her, letting her know I was awake, but other times, like now, I pretended to be asleep.

The floorboards creaked as she tiptoed over and knelt by my bed. She stroked my forehead and whispered, 'I'm proud of you, my son. Farming is an admirable Trade and I know you'll excel at it.' She sighed and her touch disappeared. 'It's hard for you, I know that. You're sensitive in a way your brothers aren't, and you get swallowed up by their exuberance. But don't ever change, Feryl, your father and I love you the way you are.'

I sat up and turned to face her. 'No you don't,' I said loudly. 'If you did, you'd make time for me, you'd be interested in me even when the others are around, but here you are again, by my bed last thing at night because finally, everyone else has let you be.'

My mother sighed. 'Do you ever wonder why you're as you are? You get your sensitivity from me, love. I get overwhelmed too. Some days, I spend my time rushing from one thing to the next, trying to please everyone, and before I know it, it's time for bed and I realise that the only one I don't know about is you. You're a good lad, you take care of the goats and of yourself with no bother, and I'm sorry that because of it, you slip below my attention. It doesn't mean I don't notice what you do or that I'm not interested. It doesn't mean I'm not proud of you.'

'YOU'RE ASHAMED OF ME, YOU AND DAD, I KNOW YOU ARE, HOW CAN YOU NOT BE WHEN I'M ASHAMED OF MYSELF?' I shouted and Jules sat bolt upright in bed. 'It's too late, Mum. It's too late to say all this to me now. I've failed at everything except looking after animals, and I've failed on my own because none of you could spare any time to tell me where I was going wrong, and help me. Just leave me alone.' I lay back down and turned away from her.

'Feryl, please, let me…'

'GO AWAY. ALL OF YOU, JUST LEAVE ME ALONE.'

My family had never been so quiet as over the weeks that followed. They were their normal selves when I wasn't in the room, but as soon as I entered – which was as infrequently as possible and only for mealtimes in the kitchen – they went quiet. My parents would ask me how I was getting on at school as they never had before, and when I answered in monosyllables, they let me be. I caught them glaring at Fratten and Jules whenever they began to talk in my presence, so mercifully I was spared both their opinions on my chosen Trade, as well as their teasing.

I gave up on school and did as little as possible to get by without getting into trouble. The other kids warmed to me once they saw I no longer had any interest in trying to impress the teachers. They even invited me to join in their ball games at break times, but I had no interest in anything other than spending time with our goats and wandering the countryside, watching and listening to the birds and staying still for hours in various hiding places I found, where rabbits, foxes, hares, badgers, deer and all manner of other wild animals were sure to pass by. Only when I was with animals did I feel that my life was worth living.

When I turned fifteen and my farming apprenticeship began, I threw myself into it. I preferred working with animals to crops, but regardless of the tasks I was given, I worked as hard as I possibly could, beginning my days before my Masters, Harris and Nia, and finishing after them.

I was second best as far as they were concerned and I knew it, since had their grownup children not shown aptitude for earth-singing and glass-singing, they would likely have apprenticed to their parents. But they had left years ago and I filled a spot for Nia and Harris every bit as much as they filled a spot for me. They were interested in me and what I had to say in a way my own parents had never had the time to be. They fed me well, offered me a bed when I was due to start even earlier than normal or finish even later, and treated me as their own. When, a year into my apprenticeship, they asked if I would like to move in with them for our mutual convenience, I leapt at the idea.

I lived with them for seven years. In that time, I reconciled myself with the idea that I would always be an outsider looking in where my family members were concerned. I was almost happy.

Then I was tugged.

I had never even considered the possibility that I might be chosen as a Bond-Partner by a horse. The Horse-Bonded were respected, looked up to and listened to – everything that I had always strived to be but had never achieved with my own family, let alone others. So, when I was helping a cow to calf and I felt a pulling sensation in my mind, I thought it was the cow broadcasting her struggles even more loudly than she was managing with her voice.

'We're nearly there, Mildred, come on, your baby is nearly with us,' I told the labouring cow. 'I've got her feet, give one last push and I'll take one more pull, and she'll be born. She'll be every bit as beautiful as you are, you wait and see.'

'You've not been wrong yet, so if you say it's a girl, it's a girl,' Harris said from behind me. I had a knack for dealing with difficult births, so he had learnt to leave me to it and watch from a short distance away. 'Come on, Mildred, one last shove, help our Feryl out, there's a girl.'

All of a sudden, the calf began to follow my pull. I leant back away from Mildred and the calf came with me. 'Clever girl, well done,' I told Mildred, opening the birthing sack and exposing her calf.

I stepped away to let the experienced mother nurture her baby, expecting to feel the pressure on my mind ease now that I had done that which she had needed me to do. But it didn't. If anything, it increased. I bent and washed my hands in a bucket of hot, soapy water that Harris had brought out for me, then accepted the glass of cold ale he held out to me. I chinked it to his glass in celebration of the new life I had helped to bring into the world, then held it out towards Mildred and her baby. 'To years of getting to know you, little one,' I said to the little calf, who was now being licked all over by her mother.

'What will you call her?' Harris asked me.

I shook my head and blinked. 'Um, I don't know. Sorry, I feel a little peculiar.'

'It's hot and you've been labouring nearly as hard as Mildred. Have a seat, Feryl.' Harris beckoned to a straw bale over at the edge of the barn. I nodded and stepped towards it – but found myself unable to step any closer.

I frowned. 'I can't seem to move. My feet won't move.'

'What is it, heatstroke? Sit down where you are, I'll get the bale for you to lean back against.'

I took a gulp of ale. 'I can't sit down, either, I need to start walking.' I pointed out of the barn and across the fields. 'That way.'

'You're not making any sense, lad. It's definitely heatstroke. Keep drinking, then I'll help you inside.'

'Harris, it isn't heatstroke. It's... I don't know, I feel as if something's pulling at me, something that won't wait. I need to go... there.' I was still pointing.

'You've always been intuitive when there are animals in trouble, but we don't have any over that way, you know we don't. I really think you need to drink more, have a lie-down and then if you're not feeling better in an hour or so, I'll call for the Herbalist.'

'My body's fine. It's my head. My mind...' My hand began to shake as realisation dawned as to what was happening to me. I turned to Harris in shock. 'I'm being tugged. By a horse. I need to go to my horse.'

Harris's mouth dropped open. 'Are you sure?'

I nodded. 'I've never been surer of anything. I'm being tugged, Harris, I've been chosen by a horse. Me! Chosen by a horse, can you believe it?'

Harris began to nod, a smile stealing over his face. 'I can believe it, lad. Aye, I can well believe it. I'll be sorrier to lose you than I can say, but I'm happy for you. Come on, we'd better go and tell Nia, then I'll go and let your family know while you pack. They're going to want to organise your Quest Ceremony.'

'No.'

'No?'

'No. Would you and Nia organise it for me, please? From here? I'll get all my own stuff, I'm not asking you to contribute anything to my quest as families normally do, but I'd like to leave from here, if that's okay?'

Harris frowned. 'I know you weren't happy at home, Feryl, but your parents are good people. They'll be proud of you and they'll want to provide everything you'll need on your quest to find your horse. They'll want to give you a good send off, I know they will.'

'In between laughing at Jules's jokes, crooning over Fratten's baby and bragging that Lance has just been made Master Herbalist over at Crowsfoot? No thanks. If they want to wish me well on my quest, they can come here and get in line with everyone else.'

'Oh, come on now, Feryl, they're busy people and they have busy lives, but they love you. You've never wanted for anything…'

'I have, actually,' I murmured, and hated that my voice shook. 'I just wanted to be heard, listened to, but there was always someone else more deserving of their time and attention, and it won't be any different now. I'm done waiting for them to notice I exist. I'm going to go and find my horse, and then everyone will know I exist, because I'll be one of the Horse-Bonded.'

Harris sighed and shook his head. 'That you will, lad, that you will. We'll give you your Quest Ceremony if that's what you really want, but I'm not comfortable with it.'

I held out my hand. 'Thank you, Harris, for this and for everything else. I'm sorry to be leaving you and Nia, you've been so good to me and I'll miss you both.'

Harris grinned and shook my hand. 'We'll miss you too, but who are we to argue with a horse? If there's one waiting for you, we'd better get you on your way as soon as possible.'

Nia and Harris insisted that if I wasn't going to allow my family to provide all of the food, and cooking and hunting equipment that I would need on my quest, then they wanted to. Once we'd enjoyed a celebratory lunch, Harris set off for the village with his handbarrow to collect everything, refusing point blank to allow me to go with him to drag it all back.

Nia fussed over me, taking all of my clothes except those I was actually wearing, and washing, drying and pressing them before she would allow me to pack them.

When Harris returned some hours later, he told me that he had passed the word around that my Quest Ceremony was to be two hours after dawn the following morning. He looked at me pointedly as he told me of my parents' joy, pride and then hurt at the news that I had been tugged but would be leaving from Harris and Nia's farm. He asked me again to allow them to give me my Quest Ceremony, but I refused. Finally, my family would be forced to notice me, and they would do it on my terms.

By the time I retired to bed that night, I found that the pull on my mind had become part of me; my intention to follow it was every bit as strong as its source's intention to draw me to itself. I smiled as I lay with my fingers interlinked behind my head. Tomorrow, I would go to find my horse. My Bond-Partner. Someone who thought I was worth something. Finally, I would have respect, purpose, and a horse with whom to share all of that.

I couldn't sleep to begin with, I was so excited. How long would it take me to find my horse? What would they look like? What would they teach me? We would have to go to The Gathering once we had found each other and bonded. My heart leapt. Finally, I would be somewhere I belonged. Then a stab of fear pierced my heart. What if, a tiny voice squeaked in my head, what if I were as insignificant there, as unnoticed, as I had been all of my life so far? What if being Horse-Bonded made no difference to how people saw me, how they related to me?

I tensed my stomach. I would make sure that didn't happen. I wouldn't tolerate it. Not again. I would be somebody, starting with my Quest Ceremony tomorrow. When I finally drifted off to sleep, I had a smile on my face.

'Feryl!' Nia's voice rang around in my ears. There was thumping on my bedroom door. 'This is your last warning before I come in and drag you out of bed. How can you still be asleep? Your Quest Ceremony is in an hour.'

My eyes flicked open. Sunlight was pouring in through the gap in my bedroom curtains. I felt the same pull on my mind as had been there when I went to sleep, and sat up, my heart thumping wildly. My horse. I was going off to find my horse today, how could I have overslept? I leapt out of bed, raced to the door and flung it open.

Nia put a hand over her eyes. 'You're a handsome young man, Feryl, there's no denying it, but that doesn't mean I need to see so much of you. At my age, you'll give me heart failure.'

I pushed the door almost closed and peered around it, grinning. 'Sorry, you washed my pyjamas and made me pack them straight away, remember?'

She returned my grin. 'Yes, well, anyway, come on down for breakfast, I've cooked you a hearty one.' Her voice trembled as she spoke.

I reached around the door and put a hand on her arm. 'Thanks, Nia. For everything.'

'Oh, get away with you,' she said. 'Get some clothes on and get yourself downstairs before your breakfast gets cold.'

I shut the door and bounded to where I had laid out the clothes I would wear – black, snugly-fitting trousers, a blue shirt that I had been told made my eyes look even bluer than they were naturally, black boots and cloak – and after donning them, checked my appearance in the long mirror attached to one of the grey stone walls of my bedroom. I ran my fingers through my black hair and nodded to myself. Dashing, that was how Nia had once described me when she'd had too much to drink. I only hoped I still looked so by the time I arrived at The Gathering.

I heaved my back-sack onto my shoulder and took the stairs two at a time. I dumped my stuff by the front door and followed the smell of bacon to the kitchen, where Nia had outdone herself.

'How many people are coming to eat all of this?' I said gazing around at the plates of fried eggs, tomatoes, bacon, sausages, mushrooms, onions and bread.

'Just the three of us, lad,' Harris said and his stomach rumbled loudly. 'Dig in, or she'll make me eat it for lunch and dinner as well today, and all of the days that follow, until it's gone.

'I won't have him going off on an empty stomach,' Nia said, gesturing for me to sit down.

'You don't want him going off at all. Is that what this is about?' Harris retorted. 'Are you hoping to weigh him down so heavily that he won't be able to move?'

Nia shook her head. 'I'll package up what we don't eat for him to take with him. Goodness knows how long it will take him to find his horse…'

'Or the terrain he'll have to negotiate, or the weather he'll encounter, or anything else about his quest. I know, love, you've churned it over a hundred times since dawn broke. He's tough is our Feryl. Whatever happens, he'll be fine, won't you, lad?'

I managed to smile at them both as I sat down, feeling anything but tough. 'I will. But thanks for worrying about me, Nia. And for all this.' I swept my hand over the table. 'We'd best get started, hadn't we?'

Harris chuckled. 'That's the most sensible thing anyone has said yet today.'

Nia swatted at him and we all laughed.

It was time. I was comfortably, but not overly, full. My back-sack was almost full of clothes and the food Nia insisted I took with me. She and Harris were waiting for me outside the front door and I could hear a cacophony of voices as the villagers of Freshtown took their places in two lines tailing away from the front door, forming a human corridor for me down which I would walk. This was my moment. Everyone was out there for me. I smiled but felt a little nervous. I just wasn't used to it, that was all, I told myself. Once I was out there, I would be fine.

I flung my cloak around my shoulders, not because I needed it – the early autumn sun was still warm – but because it was as black as my hair, trousers and boots, and would make the blue of my shirt and eyes stand out even more. I shouldered my back-sack and opened the front door.

I was almost blasted backward by the cheering that erupted. I nearly shut the door again, but then I realised that I loved it. They were cheering for me! A smile stole over my face. I was someone.

'Feryl, Nia and I would like to present you with everything you will need for your quest,' Harris said formally and gestured to the table just off to one side, on which was an array of hunting and cooking equipment, a blanket, plate, mug and cutlery. He and Nia packed what they could into the top of my already heaving back-sack and then hung everything else on the outside of it, adhering strictly to tradition as they did so by announcing to all what each item was and how it would benefit me on my quest. When they had finished, Harris helped me to get both of my arms through the straps, and heaved it onto my back.

'There you go,' he whispered. 'Come back and see us

sometime, won't you?' I nodded as I shook his hand with both of my own. 'And, lad?' I looked down into his tear-filled eyes. 'Go easy on your parents, okay?'

I drew him into a hug. 'Thanks, Harris.'

Nia couldn't speak as she stood on her tiptoes to hug me. She pulled away from me and, swallowing hard, gave me a gentle push towards where the villagers stood waiting for me. My parents stood first in line, opposite one another.

'We're proud of you, son,' my father said, holding his hand out to me.

'Better late than never, I suppose,' I said coldly. I shook his hand briefly and then looked at my mother. 'Bye, Mum.'

'Oh, Feryl, don't go, not like this,' she whispered.

'Not like what? With everyone here to cheer and congratulate me as the success I am? Would you have even noticed I was leaving without the whole village to bring it to your attention?'

'Of course we would, we're so proud of you,' my mother said, her voice shaking. She swallowed. 'Our Feryl, Horse-Bonded, it's all Pelan can talk about.' She gestured to where my thirteen-year-old brother stood hopping up and down.

'Ah, so it took Pelan to be excited about it before the news sank in, did it?'

'Feryl, stop it. Please?' my mother said.

My father stepped in front of me. 'Why won't you believe that we're proud of you, that we're happy for you? And why are you making us stand on Harris and Nia's doorstep instead of allowing us to give you your Quest Ceremony?'

'If you truly didn't know the answer to that, you'd have been here last night to ask me. You know exactly why,' I hissed.

A hand grasped my shoulder from behind. 'Lad, this isn't the time,' Harris whispered. 'Hug your parents goodbye now, or you'll regret it. Then you can carry on with your Quest Ceremony and be on your way.'

My Quest Ceremony. Mine. I nodded. He was right, I wouldn't let my parents ruin this for me. I leant towards my mother, put an arm around her and hugged her briefly.

She clung to me and whispered, 'I love you, Feryl. Be happy. Okay?'

A lump rose in my throat but I swallowed it down. 'Goodbye.' She let me go and stood, her eyes downcast, her shoulders shaking. I almost went to hug her properly, but stopped myself. How often had I felt like she did, and she had never even noticed. Let her know how it felt. I nodded to my father, then stepped away from them both and hugged Pelan as he threw himself at me.

'Stand still while I hang these on you,' he said, holding out a hand that was full of tiny metal horseshoes. 'They're for luck on your quest.'

I grinned. 'I know what they're for, Pel. That's quite a handful you have there, I don't think I can keep all of these people waiting while you hang them all on my cloak.'

'We'll help.' Jules stepped forward beside Pelan. He turned and said, 'Come on, Frat, you too, Lance.'

My brothers took great care to hang all of the good luck charms on my cloak and the blanket tied to my back-sack. None of us spoke but every now and then, one of them would look up at me and smile or nod. My heart softened and then hardened each time. When my parents took the last few horseshoes from Pelan and hung them on the front of my shirt, I nearly broke. No. I wouldn't let them in. They didn't deserve it.

I hugged Pelan and nodded to each of my family one last time, then said, 'Goodbye.'

I took a step further down the human corridor and was immediately besieged with hugs and hands to shake as more horseshoes of metal, fabric, a few of glass and some of dried grass twisted around wire, were hung from my clothes, hair and back-sack. I drank it all in. Wherever I looked, people were smiling at me and calling out their greetings and wishes of good luck.

There was humming from the Healers who began to tail me as I slowly made my way past all of my well-wishers; two Tissue-Singers sang all of the strains and excess tension out of my muscles that I had accrued from my work on the farm, and a Bone-Singer strengthened the bone I had broken in my foot the year before.

I reached the end of the corridor all too soon. I was elated by all of the attention that had been lavished on me, and wanted to do it all again. Maybe I would have found a way to string out my ceremony for longer, had it not been for the pulling on my mind increasing sharply. My horse. I needed to go and find him.

I turned back to where the human corridor had collapsed in on itself and was now a massive crowd of people. I smiled and waved to them all, then stood on tiptoe to wave to where Nia and Harris still stood on their doorstep, and blew a kiss to Nia which she returned. I turned and walked across the fields towards my horse. The cheering followed me, and every now and then, I turned and waved again, torn between leaving the adoration of the villagers and hurrying to find the cause of all of the celebration.

Full of it all as I was, I spared my family no further thought until I settled down for the night. Once my fire was lit and a pot of water set above it to heat so that I could make myself some tea, I sat back and began to munch on a tomato, mushroom and onion sandwich – my favourite, as Nia well knew. Her face entered my mind and my heart lurched. I hoped that she and Harris would find a new Apprentice very soon, one who would love them, their animals and their farm as I did. I pictured her and Harris waving to me as I walked away from them, then I remembered that my parents and brothers had been huddled together, apart from the rest of the village.

Lance had made the effort to come at short notice from Crowsfoot to be there, I realised. I remembered all of my brothers hanging the charms on me that I now picked off, one by one, as I munched on my sandwich, laying each one carefully on the wrapper that had enclosed my meal. They hadn't known how to talk to me any more than I had known how to talk to them. Any more than I had known how to talk to my parents without my anger spilling out. I felt that anger again, and quickly swallowed. I didn't want to feel that, I wouldn't let them ruin this for me. I switched to remembering the adulation of the rest of the villagers, and smiled as I continued to pick charms off my clothing and possessions.

I slept well and was awake with the dawn. I washed in a nearby stream, brushed my clothing down and combed my hair. When I was satisfied that I looked every bit as elegant and composed as the Horse-Bonded I had seen visiting our village with their Bond-Partners, I heaved my gear onto my back and continued on my way, following the pull on my mind that I found every bit as comforting as it was fast becoming familiar.

By the end of the first week of walking, I was feeling a little disgruntled. Try as I might to keep myself clean and presentable, I was beginning to look dirty and dishevelled. The weather was becoming more unsettled and as a result, my trousers and boots were flecked with mud, and my cloak and blanket were damp and grubby.

When the sun finally came out, I wanted to spend a morning washing my clothes, but the pulling on my mind made it impossible to stay in one place once I was rested; it would steadily increase to uncomfortable levels until I got myself moving again.

By the end of the second week, I was covering more ground

due to carrying two weeks' worth less of food, but I was filthy and grumpy. No matter how much I washed my hair, more dirt seemed to come out, probably because the water itself was never particularly clean – a fact that made me shudder as I splashed it on my skin. However much I washed, I only seemed to attract more dirt, and I avoided looking at my appearance in the puddles I was increasingly stepping around or over on my continuing quest.

I consoled myself with the fact that I knew, without knowing exactly how, that I was close to my horse now, even as I worried that I would be in an even worse state by the time we made it to The Gathering. I wondered if maybe we could stop off at a village on the way there, so that I could have a bath and have someone wash my clothes in exchange for the honour of hosting one of the Horse-Bonded.

No. We will not. The thought appeared in my head without me thinking it. I tripped on a bramble and nearly fell headlong. I regained my balance and looked up to see a tall, gleaming black horse rounding some trees in front of me. I gasped. He was absolutely stunning. It wasn't a matter of opinion; I had heard it said often that beauty was in the eye of the beholder, but as I stood there, I doubted anyone could deny that the stallion in front of me was anything other than breathtakingly, spectacularly beautiful.

What a pair we were, I thought to myself. My hair matched his exactly, and his eyes were as dark as mine were blue. The Horse-Bonded always caused a stir when they rode into villages astride their Bond-Partners, but this horse and I would go down in the Histories.

The stallion came to a halt in front of me. He tossed his head and snorted, then stamped his foot. He was irritated. By what? By me. I knew it as surely as I knew my own name. It was probably because I smelt – the light knew, I was irritated at that myself.

Your scent is irrelevant. It is your view of yourself with which you should be concerned. His thought was as soft as his reprimand felt harsh, leaving me unsure of myself.

I should change my view of myself? I found myself thinking back to him, although it felt as if I had said it out loud as I sensed him register it in the same way that I knew when someone had heard me speak out loud.

It would serve you to relinquish it altogether. This is a subject we will revisit often.

I was stunned. I hadn't spared much thought for what it would be like to meet my horse for the first time, so carried away had I been with the life we would live together, but had I done, it wouldn't have been like this.

'You, um, you don't waste any time, do you?' I said out loud. 'I don't even know your name and you're straight in there, telling me how it is. Flaming lanterns, you started before I'd even seen you.' It felt weird, using my voice to communicate with him, and I decided to not do it again.

I have been within sight for some time. Had you been less concerned with your appearance you would have noticed me far sooner.

I felt as if he had reached inside me and poked me firmly in a very tender place. *You felt unnoticed?* I asked him.

I was unnoticed. The fact is unequivocal. It is of no matter other than to demonstrate a point.

Which is? Immediately, I wondered why I was asking when he had already lost me.

That is for you to discover. Do not concern yourself. Anything pertinent to your learning will present itself as necessary.

Er, it will?

Consider your life so far and you will begin to understand.

I highly doubted it. I stood in front of him, taking in his beauty and his majesty, and trying to reconcile it with everything he had told me. I could make neither head nor tail of any of it, and began to wonder what I had let myself in for.

Chose.

I looked up at him as he peered down at me. *Sorry?*

You have not experienced and will not experience anything that you didn't choose.

WHAT? You're telling me I chose to grow up in a family who counted me an irrelevance?

You may explore the events in your life with which you are dissatisfied and relate them to the lesson that will be a constant during our time together when there are fewer other matters to which you must attend.

I stood back from him and put my hands on my hips. *You're bored. I can feel it. You were interested in me, and now you're bored. My life, my sadness, my loneliness is boring to you?*

He turned around and began to walk away. *Come. We have much to do.*

Anger bubbled up inside me. I tried to swallow it down, but couldn't. It spilled out of me and was fast replaced by more. *DON'T WALK AWAY FROM ME. LOOK AT ME!* I hurled my thought at him with as much force as I could muster.

You observe yourself sufficiently for us both. You have much to offer your fellow humans but you will achieve nothing remaining where you are. Come.

I found myself walking after him, my anger subsiding as I did so. How was he doing that to me? How was he making me feel invisible like everyone else did, and yet making me feel okay about it, and that whether or not he saw me was irrelevant as long as I were with him?

Do not assign responsibility to me for how you are feeling. Your emotions and feelings are entirely yours to experience as you will. You sense the bond forming between us and you are choosing to feel relief at no longer being alone over irritation that I will not indulge you in your insecurity. It is a choice I would encourage you to make often as we tread the path before us.

There's a bond forming between us? There is. I feel it, I feel our bond!

A wise choice.

I ran to catch up with him and slowed to walk at his shoulder. *What do I call you? All of the horses who came to our village with their Bond-Partners had names.*

He stopped and slowly swung his head around until one of his eyes was directly in front of my face. *Name me for that which you see in me.*

I looked into his eye and nearly fell over, grabbing hold of the long, wavy black mane that hung in front of me, to steady myself. I saw him, and not just by gazing into his eye, but by seeing right into him from somewhere deep within myself. He welcomed my mind into his with an openness I almost found too much to bear. I was swept along with him, away from the past and everything I had ever known, into a way of being that was unfamiliar to me.

Everything was possible without limit or restriction. Change swirled around me so ferociously, so tangibly that I felt I could almost reach out and grab hold of it.

You're open. You're generous with yourself. You are change. Liberal. That's your name, I thought to him, without even knowing I was doing it. He looked away and the spell broke. I gasped and let go of his mane, able to stand on my feet by myself once more. I began to feel lost without the all-encompassing sense of him I had just experienced, but then realised I could still feel it. It was like being able to smell a scent present in the minutest quantities, having first been overwhelmed by it.

Focus on our bond whenever you feel drawn to introspection with regard to the past, I was advised. Liberal turned and looked at me for a moment and then walked onward. I hurried to catch up with him and walked at his shoulder, feeling that there was nowhere I would rather be.

Having taken two weeks to find Liberal, we were together for less than two days before arriving at The Gathering. Liberal had refused all of my requests to divert to a village on our way there so that I could make myself presentable and arrive at the home of the Horse-Bonded looking my best, assuring me each time that my current state of filth and neglect was good for me. I failed to see how, yet couldn't seem to bring myself to argue with him; his thoughts were always accompanied by such a strong sense of knowing, of rightness, they left me with a feeling that I was arguing a point I already knew to be false.

So it was that as we passed between paddock after paddock full of horses, livestock and crops, I did my best to hide behind Liberal so that as few people as possible could see me.

You worry about your outward appearance when it is that which shines from inside of you with which you would be wise to concern yourself.

No one can see that and no one is interested in it anyway. If I rely on people seeing me for who I really am, I'll fade into the background like always.

You would shine so brightly with the truth of yourself that your physical appearance would be irrelevant. You would be considered for who you are rather than whom you appear to be. Hide behind me if you wish but observe that it is I who holds their attention and not you. I rolled on wet ground earlier. My coat does not shine and dirt clings to my body yet they see beauty for I do not hide the truth of myself.

I peered over his back and saw that the people attending to sheep in one paddock, and those using their voices to encourage crops to grow larger in another, were all indeed pointing and smiling at Liberal. Some noticed me and waved before immediately reverting their attention to my horse. A familiar sense of outrage began to announce itself in the depths of my belly. Invisible again.

Do not confuse visibility with worth for they could not be less related, I was advised.

And yet you are enjoying all of the attention being lavished on you, I can feel it, I retorted.

Their pleasure at the sight of me enhances my joy of the physical experience yet I do not require it in order to feel worthy of being here.

I felt as if I'd had ice-cold water poured over me, and stopped in my tracks.

Liberal halted beside me and put his nose to my neck. *We have visited this subject before and we will do so again. Many times. You experience pain because you recognise the truth in my counsel even though you do not yet understand the mistake you have made over and over. You will. Ready For Change. I name you as you named me for we are the same. In time you will believe me.* He breathed warm air onto my neck and it was as if his warmth carried his thoughts throughout my body, depositing them in my stomach, in my heart, in my throat – all of the places in which I carried the hurt of feeling insignificant. His observation had caused me pain, which he now softened with the love he had for me. In an instant, he had changed from enjoying the admiration of those nearby to directing the whole of his attention towards and into me. It was all I needed.

Thank you, Liberal. I think. No, I know. I think.

Someone chuckled, making me jump. I looked up to see a

huge man with black hair and a black beard, looking down at me. 'Sorry, I was in a world of my own,' I said.

'You don't say.' The man laughed and his belly shook. He held out a hand to me. 'I'm Mason, and judgin' by the confused expression on your face, and the fact that your mouth keeps openin' and closin', you're newly bonded. A couple of days? A week at the outside?'

I grinned and shook his hand. 'I'm Feryl. You were right first time. I found Liberal two days ago.' I put a hand to my horse's shoulder.

Mason held the back of his hand out to my horse and Liberal sniffed it. 'You're somethin' of a stunner, aren't you m'lad,' Mason said and stroked his neck. He turned back to me. 'I'm the Saddler here, so you come along to my workshop, the two of you, once you've had a chance to settle in, and I'll get you sorted. Just ask anyone how to find me and they'll point you in the right direction.' He turned back the way he had come. 'I imagine you'll be wantin' to show Liberal to somewhere he can graze and rest, so that you can have a bath and some food yourself?' I opened my mouth to reply but didn't get the chance as he was already walking away, saying, 'Come along then, the paddock nearest the buildin's is the one Liberal will be wantin', so you can get to him quickly when you have a panic at bein' away from him. Shall I ask Dili to go in with him, or would he rather be alone for a bit?'

She is open to the notion as am I, Liberal informed me.

'He's open to the idea, and he tells me that, er, Dili is too,' I replied.

'She most certainly is, we'll collect her on the way,' Mason boomed over his shoulder, then called to a grey-haired lady grooming a chestnut mare in a nearby paddock. 'One more for dinner, Turi. Feryl and Liberal bonded two days ago, and here they are.'

Turi raised a hand and waved. 'Welcome, you both. I'm the head cook here. See you for lunch in about an hour, Feryl.'

I nodded and lifted a hand back to her as a gate clicked open on my other side. A huge grey mare stepped out onto the path behind Liberal and me.

'This is Diligence,' Mason told me. 'Liberal, you've struck gold havin' Dili as a companion.' He stroked his mare's nose affectionately and I could almost see the warmth that existed between them. 'Keep goin', Feryl, until you get to the last paddock on the left. That's where we'll leave these two, then I'll show you to the accommodation block where you can choose a room and get cleaned up before lunch.'

'I'm a mess. It'll take longer than an hour to sort myself, I don't even have any clean clothes,' I said. 'I'll have to miss lunch and try to make dinner.'

'You'll do no such thing. We all provide for one another here. You'll give me a set of your clothes while you have a bath, and I'll take them to the Tailors' workshop and get a set the same size. I'll show you where to put your clothes so that they're washed by whichever lucky souls are rostered for that particular chore this week, and then I'll take you down to lunch myself. That okay with you?'

'It is, thanks, that's kind of you, but don't you have saddles to make?'

He chuckled. 'None that won't wait. And besides, I'd hate to miss your first entrance into the dinin' hall, you'll create something of a stir, young man, with those dark looks of yours. Just to the left, there, that's it, in you go, Liberal. And you, Dili, I'll be down to check on you both later.' He shut the gate behind the two horses, who both immediately dropped their heads to graze.

Liberal's contentment oozed through our bond, but I still felt guilty at leaving him in an unfamiliar place, and strangely bereft at the thought of being apart from him.

Mason clapped me on the back with a meaty hand. 'I know how you'll be feelin', I almost wept when I left Dili here when we first arrived. It's a strange time, these first few weeks of bein' bonded, but you'll get used to it. He's with you in your mind all the time, Feryl, you never need feel at a loss.'

I tried to smile. 'Thanks.'

He grinned. 'Don't mention it. Come on then, let's find you a room and some clothes.'

Everyone saw me. Everyone welcomed me. And once they had seen Liberal grazing side by side with Dili, as tall, slender and majestic as she was wide, stocky and "homely" as my mother would have called her, they saw me even more. I had never been so happy.

Mason had Liberal's saddle finished within two days of our arrival, and when we appeared at one of the riding paddocks for our first lesson with Mistral, the Master of Riding, the fence was lined to full capacity with onlookers.

As soon as I sat on Liberal's back, I felt as if I belonged there. I followed Mistral's instructions as to how to arrange myself in the saddle, and how to use my body to follow Liberal's movement and then influence it with my suggestions regarding speed and direction, but I felt as if I had done it all before and he were merely reminding me rather than teaching me. I lost myself in my awareness of Liberal's body and mine moving together, responding to one another as if we had been born doing it.

Mistral finally said, 'Okay, impressive as you both are and as

much as we've all enjoyed watching you, I think that's enough for
your first lesson.'

Immediately, cheering erupted all around us. I came back to
myself and saw that people were now standing on the fence where
they had been sitting, and they were waving and shouting
congratulations to us both. I had no idea what we had done to
deserve their admiration, but I revelled in it.

Mistral came and stood by my knee, looking up at me. 'In
case you aren't aware of it, Feryl, the two of you make an
impressive picture. It's rare for a newly bonded rider to be as
good as you are after six months of practice, let alone on their
first attempt, you should be proud of yourself. I gather you're a
Farmer by Trade?'

I nodded. 'I'm rostered to start work in the fields the day after
tomorrow.'

Mistral grinned and patted my knee. 'Is that what you want, or
would you consider apprenticing to me? In case you haven't
noticed, I'm old – seventy-three, in fact – and my Bond-Partner
has been gone ten years or more. It's customary for the Master of
Riding to take on Apprentices when they're approaching the end
of their career, then when they're ready to retire, those in
residence here vote on which Apprentice they would like as the
new Master. I'm picky. Where most Masters would have five or
six Apprentices by now, I have one. I would like you to be my
second. You have a natural talent, Feryl, and from what I've seen
of you and Liberal today, you'll progress very quickly. By the time
I'm ready to retire, you and Walter will be on an even footing, and
the rest can make their choice from the two of you. What do you
say?'

I glanced around at those still waving and cheering, and
grinned. *Liberal, is that okay?*

It is as it needs to be.

I looked back down at Mistral. 'Thank you, I would love to be your Apprentice.'

I walked back with Liberal to his paddock, surrounded by a crowd of Horse-Bonded still congratulating me and wanting to know all about Liberal. I heard the word "potential" mentioned a lot as our admirers talked amongst themselves, but it wasn't until Liberal was back grazing in the paddock he shared with Dili, and the crowd had dispersed back to their tasks for the day, that I was enlightened as to what it was they had been discussing.

I was leaning on the top rail of the fence, wondering how, exactly, I had got lucky enough to not only be chosen by a horse, but to be chosen by one who stood out so obviously from the rest. Liberal flicked an ear towards me even though I hadn't spoken.

Luck is a human invention. You and I both chose physical vessels that are seen as attractive because they amplify the issues we decided to address.

We chose them? What do you mean? I asked him.

Your body merely houses your essence. The part that is everlasting. As does mine. Before we entered them we agreed to incarnate here and share our experience so that we may advance ourselves and those around us. Consider the name you chose for me.

Liberal.

Why did you choose it? my horse asked me.

I sensed that you seek change. That you're open to possibility.

You cannot recognise that with which you are not already familiar.

Meaning?

You saw in me that which you are ready to develop within yourself. That which you have the potential to be. Your peers understand this. Their excitement is for more than merely the physical spectacle we present.

I have the potential to be liberal? Open? To introduce new ways of doing things to the Horse-Bonded? But they already know everything. They're already looked up to, listened to and respected. They don't have anything to learn from me.

On the contrary. They have as much to learn from you as you do from them. In time there will come a bonded pair who will propel us all forward in ways you are not currently in a position to imagine. We will prepare the way for them and assist them when they arrive.

The excitement that had begun to build within me at the thought that not only was I Horse-Bonded and wherever I went, people would look up to me, but that the Horse-Bonded themselves would be doing that too, was dampened slightly by the thought that another bonded pair would someday come along and take that position away from me.

You will learn the most from the situation you will find the most difficult, Liberal advised me. *Try to remember that when the time comes.*

But until then, you and I are going to set the world on fire?

It is a necessary part of your pattern. Ready For Change. Remember how I have named you even when you do not wish to. It will help.

Yes, yes, never mind that. I always knew I could be someone if only people would pay attention to me, and now they are, thanks to you. I can never thank you enough.

Liberal had turned his attention back to grazing and no answer was forthcoming. There was a sense about him that everything that was happening was very normal and mundane, but I just couldn't bring myself to feel that way. I was bursting with excitement for the future, and full of pride in both Liberal and myself.

We would make our mark on the world together, and we

would go down in the Histories as the bonded pair that changed
the world.

I was used to hard work. I had driven myself hard at school in my
quest for recognition from my teacher and family, and I had put
everything of myself into my farming apprenticeship in my quest
to cover up the pain of failure. Now that I was working towards
ever increasing acclaim and adulation, I worked even harder at my
apprenticeship with Mistral, and I loved every minute of it.

As I was constantly told, I was a natural rider. The applause
and appreciation of our constant spectators carried me to ever
greater heights whenever I was upon Liberal's back, and he came
with me, as willing as he was physically able and impressive.
When I wasn't riding him, I was working on my balance and
fitness away from him, so that whatever I asked my body to do, it
was in a position to respond. I wasn't just a good rider, I was a
brilliant one, and Liberal was every bit as remarkable.

I would be the next Master of Riding, I was sure of it – except
for when I happened to pass by the riding paddocks when Walter,
Mistral's other Apprentice, was there riding his Bond-Partner,
Adroit. I told myself that the applause he received from those
watching was muted in comparison to that which I received when
I rode, and that there were fewer onlookers than Liberal and I
drew. I looked for flaws in Walter's riding technique, in his
strength, balance and fitness, whilst trying not to notice how he
and Adroit seemed to flow around the paddock rather than move
individual parts of themselves.

I flinched whenever I heard anyone mention Adroit's name,
and told myself over and over that while it meant Walter had the
potential to be skilful, adept – a master, even – that didn't mean he

was a better choice for Master of Riding than I was. After all, I had the potential to teach all of the Horse-Bonded that which they couldn't learn without me. I had the potential to take them along with me in my slipstream. There was nothing about Walter and Adroit that suggested they could do that.

Mistral steadily became more frail. He began to need a stool upon which to sit when teaching Walter and me – the only two he would now teach, having divided all of his other students between us as his Apprentices – and as the months went by, occasionally, he didn't turn up to our scheduled sessions. I didn't mind; it meant that everyone watching could see that what Liberal and I were achieving, we were achieving alone.

When, a year into my apprenticeship, Walter received word that his mother was ill, and left The Gathering with Adroit at a gallop, I was delighted, even though it meant double the workload for me; hard work had never been a problem for me and when its reward was the constant euphoria of being appreciated and admired, I welcomed it.

Mistral died two weeks after Walter left. A myriad of emotions battled one another within me. I was devastated that the dear old man who had raised me above everyone else and taught me so much, was no longer with us; I would miss his patience, his knowledge, his wisdom and his kindness. I also worried that something may come up in my riding that without him, I would struggle to overcome, but dismissed that thought almost as soon as it arose; Liberal and I could overcome anything.

Excitement bubbled within me at the thought that The Gathering needed a new Master of Riding, and not only was I the obvious choice, I was the only one there – but it warred with anxiety that I had only been an Apprentice for a year, whereas Walter had been Mistral's Apprentice for five, and maybe, just maybe, he was more skilful.

I was aware of eyes on me wherever I went as everyone looked towards me as the only one of the Mistral-Walter-Feryl triad present, for a clue as to what should happen next. I felt bolstered by their attention and when every suggestion I made regarding Mistral's funeral was readily and unanimously accepted, I felt my position strengthening.

I led the procession of Horse-Bonded – six of whom carried Mistral's body immediately behind me – into the hills where I had been told his Bond-Partner had been buried, and I was the first to roll up my sleeves and start digging down into Prudence's grave. When we had buried Mistral with his horse and replaced the soil on top of them both, I spoke to all gathered about Mistral's talents, and looked up to the sky as I thanked him for everything he had done for us all.

It was I who shouted above all the chatter in the dining room that evening until everyone was quiet, and proposed a toast to the Master of Riding who had taught me right up until his death. I spoke in detail of every little nuance I had learnt from him – knowing very well that much of what I related went over the heads of most there, so far past their and their horses' abilities had Liberal and I progressed – and thanked Mistral for preparing me so well to take up his mantle.

When I described how I felt when I rode my horse, the emotion I expressed in my voice, in my face, in my whole body was utterly genuine. I revelled in the tears that glistened in many of the eyes turned up towards me. I took all who were there along with me as I told them how passionate I was about helping them to reach with their horses the level I had with Liberal – even though secretly, I thought that for most of them it was an impossibility. I had them in the palm of my hand.

A spike of fear lanced in my stomach at the thought that Walter could come back at any moment and take them away from me – that if it came to a vote for the Master of Riding, they might choose him over me and I would become just one Horse-Bonded amongst all the rest. It was now or never.

I smiled with a confidence I forced myself to feel as I said, 'Just as the length of Mistral's tenure as Master of Riding was unprecedented, so is his passing whilst there is only one Apprentice available to fill his shoes. But I am honoured to take up the position he has left vacant, and I promise to support you and your horses as completely, as diligently as he did. Thank you very much.'

I held my breath as I waited to see if anyone would point out that we ought to wait until Walter returned from visiting his family, and then hold a vote as was normal. But then the clapping started. Chairs were pushed back and people began to stand as they clapped, and soon there was a cacophony of voices shouting approval and congratulations. I nodded and smiled as if their reaction had never been in doubt. I thought I sensed Liberal observing the proceedings, but he made no comment and eventually returned his attention to grazing, so I threw myself into accepting the handshakes and congratulations of those crowding around me.

By the time Walter arrived back at The Gathering five weeks later, I had solidified my position. I welcomed him back, asked after his mother and then before he could bring up the subject of my having taken Mistral's position as my own, I reassured him that I would always be available to him if he needed any help advancing his riding with Adoit, thanked him for giving up his time to take on half of Mistral's students before he left, and assured him that now that all students were under my supervision, he was free to return to contributing to The Gathering with his bone-singing ability, in place of teaching.

I thought for a moment that Walter would argue. He stared into my eyes, a look of disbelief on his face, which changed to thoughtfulness and then sympathy. Then he walked away from me without comment, and avoided speaking to me again.

A small part of me felt ashamed of myself, but by far the larger part of me was so relieved to be maintaining my position and the attention, recognition and adulation it afforded me, I allowed it to continue taking precedence.

The only one who never congratulated me, never gave me any sense that he was proud of me or thought of me in any exalted way, was Liberal, and it constantly surprised me that I was okay with that. All I ever sensed from him was his enjoyment of my company, his pleasure at the level of harmony and the increasingly difficult manoeuvres our bodies were achieving together, and his contentment at his living conditions and daily routines.

Six years passed, during which, occasionally, I taught a bonded pair who challenged my knowledge and experience. When that happened, I would sense Liberal as an increased presence in my mind, observing my reaction to the situation, the procedure I adopted and its outcome. I worked through the issues I thought I could and blustered my way through those that had me floundering until the rider believed that I had put them on a track that would ultimately lead to their issue being resolved.

Every now and then, a little voice in the back of my head questioned whether I should ask Walter for his assistance, but I never allowed the voice to get any louder. I pushed back at it until I had quashed it every bit as strongly as any concerns raised by the students and horses in question.

In all that time, I never left The Gathering once. I craved the chance to go off travelling and I knew I owed Nia and Harris a visit, not to mention the fact that I was desperate to rub my family's noses in Liberal's majesty and all we were achieving; I pictured the two of us arriving at Freshtown, with me revelling in the gasps that greeted us, whilst choosing between the offers of hospitality. I would enjoy dispensing Liberal's – and my – advice to all those desperate for our help, and then soaking up all of the attention when we got back to The Gathering, of those desperate to hear of our travels and to receive instruction from me now that I was back.

But I could never bring myself to leave. The thought that I might return to The Gathering to find myself having been replaced was too much to bear. I told myself over and over until I believed it, that I couldn't leave, that I was needed too much by my students. Different bonded pairs were always leaving to travel around the villages, helping where they could, and when they returned, they needed my input to correct any bad habits into which they had fallen whilst away. And I absolutely couldn't be absent when newly bonded pairs arrived, since it was my duty to start them off as they would need to go on.

For the most part, I was happy. But then, seven years after I arrived at The Gathering, seven years after Liberal told me that he and I were merely preparing the way for a bonded pair who would propel us all forward, that pair arrived.

There was always a flush of excitement when a newly bonded pair arrived, as everyone admired the horse, got to know the person and discussed the name the horse had been given and what it meant for their potential together. When Amarilla Nixon arrived looking like she had been dragged through a hedge backwards, with her Bond-Partner whom she had named Infinity, and with a Herald hot on their heels telling of how the pair had not only escaped disaster but how Amarilla had supposedly sung her own broken arm back to health even though she was an Apprentice Herbalist, the stir was much greater than usual.

When it was revealed that Amarilla was only sixteen – the youngest person by far ever to have been chosen by a horse – I could no longer ignore the sense I had from Liberal that Amarilla's and Infinity's futures were tied intimately with our own. Fear pierced my heart. Amarilla Nixon was a threat to everything I had achieved, everything I had come to be.

I could hardly bear to look at her as she walked across the square to the dining room for her breakfast the morning after she arrived, or at her black and white mare with those pale blue eyes that caused me to shrink back inside myself when she looked at me as I observed her grazing in the paddock closest to the buildings – the very same one that Liberal had shared with Dili when he and I had first arrived.

I shuddered and then pulled myself together. When the two of them came to my riding paddock for their first riding lesson, I would be as good a teacher to them as I had been to everyone else, and they would be every bit as impressed.

So why did I have a hollow feeling in the pit of my stomach?

Ready For Change. Remember. Liberal's thought was so faint, I almost missed it, and then wished I had. I didn't want anything to change. I loved the life I had created for myself; I loved my position, my status, my relationship with Liberal and our prowess whenever I was on his back. I had everything I wanted, everything I needed.

You are mistaken. Our situation to date has served its purpose and now the time is upon us for you to use it to surpass yourself. I will assist where I can but the opportunity is yours to resist or accept.

Fear exploded within me. *I'm not mistaken, Liberal. You didn't grow up as I did, ignored and made to feel insignificant. Despite it*

all, I've risen to where I am now, and I won't give it up, whoever
Amarilla Nixon thinks she is and however that mare looks at me.

Infinity raised her head from grazing and peered at me. Then
she merely blinked and dropped her head back down to the grass,
dismissing me as inconsequential. I clenched my fists, trying to
stop myself trembling. What was happening to me? All horses
loved me just as much as their Bond-Partners did. I was imagining
things, that was all. Amarilla's arrival and the name she had given
her horse had thrown me, and I was creating monsters where there
weren't any.

I sent word to Amarilla that I would be expecting her and Infinity
– I could barely bring myself to think the horse's name, let alone
speak it – for their first lesson mid-afternoon, and then spent the
morning teaching one student after another. By lunchtime, I had
managed to dispel my nagging fear that for some reason I couldn't
even imagine, I wouldn't be good enough to teach the newly
bonded pair.

I laughed and joked as loudly as I always did as I sat with my
admirers in the dining hall, enjoying and returning all of the
smiles and nods afforded me as people caught my eye. But when I
passed Infinity's paddock on my way to my teaching paddock, my
unease returned. She didn't look at me, but there was just
something about her existence, her presence, that gave me pause.

By the time I saw her and Amarilla approaching my teaching
paddock with loud-mouthed Rowena Harrol, of all people, in tow,
my heart was thumping so loudly I was terrified everyone
watching would hear it.

'Amarilla and Infinity, right on time,' I said loudly, relieved
that my voice had made it past the tightness in my throat. Now to

get this over with as quickly as possible. 'Come in, come in, I've got some saddles here, I'm sure there'll be one we can use until your own is ready.'

In my haste to get Infinity saddled and moving away from me so that she would stop looking at me with those perplexing eyes of hers, I allowed her only a very brief sniff of my hand by way of introduction, before placing the first of the saddles on her back. She laid her ears flat back and snorted at me. I was mortified, even more so because the fence surrounding the paddock was even more packed with spectators than usual as those curious about Infinity's name watched her intently, hoping for a clue as to what she and Amarilla had the potential to achieve.

I turned away from the mare so that she couldn't unsettle me any more, and tried to distract our onlookers by explaining at the top of my voice why the saddle currently on Infinity's back wouldn't suffice. I turned back to the mare and removed the saddle, then approached her with one I thought would be more suitable. Infinity flattened her ears again and stepped away from me, swishing her tail.

'Just stand still, there's a girl,' I said cheerfully, almost unable to hear myself for the blood pounding through my ears. The mare glared at me. I frowned at Amarilla, hoping to embarrass her into helping me out with her Bond-Partner's behaviour. The girl had the audacity to look straight back at me whilst doing nothing. I propped the saddle on my hip and held my hand out to Infinity, trying to stop it shaking.

The bloody horse looked away from me. I bit my lip as all of the times that had happened to me before flooded my mind, almost blinding me to my current situation. I heard the nearest spectators whispering to one another, and felt my cheeks redden. My situation was unbearable, but there was nothing I could do other than wait for Infinity to accept my second attempt at introducing myself. Eventually, she did. I breathed out slowly and felt my body relax to the point that my knees almost gave way.

'Right, now, Infinity, I'm just going to put this saddle on your back to see if it fits. Stand there for me, there's a girl,' I murmured, hoping upon hope that she wouldn't prolong my humiliation.

'She'll allow it,' Amarilla said.

I was so grateful, I couldn't even find the wherewithal to be angry at being "allowed" to fit the infernal horse with a saddle so that I could give up my time to help her and her Bond-Partner.

The saddle was fine, so I proceeded with the lesson. I was more relieved than I cared to admit that while Amarilla learnt quickly and Infinity responded to her rider quickly and willingly, the pair was unremarkable. I wondered whether I had been wrong to fear them so much, whether they weren't the ones about whom Liberal had warned me seven years earlier – yet still something about them, Infinity in particular, bothered me.

That feeling only increased when during their lesson with me the following day, Amarilla had the nerve to question my instruction. Infinity's lack of balance when carrying a rider was expected and something I could help them both to work through, but even when I explained that to them, Amarilla didn't look convinced. Annoyingly, doubt began to swirl around in my stomach. Why did I care what she thought? I had taught hundreds of horse and rider combinations over the years. I was good at what I did, and she would come to realise that.

But she didn't. In fact, after mounting Infinity for their third lesson with me, Amarilla promptly dismounted and then refused to ride at all. Nothing I said made any difference. I felt myself shrinking where I stood, until I was convinced I would become as invisible as she was rapidly making herself visible to those who continued to watch her and Infinity wherever they went and whatever they did. In my desperation to assert my authority and talent over her lack of both, I called Liberal to me.

As soon as I saw him cantering down the track, my heart slowed back to its normal rhythm and I stopped sweating. My boy was here, everything was okay. I quickly saddled him and then leapt from the ground onto his back, landing softly in the saddle. The collective gasp emanating from my spectators bolstered me and calmed me further, and when Liberal and I proceeded to remind them, and show Amarilla and Infinity, exactly what we could do, why they should look up to us and what I could teach them, I felt back to my normal self.

My beautiful boy cantered up to where Amarilla stood with Infinity, Rowena, and Rowena's Bond-Partner, Oak, and came to a graceful halt in front of them. My heart lurched as I saw that far from looking up admiringly at me, Rowena was rolling her eyes, and Amarilla appeared to not even have noticed me, but was staring at Liberal's face as if there were something wrong with it.

No. It was my imagination, I was sure of it. They couldn't help but be impressed by what they had just witnessed. I rallied. 'Any questions?' I asked Amarilla. Amarilla blinked and looked up at me as if only just remembering I was present.

Rowena glared at me and said, 'I was just wondering, Feryl, whether Liberal struggles at all under the weight of that enormous ego of yours?'

It was more than I could tolerate. Liberal spun around beneath me in perfect and immediate response to my request, and cantered away from them. I shouted over my shoulder, 'I'll see you and Infinity here tomorrow afternoon at the normal time, Amarilla. I hope that you arrive in a better state of mind.'

Liberal jumped the paddock fence and then took me down to the river. Once there, we raced alongside it until I could convince myself that the tears streaming down my face were as a result of

the air through we which we had blasted, rather than from the fear
and agony that pounded through me.

Ready For Change. That is who you are, Liberal reminded me
as he slowed gracefully to a trot and then a walk.

*You've told me that over and over since Amarilla and Infinity
arrived. But I don't want to change. I'm happy, I want things to
stay as they are,* I told him.

*Were that true then you would not have heard my call. You
would yet be tending crops and animals in your home village.*

*You said we would introduce new ways of doing things, well
we have. Never has there been such a naturally talented bonded
pair as we are, everyone says so. They see us and they aspire to
achieve more with their own horses. We did that, Liberal, you and
I. I don't need some child coming along and telling me I'm not
good enough to teach her and that awful horse of hers with her
horrible eyes. I know what I'm doing, I've helped everyone who
has needed it since I've been here. I've always done my best.*

*That is a falsehood. You have done what you needed to
maintain your standing and reputation. There have been occasions
when He Who Is Adroit would have been better able to help than
you yet you refused to ask for his assistance. There have also been
occasions when you convinced your students that a problem they
brought to your attention was of their own imagining. In both
situations those in question found a way forward despite you
rather than because of you.*

I jumped down from Liberal's back and stepped away from
him, hardly able to believe what I was picking up from him. *Why
are you being like this? Why are you belittling me? You know how
much I've achieved since we arrived here.*

*And now we are in a position to achieve more. You have a
choice. Acknowledge your mistakes and open yourself to learning
from those who are here to help or continue to resist change and*

have it forced upon you. Our destination is assured but you may choose how we reach it.

Open myself to learning? From Amarilla? She's a sixteen-year-old child, Liberal, I have nothing to learn from her.

Liberal turned and began to walk back to The Gathering.

Where are you going? Liberal, don't walk away from me, you know I hate it when you do that.

He continued to walk and I was forced to run to catch up with him. When we were almost in sight of the first paddocks, I put a hand to his neck and asked him to stop so that I could mount; I needed the admiring looks we would receive, in order to gain enough strength to face everyone and the questions I would surely be asked regarding Amarilla's refusal to take instruction from me. Liberal did everything I asked, as he always did. I could sense him in my mind, as kind and level as ever, yet he seemed a little more distant than normal.

The weeks and months that followed were a nightmare. Not only did Amarilla refuse to have any more lessons from me, but she enlisted the help of Rowena and a friend of theirs, Justin, to help her to ride instead. She completely dismissed my talent and experience in favour of instruction from two who themselves had given me trouble when I taught them to ride.

Whenever I saw the three of them together, fear roiled around in my stomach, which only got worse when people began to watch them ride. After a couple of early retorts, Justin and Rowena kept their mouths shut whenever I challenged them over their actions, and I have to admit, every time I railed at Amarilla and saw her shrink inside herself, I enjoyed it. It was small consolation for how I felt most of the time though. It was as if the seven years I had spent building my reputation were reversing, and then time was reversing even further, taking me back to my home village where no one saw me other than to tease me or tell me I was stupid.

When a group of Woeful attacked some of the horses at The Gathering, I was ashamed to find myself relieved to see Infinity on the ground and covered in blood while Amarilla crouched beside her, apparently helpless to save her horse. I thought – I actually believed for a few minutes – that I could use the situation to reassert my authority. But when I tried, as was only right and proper in my position, to organise everyone to get Infinity moved into one of the field shelters where the Healers could tend to her, Amarilla got to her feet and yelled at me to go away. In front of everyone! She had ground me down to such a shadow of myself by then that I could think of nothing else to do but comply.

As I hurried away from them as fast as I could, I hoped that Infinity would die. That's the first time I've admitted that to anyone – even to myself. Liberal knew, of course he did, but I clamped my mind shut to him so that he couldn't lecture me for the thousandth time that I should be working with Amarilla rather than against her.

When news reached me that not only had Infinity survived but that Amarilla had been the one to heal her horse's bones and tissues with no training whatsoever, all of the pain and fear of the past months disappeared and was replaced by a numbness that was even worse.

By the time Infinity returned fully to health and Amarilla started riding her again, they, Justin and Rowena and their horses had been joined by more horses and riders, all attempting to ride in the same way as were the original three. All defying me and my methods. The numbness that had carried me through each day slowly began to be replaced by anger. When my anger turned to fury, it gave me the strength to march along to where they were riding, with every intention of giving them a piece of my mind. I was completely unprepared for what I found when I got there.

Amarilla and Infinity were a vision of perfection. Infinity was lifted in front, both her weight and Amarilla's balanced on her hind legs as she powered them both around the paddock – yet they weren't two at all, but one. Infinity barely seemed to touch the ground when she landed on it, even though I knew she had to be pushing down hard into it in order to create the amount of lift and forward movement she was achieving while hardly seeming to be moving at all.

I was spellbound, so much so that I forgot how much I hated the two of them for everything they were putting me through. But then Infinity roared and began to throw herself around, finally depositing Amarilla on the ground. I flicked back to myself. It felt odd to smile after all of my misery of the past weeks, but sure enough, a grin spread slowly across my face as Infinity galloped away from Amarilla and towards where I leant against the fence.

When those nearby turned to look at me, their questions as to what was happening written all over their faces, I stifled my grin. I had no clue either, but I couldn't tell them that and I couldn't let them know how happy I was at the scene playing out in front of us all. I shrugged, raised my eyebrows and said, 'It was bound to happen eventually.'

It looked as though one of Amarilla's friends performed some sort of healing on her, then she was helped to her feet. She walked over to Infinity and managed to calm her horse enough to get Infinity to come over to the fence where I continued to lean, with the apparent intention of remounting. I couldn't let that happen. If she stopped now, everyone would realise how foolish she had been to refuse my help. If she remounted and managed to recreate what she and Infinity had just achieved, it was well and truly over for me. Liberal and I had a natural talent on which we had built by years of hard work. Amarilla and Infinity had been naturally awkward, yet had achieved a level of balance and lightness that I had no idea how to achieve, even with a horse of Liberal's calibre.

'I see you've finally managed to drive that horse of yours mad, Amarilla,' I said loudly enough that everyone except for those at the far side of the paddock could hear.

Amarilla raised her eyes and gazed into my own. There was no sign of fear or worry within them, instead they were full of a determination that I recognised as once having possessed, but that had withered away since her arrival. 'Excuse me,' she said.

A quick check of my peripheral vision told me that everyone was watching us both, keen to see what would happen next. 'No, I'm afraid I won't excuse you and I can't allow this to go on any longer. By all accounts, you've already suffered one injury and it's my responsibility…'

'I don't have time for you right now, Feryl, I just need you to move so I can get on and help my horse.' She was so calm, I could have throttled her.

'Help her? You call this helping her? You drove her to the point where she threw you, Amarilla. I'm very happy to get on and ride her myself, that way I can show you…'

'How to produce a shut down, unfulfilled horse like Liberal? You don't have a clue what's happening here, Feryl, and I don't have the time to explain it to you because my horse needs me, so if you'll excuse me.' She began to climb the fence, and I had no option but to take a step backward.

The numbness that had been my constant companion for the past weeks returned as her words swam around and around in my head. Liberal was shut down? Unfulfilled? What did she mean? I reached for him and found him exactly where he always was in my mind – yet, as he had for the past weeks, he seemed smaller there than he used to be, as if he took up less space. Why had I not looked into that further in all this time? *Liberal? What's wrong?*

Nothing that cannot be rectified. Observe the bonded pair before you for they are the way forward for us all.

No. You and I are that, I told him.

We are part of the process and there are many we can help but first you must learn that there is more to riding a horse than merely moving well together. There is a level of balance that horse and rider can help one another to reach that will propel both partners forward. You have just witnessed it and now you will witness it again.

I looked up to see that Amarilla and Infinity had once more disappeared into one another. They glided around the paddock for a short while and then Amarilla dismounted. I was nearly deafened by the cheering and clapping that erupted all around me. I couldn't bear it. I ran for my room, dived into bed and covered myself with my quilt, trying to make myself believe that it was the reason I was invisible this time, rather than that of which I had just been a part.

I barely left my room over the weeks that followed. I went to see Liberal before everyone else was up in the morning, and after they had all gone to bed at night. I drifted into the dining hall when most people had left it, and sat by myself, aware that my unwashed scent and appearance held everyone away from me as surely as my glare.

I kept my mind clamped shut after Liberal requested the first few times that we join the riding sessions an ever increasing number of people had already joined, in which Amarilla and her friends had begun to teach everyone to ride the way they were, presumably with the aim of achieving the same level of balance she and Infinity had achieved.

So many emotions fought for prevalence within me; the pain of once more being invisible and irrelevant; the fear that I wasn't all I knew I should be as Master of Riding, that I wasn't good enough; the misery of spending so much time apart from Liberal; the fury that not only were some of those who should have been my students not accepting my instruction, but they were giving their own to more of those who used to look up to me. I couldn't cope with them all and chose numbness instead.

It was when I was sitting, eating a late lunch alone as had become usual and as I was continuing to ensure with my glare and lack of personal hygiene, that finally someone found the nerve to ignore my overtly expressed wishes, and came and sat opposite me. I looked up from my plate of toast and butter, to see that it was Salom, the Herald. That figured. I had long since decided that she must have no sense of smell in order to spend as much time as she did with her Pedlar friend, Pete.

'Hi, Feryl, I'm surprised you're not at the riding paddocks with everyone else,' she said.

I glared at her. 'Are you indeed.'

She gazed levelly back at me, as thick-skinned a Herald as I had ever met. 'I suppose it must be a little galling, having all your students going to Amarilla, Justin, Rowena and company for their riding instruction, instead of coming to you?'

I couldn't stop my face reddening. 'Do you.'

'Yes, and I guess you must be worried about Liberal? He doesn't look great at the moment, does he? His eyes and coat are very dull and he looks as though he's lost weight.'

I slammed my beaker down on the table so that water shot up and out of it, landing on the table in front of Salom. 'What do you want, Herald? As if I didn't know. You want gossip to take away with you when you leave here, so you can barter it for your food and lodging. You're a parasite.'

Salom's eyes hardened. 'If you had taken the time to notice anyone other than yourself, Feryl, you would have seen that I'm not wearing my bandanna. I'm off duty and anything you say to me is confidential. I've watched you wallowing in self-pity for weeks now and I can't stand it any longer. I just wanted to put a bit of fire in you.'

'Well, you've certainly done that,' I hissed and stood up. I stalked towards the door and then once I was on the cobbles of the square, turned for the paddocks with Salom hot on my tail. The anger I had been holding at bay strengthened with every footstep until it was a wild fury.

When I saw Infinity cantering around with an insane level of balance and power, carrying Amarilla as if she were the weight of a petal, my anger almost fled, but I grasped hold of it, pushed it back down inside of myself and focused on it to the exclusion of all else until it gave me the strength I needed. I marched up to the fence and began to clap slowly and loudly.

I almost laughed out loud when Infinity spun away from me, nearly unseating Amarilla. I climbed between the railings, still clapping, and walked towards where Infinity stood staring at me, her blue eyes as calm and disconcertingly all knowing as ever.

'Well, at least this time, you didn't fall off, let's have a round of applause for Amarilla, everyone,' I said. A few people clapped half-heartedly and then were silent. Amarilla joined Infinity in gazing at me calmly. It was too much to bear. 'Tell us, Amarilla, in front of the captive audience that we all know you crave, tell us all, what gives you, who hadn't even sat on a horse this time last year and who – let's be honest – still finds it hard to sit on one for any length of time without hitting the deck, the right to TEACH MY STUDENTS?'

Just let her try to justify her actions, just let her. I would shout her down until she was on the verge of tears, just as I had caused her to be so many times before, then I would keep shouting until she admitted she was wrong, until she agreed to leave here. To leave me in peace.

Amarilla didn't say anything. She dismounted and then walked over to me, Infinity at her side. I stepped backward. I didn't want them anywhere near me, any more than I ever wanted to see them working together again, demonstrating to all as well as me that they had achieved that which no one else – not even Liberal and I – had achieved, that which was so beautiful, so mesmerising, so... true.

What... was... happening... to... me? My anger was dissipating and I couldn't get it back. And why did everyone, everything look hazy, as if I were looking through a white mist? I felt my face relaxing out of the scowl into which my fury had contorted it, and found my shoulders relaxing too.

Amarilla began speaking to me softly, so that only I could hear her. 'Feryl, there's no need to be frightened. Everything you've always taught was right and is still needed by everyone here, it's just that we've found a few extra things that can really help the horses. I know you can see how Infinity can balance now and the effect it has on us both, and we couldn't have got there without some of the things you taught me. We couldn't have done this without you, Feryl.'

Her gaze was steady as I looked from one of her eyes to the other, trying to find the lie, but hoping upon hope that I wouldn't. Could it be true that I had contributed in some way to that which Amarilla and Infinity were achieving? Why did it matter so much to me all of a sudden that it was? What was this mist that calmed me as it surrounded me, that seemed to be emanating from Amarilla herself?

'Feryl, please come and ride with us. Between your knowledge and what we've learnt from our horses, we can help so many more people and horses so much more quickly, including Liberal. He misses you as much as you miss him, you know he does.'

Liberal. I could help Liberal. And between us, we could help more people and their horses. That was what he had told me when we bonded. It was all that mattered. How could I possibly have thought otherwise? Infinity moved closer to me and rested her head on my shoulder, her warm breath wending its way into my ear and with it, a sense of love and acceptance.

I lifted a hand to stroke her muzzle. 'What have I done?' I whispered. 'Liberal, what have I done?'

He whinnied in the distance and I heard him pounding his way to me even as his thoughts settled in my mind. *You have fought your way through the pattern of craving attention and recognition that has held you back. You have allowed yourself to be shown that your worth is inherent and need not be earned or stolen.*

I saw a dark shape rise into the air to my left, near the paddock gate. There was a thump, a further pounding of hooves and then Liberal skidded to a stop in front of me. *You have done well,* he told me.

I haven't. I've been an idiot. I used you to make myself look good. I cared more about what my spectators thought of me than I did about the students I was teaching. I've been arrogant and negligent. I've been selfish and I don't deserve to be the Master of Riding. I'll resign and let Walter take my place as he deserved to in the first place. We can leave here and travel around all of the villages, we never need return here if we don't want to. I'll devote myself to passing on your teachings so that other people don't need to be such monumental idiots as I've been.

He Who Is Liberal. We will stay here. We have much work to do. Your riding and teaching experience will combine with that of She Who Is Infinity and her peers to propel forward the advancement of both your kind and mine. It is all as we agreed. My horse's thoughts settled within me as surely as the white light that still surrounded me, and with them settled a clarity of purpose that transcended all thoughts and feelings I had ever had about anything else. I reached a hand to Liberal's face, relieved to see that his eyes shone once again where they had grown dull. I stepped closer to him and put my arms around his neck, burying my face in his mane.

He and I were all that existed. As he swirled from one moment to the next, never static, always changing, I now joined him.

Liberal came to a standstill as we caught sight of the grey stone cottages of Freshtown. I had planned to go and see Nia and Harris first, but now that we were so close to my family, I realised how much I had changed. All desire to hurt them had fled along with the insecurity that Amarilla, Infinity and Liberal had helped me to release. Liberal snorted and stamped a foot.

I grinned. *I know, we're needed back at The Gathering where it's all happening, as soon as possible. Come on then, let's go.*

We flew across the pasture. Where once the shouts of delight that began to erupt from the nearest cottages at the sight of the two of us would have fed my craving for just such a reaction, now I smiled as I recognised those around whom I had grown up. I looked forward to being able to help any of them needing Liberal's advice, and I looked forward to introducing my beautiful, wise Bond-Partner to my parents and brothers.

Liberal slowed to a trot when his hooves touched the cobbles, but didn't stop. He knew exactly where I needed to go first. I lifted a hand to everyone we passed, calling out greetings to each and telling them to visit Liberal and me at my parents' house during the following few days if they needed Liberal's help. Liberal followed his sense of my family until we rounded a corner and their house, the home in which I had grown up, was just in front of us. I felt nervous.

Worry not. You have changed much and this they will see.

I sighed and relaxed. *Thanks, Liberal. I'm glad you're here.*

I would be nowhere else.

The front door opened and my mother flew out of it, followed by Pelan, Jules and then my father. They all stopped in their tracks at the sight of Liberal and me at the front gate. I rubbed my horse's neck and dismounted.

'I'll say this for all to hear, because it concerns everyone,' I said, looking around at those now crowding behind me and Liberal, and then back to my family as Fratten joined them on the front step. 'I'm sorry I've spent so much of my life being such a chump. I had a whole lot wrong and I know that now thanks to Liberal here, and a few others. We can't delay here for very long, but if you'll have us, we'd love to stay with you while we help wherever we can?'

My mother put a hand to her heart and smiled at me, her eyes holding mine. Fratten and Jules both nodded and grinned. Pelan raced down the path towards me. My father's eyes glistened as he called out, 'Welcome home, son.'

Salom

*E*veryone always said I was a gossip. My parents said it fondly and, with hindsight, over-indulgently. My friends said it in the nicest possible way to my face in the hope that they wouldn't become the subjects of it, but when I heard them whispering behind my back, they weren't so kind. My teachers constantly berated me for my "tittle-tattle", often advising me that if it weren't for my incessant nattering during lessons, I would have been at the top of my class.

Few of my school lessons held any interest for me, however; people watching was so much more interesting, especially when the people in question had been stirred up by one of my well-placed comments. A little observation here, followed by a little snippet whispered there, and boof! I could stand back and enjoy the results of my efforts.

If I'd had to choose lessons that held even mild interest for me, it would have been those dedicated to the Histories, especially those that involved the Horse-Bonded – the reverence afforded them by my teacher and classmates fascinated me – but aside from those, I put all of my effort into ensuring my reading and writing were fast and accurate, for I knew exactly which Trade I would adopt when the time came to choose.

When I reached fourteen, I had to participate in testing for the Skills, the same as everyone else. To say I was bored is an understatement. Who wanted to devote time and energy to serving the community when there was a whole world out there full of people with interesting secrets to discover?

I didn't know if I had any aptitude for any of the Skills, because I didn't attempt to find any. When the Testers looked at me for any sign I could sense what they were guiding me to sense, whether it be the ability of the fresh herbs lying on the table in front of me to reduce inflammation, or which of the tones they hummed resonated with an animal bone placed in my hand, I kept my mind and face completely blank.

My parents – one a Tissue-Singer and the other a Weather-Singer – tried not to look disappointed when I told them I hadn't shown aptitude for any of the Skills. I almost felt bad, but then excitement rose within me as I waited for them to ask me in which Trade I would seek apprenticeship instead.

'You want to be a Herald, don't you?' my father said.

I was furious. I had so been looking forward to telling them that bit of news and seeing their faces, and he had ruined it for me.

My father laughed. 'You can't honestly think we didn't know, Sal? You can't believe everyone in the village doesn't know you've wanted to be a Herald ever since you could talk?'

'I thought you wanted me to follow you both into the Skills,' I said sullenly.

'What parent doesn't want to take on their own, dearly beloved child as an Apprentice?' my mother said. 'But that doesn't mean we don't know you and that we don't want you to be happy. We saw this coming, and we're happy for you that there's a

Trade you're so well suited to and that you'll love doing. I'm thinking that you really have no idea whether you would have shown aptitude for any of the Skills had you actually tried?'

This time, both of my parents laughed as I opened my mouth and then closed it, over and over again, for once unable to find any words to say as shock and anger vied for my attention.

My father put an arm around my shoulders and tried to draw me into a hug, which I resisted. 'You're as astute as they come in most ways and you'll be a credit to heraldry, but you have a blind spot that I don't need to be a Master Herald to point out to you. I'm telling you now, because I'm your father and I want my words to protect you when I won't be there to watch out for you myself, so please, listen to me.' I turned to him with a glare that challenged him to tell me something I didn't already know. He said, 'For your own sake, don't assume you're the only one who can read other people and see straight to the heart of things, even if there'll be few who are as good at it as you are. Okay?'

I rolled my eyes. What did he know.

As it turned out, he knew a great deal.

I was apprenticed to the next Herald to pass through our village, a woman named Janni, who accepted me as her Apprentice as soon as my parents approached her about it, as any Herald should.

Unlike the apprenticeships for the Skills and many of the Trades, that for heraldry was short; a year at the most. All it required was the ability to read and write so that messages could be taken down and carried to recipients in other villages along with sealed letters; outstanding observation skills so that news could be accurately gleaned; an exceptional memory so that news and messages could be correctly repeated on arrival at each village; an eloquent manner of speaking and a flair with people so that when we spoke, everyone wanted to listen.

As far as I was concerned, I had all of those attributes in spades, and didn't plan on being apprenticed for anywhere near the year taken by those with less ability. I was furious, therefore, when after six months of travelling between the villages, Janni refused to pronounce me a qualified Herald, instead informing me that I still had a lot to learn.

I took far more notice than she did of what went on in the villages whose residents put us up for the few days it usually took to deliver and gather news, messages and letters. In fact, after we arrived at the next village on Janni's list, and she had delivered her announcement of the news we carried and where we would be staying so that people could both collect and deliver their messages and letters, I had to make a follow-on announcement to hers, containing all of the bits she had forgotten.

I loved the way my voice rang out over the hushed crowd, bouncing off the grey stone cottages typical of the villages, so that my words returned to me. I loved the villagers' rapt attention and their glances between Janni and me as they clearly wondered why she hadn't just allowed me to do the whole announcement when I was by far the more accurate and eloquent of the two of us.

Once we were alone in the shared bedroom provided by the family who had offered to host us for our stay, Janni asked me to sit on my bed. When I complied, she sat down opposite me on her bed, and sighed. 'Salom, you can't go on like this.'

'Like what?' I said. 'Showing you up? I know it must have been a little embarrassing, but you left out the bit about Erami Nelson tripping on her wedding dress and falling flat on her face while walking down the aisle, you forgot to mention that Aron Wilson is at death's door, and you rushed through the names of everyone who is newly qualified in the Trades and Skills in all of the surrounding villages.' That would do it. Surely she would pronounce me qualified now?

Janni shook her head. 'I chose to focus on the beauty of Erami's wedding for all of those who watched her grow up in this village and couldn't make the journey to Sandtown to see her marry the love of her life. Aron's family asked me to merely pass on the news that he is ill without stressing the severity of his situation until they have come to terms with it themselves. And as always, I will pin a notice of all of those who are now qualified in the Trades and Skills, on the village noticeboard. I always make the announcement out of respect to those who've worked hard to gain their qualifications, but no one remembers the details, they go and look at the list if they're thinking of taking anyone on or apprenticing to those who may need help setting up practices of their own.' She stared at me as if needing a response. I just looked at her. 'Being a Herald isn't just about having people hanging on your every word while you spread gossip, Salom, the job requires integrity.'

I frowned. 'I have integrity.'

Janni smiled sadly. 'Maybe you do, somewhere deep inside you. The trouble is, you can't find it because it's swamped by your need for attention. You focus on reporting news that you'll enjoy delivering the most, instead of on what will provide the highest level of service.'

'I just know what everyone wants to hear,' I retorted. 'I'm not arrogant enough to choose which bits I think people should hear and which bits they shouldn't, I just tell it all and then people can decide for themselves.'

Janni's voice hardened. 'By which time, you're too drunk on the euphoria of having everyone listening to you with rapt attention, you fail to notice how many people have been hurt by your lack of empathy. You have it in you to be an excellent

Herald, Salom, but I absolutely will not qualify you until you can consistently show me that you will put the needs of others over your insecurities.'

I stood up and glowered down at her. 'Insecurities? First I have no integrity and now I'm insecure?'

Janni stood up and met my glare straight on. 'I'd say that pretty much gets to the heart of it. I suggest that you take a long, honest look at yourself, or in six months' time, it'll be you who'll be the news carried by all the other Heralds. Do you think they'll spare your feelings in the slightest when reporting that you're still in training long past when you should have qualified, as a result of bringing our Trade into disrepute?'

I couldn't speak. My heart felt as if it were thumping in my throat, which had gone completely dry at the thought of those things being said about me.

Janni nodded. 'I see I'm finally getting through to you.'

I didn't speak for the rest of the day. I didn't even leave my room, not even for dinner, which Janni brought up to me on a tray and at which I picked while thinking about what she had said to me. I couldn't believe she had threatened me, but moreover, I couldn't believe that I was in this position – me! I was cleverer than everyone else, I saw to the heart of things quicker than anyone, I knew which snippets to pick out of a situation and say at the right time to cause a stir and enough of an appreciation of my abilities that no one would dare come back at me. I hadn't foreseen this happening to me, not ever. How had Janni done it? She wasn't cleverer than I. I could outsmart her, and I would.

Finally, as the sun went down, a smile began to lift the edges of my mouth. I would do exactly as she had said until she qualified me. Then she would know what it was to feel threatened.

Janni pronounced me qualified three months later, and then duly went to the village square and announced it at the top of her voice for all to hear and congratulate me. I loved the spectacle, and almost forgave her for browbeating me into being as dull a Herald as she was. Almost. She ruined my improved feelings towards her by taking me to one side just before we left the village later the same day to go our separate ways.

'Here you go,' she said, holding out a folded piece of yellow cloth. 'I had one of the Tailors make it for you. As you know, you must always wear it when you're on duty so that everyone knows you're available to give and receive messages, news and letters, and that anything they say to you is eligible to be repeated. While all of us Heralds love our job, we also need our rest, so when you don't want to be approached, take it off and you'll be left alone.'

'Thanks.' I took it and immediately began to tie it around my neck.

'Salom, please look at me,' Janni said softly.

Shocked by the different tone of voice from the loud, cheerful one she usually adopted, I stopped tying the bandanna and looked at her.

'You're a talented Herald, I wouldn't have qualified you if you weren't,' she said. 'But I know you've been tempering your behaviour in order to reach this moment. Before you leave me, I'd like to reiterate what I've already told you. An observant eye, an excellent memory and the ability to hold the attention of a crowd are only half of what makes a good Herald. Integrity accounts for the other half. During the last three months, you've shown me you know the difference between reporting and gossiping. From this point onward, it will be up to you which of the two you choose to do. If you gain a reputation for merely being a gossip, people will hide both their lives and their news from you and in time, you'll find yourself redundant. If you make yourself known as a fair and decent Herald, people will open their lives to you and you'll have an enjoyable, fulfilling life. You'll also have the respect of your fellow Heralds, which, believe me, you'll need if you are to thrive in our Trade.'

I narrowed my eyes at her. 'You're threatening me again.'

'I'm stating a fact. My advice to you, as one Herald to another, is to remember that you aren't the only one who is perceptive. You are just one of many Heralds, all of whom can and will band together to ensure your failure if they catch so much as a whiff that you are damaging the reputation of our Trade. Without it, none of us can live the lives we love. Without us, neither can you.' She smiled warmly as if she hadn't just moved the earth beneath my feet, and said, 'I wish you well, Salom. Be happy.' Then she turned and walked away, leaving me staring after her.

I wanted to scream and shout, to threaten to use the weaknesses I had picked up in her, against her, but I found myself unable to; her warning had taken root within my mind.

I would never have believed it possible that my abilities could be curbed as a result of a single conversation, but that is exactly what happened. There were times when I was by myself, travelling between villages, that I would shout and scream with frustration at not having been able to say everything I wanted to when reporting news to the village I had just left. There were also times when I found myself reflecting on Janni's accusations that I lacked integrity and was insecure. I hated her for having insinuated herself into my mind in such a way that I couldn't get her out, and I hated her for causing me to look more closely at myself, to doubt myself. I suppose it was a combination of both of those things that caused me to gradually mellow over the months that followed.

Without my brashness and confidence to bolster me and drive me from village to village, I began to feel lonely. I tried to cheer myself up by dressing in bright clothing and adopting an overly positive attitude, but it wasn't until I happened upon a Pedlar sitting around his campfire one evening while four donkeys grazed nearby, untethered but clearly keen to remain in his company, that I realised what I really needed. For the first time in my life, I needed a friend.

It was common for those of the Travelling Trades, as ours were known, to team up and travel together, and I began to see why as Pete, as he introduced himself, welcomed me to his fire, fed me from his stores and introduced me to his donkeys, each of whom snuffled my hand before allowing me to stroke them. It was strange to feel so instantly accepted by the animals. They had no interest in what I knew about anyone, or indeed anything, but seemed to enjoy my company nevertheless.

'They like you, tha's a good star',' Pete told me.

'A good start? To what?' I asked him.

'To your relationship with them, tha's wha',' he replied. 'You're welcome to travel with us until you tire of us?' His pale blue eyes held no challenge, no agenda, just anticipation for the answer to his question.

'You don't even know me.'

Pete nodded to the donkeys. 'They do. They like you, an' tha's good enough fer me.'

Warm breath on my stomach preceded a heavy weight being placed into my arms. I looked down at the donkey nestling against me as I rubbed her ears, and something shifted inside me. Where I had always felt so driven but in recent months had just felt emptiness, now I felt warmth. Tears welled in my eyes, and I was powerless to stop them. I blinked furiously and only succeeded in causing them to spill down my cheeks where Pete couldn't miss them. I appreciated his apparent lack of need to comment even though I didn't understand it. He left me cuddling his donkey and went and sat back down by the fire, where he remained until I joined him some time later.

'I'd, um, I'd love to travel with you and your donkeys,' I said as we both stared into the fire.

'Righ' ye are. T'will be grand to have company,' was all he said for the remainder of the evening.

Nearly two decades later, Pete and I were still travelling companions. He was a naturally quiet, thoughtful man whose company I found as comfortable after eighteen years as I had on that first evening; I never had to watch what I said in order to avoid being accused of gossiping, because we tended towards companionable silence when alone together. When Pete did opt to speak unprompted, I learnt to listen, for the years taught me that he never said anything without good reason and the best of intentions.

Sometimes, he would point out something he thought I might have missed, whether it be a fleeting view as we travelled between mountains, or a different angle on news I'd gathered that had relevance to whether or not I would choose to pass it on. Other times, he would smile at me and congratulate me on a job well done after I had reeled off news to a listening crowd that would have been impossible for most to take in, let alone remember. Occasionally, he would share his opinion that I had said a little too much, or delivered news without the empathy or consideration it warranted.

I was often surprised at my inability to take offence at his criticism, but it was as if his mellow presence absorbed any spikes in my mood so that I found myself nodding in agreement with everything he said. Eventually, I began to believe that I had become the Herald Janni had hoped I would be – that my love of gossiping had been replaced by responsible reporting. My view of myself changed, however, when I met Amarilla Nixon, and as a consequence, Rowena Harrol.

Pete and I were almost upon The Gathering one autumn day, after weeks of travel, when Amarilla and her horse, Infinity, happened upon us mere days after their having met and bonded. Amarilla seemed impossibly young to be Horse-Bonded, but her age was the least shocking detail of the tale she proceeded to tell us, unprompted and whilst I was wearing my bandanna, so very clearly on duty.

What was I supposed to do when Pete and I arrived at The Gathering? Keep the juiciest story I had heard in years to myself? Of course not. The Horse-Bonded deserved to know all about their newest member.

I felt a thrill such as I hadn't experienced in years as I stood on Pete's cart in the cobbled square of The Gathering, and related everything Amarilla had told me about the drama that unfolded when she was on her way to find Infinity, and the even bigger drama that befell them once they had met and were on their way to The Gathering. I drank in all of the gasps, wide eyes and looks of disbelief as the Horse-Bonded – revered and listened to by all – hung on my every word.

I barely noticed that Pete was even quieter than usual when I had finished, so busy was I with answering all of the questions of those wanting me to repeat bits of my story and confirm that they had heard other parts correctly. It was hours later, when I had finally finished answering questions and delivering messages and letters to those queueing to see me, that I noticed that my travelling partner, the donkeys and the cart were no longer in the square. It was only when we sat down to dinner in the enormous dining hall of The Gathering, both of us minus our bandannas so that we would be left to eat in peace, that I noticed a slight tightness around the corners of his eyes. My heart sank slightly; I knew what that meant.

'Everything okay?' I asked him.

He merely raised his eyebrows and looked at me whilst continuing to chew his mouthful.

'Come on, Amarilla volunteered that information voluntarily and while I was very obviously on duty, you know that, you were there,' I said. 'She's the youngest Horse-Bonded in the Histories by a long way and she's already proved that her lack of life experience will get her into trouble, the Horse-Bonded here deserve to know who now walks in their midst.'

Pete's eyebrows stayed where they were.

I tried again. 'Don't you think it's a good thing they all know how accident prone she is, so they can look out for her and keep her out of trouble?'

'Don' ye think the lass has bin through enough recently tha' she would've preferred to settle in here without any fuss?'

I sighed. 'You clearly do.'

Pete returned his attention to the plate of salad in front of him, his point made.

'Okay, fine, if anyone else asks me any questions once I'm back on duty, I'll divert them onto other news.'

Pete munched on in silence and the discomfort I had felt at his disapproval faded away.

The following morning, I did as I had told Pete I would, and expertly redirected the attention of those wanting more details of Amarilla's and Infinity's exploits, to other topics of news.

I saw no sign of Amarilla, and couldn't help looking around for her from time to time whilst wondering what she was up to and whether I was missing anything important; there was something about the girl, sweet as she was, that tweaked my intuition, as if her exploits so far were the thin end of the wedge.

When lunchtime came and there was no sign of her in the dining hall, I decided that she was probably spending a lot of time with Infinity, and made my way to the paddocks nearest the buildings, where newly bonded horses could always be found.

I arrived at Infinity's paddock on the heels of a tall, black-haired young woman who matched the description I had gleaned from some of the other Horse-Bonded of Rowena Harrol, the Horse-Bonded who had apparently taken Amarilla under her wing. She appeared to be carrying food and was struggling to open the gate whilst keeping hold of it all. I rushed to open the gate for her, and followed her into the paddock where Amarilla was sitting under a tree with a very muddy Infinity grazing nearby.

Rowena rounded on me as I was pushing the gate shut. 'Can't you leave Amarilla to eat her lunch in peace?'

I flinched at the fury in her almost black eyes but collected myself instantly, as any Herald should when challenged. 'I won't keep her for longer than a few minutes, but I do need to see her now.'

She turned to Amarilla and made no attempt to hide the rolling of her eyes as she said, 'Salom wants to talk to you, can't wait apparently.'

I completely ignored her. 'Settling in well, Amarilla?' I asked in as cheerful a voice as I could muster.

Polite girl that she was, she smiled and said, 'Yes, thank you, how is Salsh?'

I was impressed by her decision to ask after one of our donkeys, whose lameness she and Infinity had helped to ease when they had caught up with us the previous day, rather than mentioning that I'd shared everything she had told me with most of the other Horse-Bonded. 'Fit as a fiddle, thanks to you,' I said. 'We're off in the morning, so I just wanted to check if you had any letters or messages for me to take to your family.'

'So you can have more gossip to spread around?' Rowena said. 'Amarilla's not that stupid.'

Gossip. The word took hold of my heart and wrenched it. 'Gossip?' I managed to say. 'How dare you, I'm no gossip, I'm a Herald and a very good one.'

Rowena took a breath and drew herself up to stand even taller than she was, her dark eyes now filled with hurt as well as anger. 'How do you expect Amarilla to trust you after you announced everything she told you to everyone in the square? Do you have any idea how upsetting it is to hear people talking about you?'

Old habits died hard. I found myself staring avidly into her eyes, trying to work out how to draw out of Rowena what this was really about, because it certainly wasn't just about Amarilla any more. When the pain in her eyes faded and was replaced by rage, I thought better of it, instead deciding to plead innocence before things got really nasty.

'Amarilla told me what happened to her whilst I was wearing my bandanna, just as I am now,' I said. 'Any information given to me whilst I'm on duty is for me to part with as I see fit, whereas any letters or private messages I carry remain private between sender and receiver. Rowena, you know all this, why must I justify myself to you?'

Rowena looked away towards where her horse, Oak, grazed

near Infinity, and studiously ignored me until I left the paddock a few minutes later with Amarilla's assurance that she would bring letters for her family to my room that evening. I would have preferred it had she expelled all of her rage at me; her silence reminded me of Pete's disapproval the previous evening, and gave me no other words onto which I could hang so that I could distract myself from the one that had lodged itself in my heart and was refusing to budge – the description that had accompanied me throughout my life, that had bolstered me until I apprenticed to Janni, and had terrified me since Janni attached it to the threat of me losing my position. Gossip.

I couldn't get away from The Gathering quickly enough the following morning, after a sleepless night. As always, I was grateful for Pete's companionable silence as I tried in vain to shake off Rowena's accusation, to find where she was wrong. When I couldn't, I focused on the emotions her eyes had given away to me, and tried again to discern what her reaction could have been about. I racked my memory for any mention I might have heard of her anywhere, but could find nothing.

I found a new strength that replaced the feeling of weakness she had placed in me, by deciding to dig up anything I could on her on my travels, so that by the time I returned to The Gathering, I would be armed with the knowledge that it wasn't my actions with which she had a problem, but those of another, of whose actions I had reminded her. I was no gossip.

It was the following spring before Pete and I made it back to The Gathering, following an interesting winter for me of collecting snippets of information about Rowena whilst we were on our travels. It had taken all of my skill to draw tiny bits and pieces of her story from many different people, so that none noticed what I was doing and more importantly, I couldn't be accused of digging for gossip.

Once I had put all of the pieces together and formed an understanding of Rowena's reaction to me, I convinced myself that the issue was all hers. I hadn't acted even remotely inappropriately in my sharing of Amarilla's story, and if she confronted me over it again, I would be forced to point out that the anger she had directed towards me was as a result of her hatred of one particular Herald, and nothing whatsoever to do with my actions.

Yet I hadn't told Amarilla's tale anywhere else. I had yearned to; every time Pete and I arrived at a new village and everyone rushed to gather around the cart upon which I would stand to deliver my offerings, I remembered the thrill I'd had while telling the Horse-Bonded all about her, and was desperate to feel that way again, but something always stopped me – I still couldn't shake that cursed word loose from me. It was as if Rowena had smeared it in a glue made of her hurt and anger before hurling it in my direction, and whenever I thought of Amarilla's story, it joined with my fear of losing my position, and my jaw clamped shut until I remembered all of my other news.

As we approached The Gathering, I found myself desperate to catch up with whatever Amarilla had been up to in my absence, but also nervous. I counted it unlikely that Rowena would have mellowed towards me, and dreaded hearing the word I feared above all others.

As it happened, my fears of what Rowena would say about me were eclipsed by shock that rendered me speechless for the first time in my life, when the first Horse-Bonded Pete and I came across on our arrival in the square told us that a group of Woeful had attacked The Gathering, killing a horse and two people, and seriously injuring Infinity. Once I had heard her out and then, as always, stood on Pete's cart to deliver my news, I was desperate to find Amarilla and hear what had happened to her and Infinity first hand. Happily for me, I had some letters for her from her family, giving me an excellent reason for seeking her out.

I found her sitting at a table in the dining hall with Rowena. My heart plummeted at the sight of my black-haired, black-eyed nemesis, but I was full of what I had heard about the Woeful, and the drama of it all fuelled both my confidence and my legs as I strode over to them both, tucking my bandanna in my pocket so that everyone else could see I was off duty and would leave us alone.

'Amarilla, Rowena, how lovely to see you again,' I said cheerfully. 'Amarilla, I have letters for you from your family and I must hear all of your news, it seems you and Infinity have continued to create a stir since my last visit.'

Rowena leant back against her chair, folded her arms, and narrowed those black eyes at me. 'I thought you were off duty.'

A shard of panic pierced my heart, but then everything I had been told came raging back into my mind, blocking her out. 'To the world at large, I am, but I always have time for my friends, and Pete and I both count Amarilla as one of those,' I replied.

'It's funny how your friends always seem to be the people you think can give you the most gossip, isn't it,' Rowena said. She muttered something to Amarilla and then left, leaving my heart and my stomach feeling as if they were full of ice.

Your friends always seem to be the people you think can give you the most gossip. Your friends always seem to be the people you think can give you the most gossip. Your friends always seem to be the people you think can give you the most gossip. The words went around and around in my mind, blocking me from calling after her my well-practised retort about the reason for her attitude towards Heralds.

When Amarilla looked back at me, I managed to say, 'I'll just grab some shepherd's pie and then be back, if that's alright with you, Amarilla? Pete'll be along soon, he's just checking that the donkeys have everything they need for the night.'

She nodded, and I hurried towards the food table as fast as I could without actually running, catching my shirt on the back of a chair on the way, and sending it flying. *Your friends always seem to be the people you think can give you the most gossip.* I held my hands to my head, trying to squeeze the words out, to no avail. If Rowena repeated her accusation to even one of the other Heralds, I could lose my job, my standing in society – my life.

But I hadn't done anything wrong. I stopped just short of the food tables as the realisation hit me. I hadn't done anything wrong. Rowena had a grudge against Heralds, and everyone knew it. I just had to behave impeccably so that no one else could accuse me of the same thing she had.

I spooned some shepherd's pie onto a plate with a trembling hand, took a deep breath, and made my way back to where Amarilla sat.

I wished Pete had been there to give me credit where it was due for my restraint when I sat down, expecting to hear, in all its gory detail, exactly what had happened to Infinity, while Amarilla instead proceeded to relate how fantastic it was that so much good had come out of the Woeful attack, and to tell me of her plans for the future – which involved helping the very monsters who had caused all of the pain, death and misery.

I was incredulous, and increasingly so when I pointed out that Pete and I had lost two of our donkeys to Woeful attacks in recent years, only for her to retort that it wouldn't have happened had we humans seen fit to welcome the Woeful into our communities earlier! When I could see no way to make her see sense, I allowed myself to be distracted by her excitement over what she and some of her friends were apparently achieving with their horses.

When I asked her to tell me more about it, she winked at me and said, 'You'll just have to come along and see for yourself. The far riding paddock after lunch every day is where you'll find us.'

The cheek of her! Gone was the meek, sweet girl I had met the previous autumn; in her place was someone who had skilfully, and to my chagrin, effortlessly, directed the course of our conversation.

Rowena's words still rang in my ears, preventing me from being able to think of a way to press Amarilla for more information, so I resolved to bide my time and do as she had said. I would stay at The Gathering for as long as it took me to pick up the little snippets about the Woeful attack that I was missing, and I could think of nowhere that was more likely to happen than in the vicinity of Amarilla and Infinity.

At the appointed time the following day, I found the paddock to which Amarilla had directed me, and sat on the top rail of its fence just as Amarilla and her friends appeared with their horses.

Amarilla smiled and waved before mounting Infinity. As soon as she was in the saddle, her expression changed from warm friendliness to intense concentration. I watched the black and white mare walk away from me, and craned my neck around the dark shape that appeared in front of me, in order to continue my observation. When it blocked my vision entirely, I blinked and looked directly at it to find that it was Oak, the huge, black horse who was Rowena's Bond-Partner.

She glowered down at me from his back. 'You may have

Amarilla fooled into thinking you're a decent person, but you don't fool me,' she said stonily. 'You're not here to observe and report on what we're doing with our horses, you're here to try and get more gossip about what happened during the Woeful attack. I imagine you've exhausted all your other leads, so you're going to hang around Amarilla and try to trick her or one of us who were with her into telling you exactly how horrific it was when her horse was attacked and her friend died at her side?'

My eyes widened only very slightly at the very thought before I managed to drain my face of all emotion, but it was too late; Rowena had seen the evidence of her suspicions for herself.

She leant down and hissed, 'Instead of hanging around, watching Amarilla for the first sign of an opening you can exploit, why don't you look at yourself? Why don't you ask yourself what it is, exactly, that's missing from your life that you need to live it through what's happening to other people, and use their lives, their news, their personal information, to keep a constant stream of attention coming your way? In fact, don't bother to answer, it'll save us all a lot of time and grief if I just tell you. You're addicted to attention and creating problems for other people because it fills the gap where your regard for yourself should be.'

I reeled as her tongue stripped me down to the bare bones of who I was, swaying where I sat and almost falling backwards off the fence. I grabbed hold of it tightly with both hands, feeling as if I were going to cry. 'That's rich coming from you,' I said, my voice trembling, 'with all the attention that comes your way just because a horse chose you as his Bond-Partner. The rest of us don't have that luxury.'

Rowena sat up straight and appeared to be listening to a voice I couldn't hear, like the Horse-Bonded always did when their horses were counselling them. Then she looked back down at me, all traces of her anger gone. 'What you do have is a responsibility to do your job with kindness and integrity. You can help Am and Infinity with what they're trying to do, or you can hinder them. The choice is yours, but if I ever catch the slightest hint that you're gathering news of Amarilla's experiences here in order to fuel your flaws instead of to help her, it will be me standing in the middle of the square on Pete's cart, reporting on exactly what it is you're about. Do you understand me?'

Oak stared at me, fuelling Rowena's words so that they reached me in a way no one else's had ever managed to do. While Janni had frightened me into behaving myself, Rowena and Oak had, between them, flayed me alive, leaving me feeling exposed and vulnerable – exactly, I suddenly realised, as I had done to so many others.

Oak nuzzled my hand as it gripped the fence, and my reply tumbled out of me. 'I understand you perfectly,' I said miserably. 'I'm sorry, I…'

I never got to complete my apology. Oak spun around at a horrible roaring noise, and he, Rowena and I watched Infinity as she bucked and leapt around as if Amarilla weren't astride her, which she very soon wasn't.

Rowena leapt down from Oak's back and ran to her friend as Infinity galloped off. I remained sitting on the fence, not daring to move as Oak's big bulk in front of me continued to remind me what his Bond-Partner had just said. I watched helplessly as Amarilla's friends gathered around her where she lay. Rowena knelt by her head next to a man I recognised as a Bone-Singer – Marvel, I thought his name was – who proceeded to relocate her shoulder.

I winced, almost feeling Amarilla's agony for myself, before she was helped to her feet. Stripped bare as I had so recently been, I was surprised and not a little disconcerted to find myself vulnerable to the emotions with which Amarilla practically blasted her spectators as she ran to where her horse continued to throw herself around. She was shocked and hurt by the fact that Infinity had thrown her, but far more than that, she felt sorrow for whatever was causing her Bond-Partner to behave in that way, and she felt love for her mare with a force that I had never even dreamt was possible. Any fear she might have felt as she approached her bucking, heaving mare was obliterated by the love she felt for her, and her determination to help Infinity through whatever it was that was bothering her.

For the first time in my life, I watched a story unfold in front of me with no thought of how I would retell it, no anticipation of the rapt attention I would receive as I did so, and no delight at having the hole inside me – that had so accurately been identified by Rowena – temporarily filled in place of that which should have been there. I watched a young girl put her pain and fear to one side, mount the horse who had just hurt her, and ride her until I stopped seeing them as a girl and her horse, but instead as simply a vision of breathtaking beauty.

Everything on which I had ever reported paled into insignificance as more of Rowena's words, that now held even greater significance to me, reared back up in my mind. *You're addicted to attention and creating problems for other people because it fills the gap where your regard for yourself should be. You can help Am and Infinity with what they're trying to do, or you can hinder them.*

My way forward was suddenly clear. I knew exactly how to fill the gap where my regard for myself should have been.

When Rowena had congratulated her friend on the vision of perfection Amarilla and Infinity had presented to us all, she made her way back to where Oak still stood with me. I amazed myself for feeling a sudden fondness for her. She frowned suspiciously at me when I smiled at her and said, 'I'll help them. I'll help you all.

Thank you for telling me what I needed to hear, even if it was the worst bit of news anyone has ever told me.'

She stopped in her tracks and stared at me. Then corners of her mouth twitched. 'You're welcome.'

I never told Pete exactly what had transpired between Rowena, Oak and me, but I knew he realised that something in me had changed. His voice sounded different when he spoke to me, and I often caught him watching me when I was chatting with people, wearing an expression I had never seen before. It was some days before I managed to pin it down in my mind to a combination of approval and pride. He didn't question me when, for the first time since we had begun travelling together, I made no mention of moving on. Where usually, I was itching to leave wherever we had spent a few days, a week at most, so that I could share what I had learnt with a new audience, I was content to stay and be a part of the change that was happening in the people and horses at The Gathering, and Pete seemed every bit as content.

I never missed a riding session involving Amarilla, Infinity and their friends, despite the fact that Rowena glowered a warning as soon as she spotted me. I didn't need it. She had opened me up to myself like a crow tearing open a carcass and exposing all of the maggots wriggling around inside. I couldn't hide from the unpleasantness that had been revealed any more than I could from the emotions I had continued to both see and feel from those around me since Rowena and Oak had stripped my thick skin of insecurity from me.

I found myself revelling in the beauty before me as I witnessed more horses and riders following in Amarilla and Infinity's footsteps, as well as wincing at the riders' frustration with themselves when they made mistakes, rooting for them to improve, and celebrating when I could see and feel that they had.

I also found myself vulnerable to the fear that still hung over The Gathering as a result of the Woeful attack. Much of it had dissipated due to the excitement at what so many of the horses and their Bond-Partners were achieving, but some of the Horse-Bonded were still traumatised by what had happened, and despite urgings from their peers to desist, were planning to leave The Gathering and hunt down the perpetrators of the attack.

I could feel who they were, and often was aware that they were near me before I saw them, so strong was the fear that emanated from them. I found myself employing some of the tactics I had developed in order to gather news that wasn't necessarily freely given, in order to keep a close eye on them. I questioned myself occasionally as to my motive for doing so, desperate not to return to my previous way of being, and worried that it might happen without my realising it. But each time I questioned myself, I thought of Rowena's warning and of what she, Amarilla and their friends were achieving with their horses, and I had a strong feeling that those planning to hunt the Woeful were a threat to what Rowena and Amarilla were about. I had promised to help Amarilla and Infinity, and I hoped that was what I was doing.

So it was that I was sitting close by the table at which sat the core members of the hunting group, listening in to their conversation while appearing involved in a conversation with those at my own table as we all ate lunch. My ears strained to pick up the whispers from the table behind me, and I managed to string together the snippets I heard into a picture of exactly what it was they were discussing. Anyone else may have questioned whether they had put together the snatches of conversation correctly, but long experience was backed up by a solid feeling in my gut. Those planning to hunt the Woeful would be leaving to do so that evening.

I was wearing my bandanna in full view of everyone nearby, so technically, the information I had heard was mine to distribute freely. I could almost feel the old me wringing my hands with glee in anticipation of announcing to the rest of the Horse-Bonded that their esteemed peers would be leaving that evening, and assuring them that I knew how much they would all want to wish the hunting group well on their mission... and then stepping back to enjoy the fallout. I felt sick at the person I had been. The hunting group needed help, and my best guess was that Amarilla, Rowena, their horses and friends would be best placed to give it.

A thrill shot through me at the thought, shocking me to my core. Could it really be that using my talents to help people was becoming more enjoyable than using them to cause upset? Worry caused my stomach to flip over. Would I be accused of causing trouble if I passed on that which I knew, despite my good intentions? Was Rowena's opinion of me so low that she would think the worst of me whatever I did? I decided that I would have to take the risk.

I found Amarilla sitting on the fence of one of the riding paddocks, watching Feryl, the Master of Riding, and her friend Justin, instructing some of the other Horse-Bonded astride their horses. I sat down next to her and was pleased and surprisingly reassured when Pete sat down on my other side. Even so, I felt uneasy at how what I said would be received.

Amarilla looked at me. 'What's wrong, Salom?'

I took a breath and before I could talk myself out of it, said, 'I'm not a gossip and I'm not here to cause trouble. Whatever a certain person thinks, that isn't my role. I just gather information and give it to whoever wants it.' I made a show of rearranging the bandanna around my neck, emphasising that I was on duty.

Amarilla took my hint and said, 'Salom, please tell me the latest news around The Gathering.'

I nodded gratefully. 'Those who intend to hunt the Woeful will be leaving The Gathering this evening.'

'Tonight? They're leaving in the dark? Why?'

Amarilla listened intently as I explained about the hunting group's reluctance to risk being stopped. She looked over to where Justin was teaching, and I could have sworn he read her mind, as he spoke briefly to Feryl and then came over to us.

My suspicion was confirmed when he said to Amarilla, 'You and I are going to have to find a way to shield one another if we're ever going to be able to concentrate in each other's presence. What's up?'

Amarilla whispered to him what I had told her, and he said, 'We can't let them leave, they'll destroy themselves and cause a great deal of harm.' He looked at me suddenly. 'Salom, you didn't just hear that, okay?'

I didn't think twice. 'You know I can't withhold information, but I feel a headache coming on.' I removed my bandanna, folded it and put it in the back pocket of my trousers. 'I'm going to my room to lie down, and won't be available for the rest of the day. Pete will bring a dinner tray to my room, won't you, Pete?'

Justin nodded to me. 'Thanks, Salom.'

I nodded back, climbed down from the fence and hurried to my room. At the sound of footsteps behind me, I turned to say that I was off duty, only to find that it was Pete who was following me.

'Oh, thank goodness it's you,' I said. 'Everything okay?'

He smiled. 'S'more than okay, actually. S'wonderful. I wanted to tell ye that I'm proud of ye.'

I smiled back at him and realised that I was proud of me too.

When Pete and I left The Gathering a few weeks later, I was touched that Amarilla and Justin came to see us off, and a little nervous to see that they were accompanied by Rowena.

Amarilla hugged me and said, 'Thanks for being such a good friend to all of us here, if it hadn't been for you, there would have been Horse-Bonded hunting Woeful, and everything our predecessors worked so hard for would have been at risk. You're really okay with not mentioning what they were planning to do until you helped us to stop them?'

I smiled. 'I never thought I would be, but yes I am. If there's one thing I've well and truly learnt in the past few months, it's that there are times when it's better for everyone if I keep my mouth shut.' I glanced at Rowena, who raised an eyebrow. 'And besides,' I continued, 'I have a whole heap of exciting news to tell everyone about everything you guys have achieved and what it will mean for us all. I think my time will be much better spent focusing on that. Thank you, all of you for allowing me to be a part of it.'

Justin grinned and nodded to me. Amarilla hugged me again. Rowena gazed evenly at me and then smiled.

Frank

*O*f all my children, Robbie was the most obvious candidate to make me doubt myself as a father. He was the eldest, the loudest, the most confident and by far the least likely to consider the consequences of his actions, or to care what his mother and I thought or told him. Sure, Con was often up to his neck in just as much mischief as his older brother, but that was more due to his desire to be Robbie's best friend than out of any real waywardness of his own.

Then there was Katonia. She was born in the depths of a grey, cold winter but the moment she came into this world, the sun appeared seemingly from nowhere, and beamed through her forever after in her smile, her laugh and her warm disposition.

When Amarilla was born, Mailen and I couldn't have been more delighted to welcome another daughter. We hoped that she would be as close to Katonia as the boys were to one another, and would maybe help to balance the force of nature that Robbie and Con were rapidly becoming.

It was soon very clear, however, that Amarilla was nothing

like Katonia; where our elder daughter had spent most of her waking hours as a baby smiling, Amarilla spent hers screaming as if she'd been dragged into her tiny body against her will and wanted the whole world to know it.

All three of our other children had allowed themselves to be settled into a routine, allowing Mailen to rest when she needed to, as well as tend to everyone and everything else that needed her attention. Amarilla resisted, well, just about everything. It was normal for our new daughter to throw up all over herself just after she had been bathed and dressed. She would fall asleep when she was supposed to be feeding, and stay awake, screaming, when she was exhausted and needed to sleep. Most disturbing of all were the times when she would scream whilst asleep, as if reliving horrors that she couldn't possibly have experienced.

Where Mailen continued to thrive at mothering the other three, she seemed to shrink in on herself when it came to Amarilla. She tried everything to help our baby to relax into the happy, content babies her sister and brothers had been, to no avail.

'She'll settle soon, love,' I tried to reassure my wife as she sat, exhausted, whilst trying in vain to rock a six-month-old Amarilla to sleep. 'Let me take a turn, so you can get some rest? It's not failure to let me help, you let me do my share with the other three.'

But she wouldn't allow me to intervene. Mailen was vivacious, loving and had a tendency to be overly dramatic, but when it came to being a mother – all she had ever wanted to do – she was a natural. She took pride in the fact that she excelled at it with our other three and she took it personally that Amarilla defied her at every turn. The two of them seemed to be locked in their own private battle of wills, and my wife was determined to persevere until she had loved and nurtured Amarilla into a happy, content little girl like Katonia.

Everyone advised us that Amarilla would grow out of being so fractious, but it was a long three years until she did. When the dark cloud that had seemed to hang over her finally lifted, we could hardly believe it. She began sleeping the night through and without the nightmares that had plagued her since she was too small to be having them. She settled into eating proper meals at normal times and she smiled and laughed, sometimes for me, often for her mother, but usually for her big sister; Katonia had always adored her little sister and the feeling became increasingly mutual. When Amarilla began to follow her sister around and copy everything she did, it was as if the sun came out for a second time.

Where Amarilla had always held us at arm's length, as if we couldn't be trusted, she began to hold her tiny hand up to be taken in ours, and even began to snuggle up to us all for cuddles – such a welcome display of affection that even her brothers allowed it. Watching a ten-year-old Robbie on a cushion in front of the fire with his arm around his little sister while she wriggled ever closer to him, I could almost imagine that the previous years of him and his brother running wild whilst his mother and I were occupied trying to calm our eternally shrieking baby, hadn't happened.

From that point onwards, Mailen and I were able to relax more and return to enjoying bringing up our children. Predictably, it was always Robbie who required the most correction, and Katonia the least. Con could be frustrating in that he was frequently in trouble of his brother's making, of which Robbie had an ever increasing knack of appearing innocent, but both he and Robbie behaved in ways that, to me at least, were to be expected of two lively young boys. Amarilla, however, retained the ability to confound her mother and me.

On the face of it, our youngest child was like her sister; happy, loving and cooperative. Unlike her brothers and sister, who all thrived in company, however, she was more than content to be on her own. In fact, she often seemed to prefer it and if interrupted, would withdraw into herself, unwilling to tolerate any deviance from her plans for herself.

She rarely answered back or got into mischief, and she did everything she was asked – as long as it was in line with what she already wanted to do. If she hadn't yet decided on a course of action, she would happily receive her share of the tasks we gave all our children to help them learn responsibility, as if helping and pleasing others was at the top of her list in the same way that it was at the top of Katonia's. But often – usually when Mailen and I were distracted by Robbie's and Con's constant need for discipline – we would realise hours, days or sometimes even weeks later, that Amarilla had slipped away from what she had been asked to do, in favour of what she had already decided to do. When she was brought to task over her disobedience, she would immediately set to work rectifying her misdemeanour with enthusiasm, making it impossible for us to stay angry with her.

As they grew up, everything about our three older children's personalities remained obvious and easy to deal with while Amarilla continued to operate in her own little world. She never openly defied us, yet seemed unable to give us her full attention until whatever occupied her complicated little mind had been seen to first – building a house out of sticks and moss for the night animals who visited the garden, complete with a water bowl made from a baked potato skin lined with leaves; collecting the heads of wildflowers to lay over the grave of a sparrow who had flown into her bedroom window; planting a row of acorns in a carefully dug little patch in the paddock to see if any would sprout. Anything else, be it a chore, homework, even a conversation, was quietly resisted and ignored until her head was clear of whatever burning mission had filled it.

When, aged seven, Amarilla announced that she would become one of the Horse-Bonded when she grew up, I was unconcerned, despite Mailen's immediate and excessive panic that her worst fear would be realised and one of her children would move away from our home village of Rockwood. Even knowing how difficult it was to deter Amarilla from a course on which she had decided, I really thought that, like her brothers and sister – who had all reacted in the same way when they learnt of those revered by the rest of us for the fact that they had each been chosen by a horse as a Bond-Partner – she would realise how unlikely it was and how far in the future it would be even if it were to happen, and move her attention on to something else. I was about to discover just how single-minded Amarilla really was.

It was a source of amusement to everyone in the village except us that in turn, they opened their front doors to find our previously introverted younger daughter standing on the doorstep, pen and paper in hand, intent on interviewing them in the hope of learning any detail she didn't already know about the Horse-Bonded.

Some of our friends were woken by Amarilla tapping on the door at dawn, others were prevented from going to bed at night or disturbed whilst trying to work. Every time, she was returned to us having been given the interview that she so politely requested. We were constantly implored not to be too hard on her for slipping away, and congratulated on a child so desperate to educate herself.

We grew increasingly exasperated when tasks that she had been set were left undone whilst she was off hunting for yet another interviewee, though we knew that once she had the relief of another set of information about horses and the Horse-Bonded in her possession to mull over, she would, as always, set to whatever she was supposed to have been doing, with gusto.

Once she was old enough to use the library, we barely saw her and when we did, she was full of everything she was learning from the Histories – how the Horse-Bonded came to be, why they came to be, and how, through them, their horses had influenced our communities so that we now thrived.

'She's too young to be learning about the past,' Mailen said to me one evening as we sat out in the garden with glasses of ale, watching the sun go down. 'Everyone tells us how proud we should be that her reading and writing are so advanced for her age, but she's learning things about the people of The Old that sometimes it's hard for us adults to understand, let alone someone so young.'

'And yet she does seem to understand it. She's so driven to know everything about the Horse-Bonded and their horses, she won't let go of any detail about them until she's found a way to make it sit right in that mind of hers.'

'It's not healthy though, Frank. Her obsession with learning everything there is to know about the Horse-Bonded, I can just about get my head around. But her insistence that she knows she'll be Horse-Bonded herself, that she even knows what her horse will look like – I mean, it's Bertha Matti all over again, isn't it?'

I sighed as I remembered. Bertha Matti was a middle-aged spinster who lived in the village. She was a few years older than Mailen and me, but we had both been witness to her humiliation during her childhood years.

Bertha was an only child and, spoiled by her parents, grew up always expecting to get her own way. Unpopular with children her own age, she tended to try to bully younger children into being her friends – Mailen was one of them until Bertha learnt better of it – and as such earned the enmity of much of the village, although many felt sorry for her, realising that her upbringing was largely at fault.

Bertha was furious when at fourteen, she showed no aptitude for any of the Skills during testing, and she flatly refused to train for any of the Trades. Her parents continued to indulge her and after she had finished her final year at school, announced that they would be training her to be a homemaker, ready for when she had a family of her own. The fact that she was learning to do the chores that all of the other village children had begun doing before they even began school was lost on very few, but as was the usual way, kindness prevailed and nothing was said.

A few years later, one of the Horse-Bonded, a woman named Joss, visited the village with her horse, a fine-boned, bay mare named Flair. Joss stayed with the family next door to the Matti family for the duration of her visit, while Flair grazed in the paddock behind their house. Bertha saw the respect shown to Joss and Flair, and observed many of the villagers visiting Joss to ask her for Flair's advice on various matters.

A week after Joss and Flair moved on, Bertha announced that Joss had told her she was "just the sort" that would be chosen by a horse, and that she should prepare herself for when the big day came. She spent her days being even more idle than normal, telling anyone who would listen that she would have the respect she deserved once she was Horse-Bonded. Her parents despaired of her, but, ever indulgent, they believed their daughter that one day, she would indeed be tugged by a horse, become Horse-Bonded and adored by all.

Five years later, Bertha was still waiting. Her name became synonymous with being work shy. Those in need of a day off from contributing their Skill or Trade to the village would say they fancied "doing a Bertha".

No one was directly unkind to Bertha or her parents, but her continued insistence that she was spending her time preparing for the day that a horse would call for her invited a fair measure of good-natured teasing. Suggestions were made that maybe her horse had already tried to tug her, but she had slept through it; that the other Horse-Bonded would need to look out when Bertha finally joined them, because with all of her years of preparing to join them, she would know more about being Horse-Bonded than they did; that maybe she'd had the misfortune to have been chosen by the most forgetful horse ever, who had simply forgotten to let her know about it.

Then, one bright spring morning, she announced that she was being tugged – that she could feel the pull of a horse's mind on her own and that she would be leaving to find her Bond-Partner. Her parents were overjoyed and threw a lavish party to celebrate. Unpopular she may have been, but still the entire village attended her Quest Ceremony the following morning, and of course she relished the attention. She was waved off partly with astonishment that the tugging she had spent the past years forecasting had actually happened, and partly with relief that her brash, selfish presence would no longer hover around Rockwood.

A few weeks later, she returned to the village bedraggled, a good deal thinner and accompanied by Navo of the Horse-Bonded and his horse, Charm. Navo informed Bertha's parents on their front doorstep while ears flapped nearby, that he had found Bertha harassing a herd of wild horses. She had apparently been stalking them for days and had resorted to trying to catch one of them with a lasso. The horses had reached out to Charm, he being the closest bonded horse to where they were grazing, and asked for his and his Bond-Partner's help.

Navo and Charm stayed with Bertha and her parents for several weeks. Nobody knew what transpired, exactly, but there was a marked difference in the way Bertha's parents behaved towards her from that time forward. Finally, they established boundaries for her behaviour, and Bertha humbly approached the village Chandler to ask if she would take her as an Apprentice.

Navo, Charm and Bertha spent a lot of time together in those weeks. They would often leave the village for long walks together and a couple of times, they returned to the village with Bertha riding Charm. As the villagers began to see the obvious mutual affection between Bertha and the gentle bay stallion, their feelings toward her softened. By the time Navo and Charm left the village, Bertha had started to make a few genuine friends.

She was now well regarded in the village and a Chandler in her own right, producing candles with the most amazing and novel scents. Her story would be a long time in being forgotten, however, and I had to agree with my wife; there were definite similarities between her behaviour and that of my younger daughter. But there were also many differences. Where Bertha had craved attention, Amarilla was oblivious to it. She did what she did because she believed in her feelings, in herself, and, it seemed, in the black and white mare with blue eyes whom she saw in her many daydreams as well as those that came to her at night. Where Bertha had avoided chores and anything else that didn't interest her because she was lazy, Amarilla avoided them because she had more important things to do – things that, when questioned about them, she spoke about with such passion that she would almost convince me of their importance.

As the years went by and Amarilla's obsession with horses increased in exact proportion with Mailen's resulting distress, I found myself constantly consoling my wife that our daughter would grow out of her insistence about the course her future would take, while secretly hoping that she didn't; that she was right, and that one day, she would be everything she was so determined to be. And although I never admitted it to anyone, deep down, I had a feeling that she would.

I didn't understand my younger daughter at all, and it continually flummoxed me that out of all of my children, it was she – quiet, polite Amarilla – who constantly caused me to question my ability as a father. But when I stopped trying to fit her into my idea of what a normal child should be, her behaviour didn't seem so strange – in fact it felt oddly necessary in a way that I couldn't explain to myself. So, where my wife stormed and fretted, I found myself content to console, watch and wait while hoping upon hope that I was right.

It was a welcome surprise when Amarilla decided to test for the Healing Skills, and an even happier one when she was found to be a natural at herbalism. Mailen and I agreed readily to her leaving school a year early to begin her apprenticeship, and she spent the next two years throwing herself into her studies, determined to be able to use her Skill to good effect once she was one of the Horse-Bonded. Mailen chose to focus on the fact that she was following in her brothers' and sister's footsteps and that all four of our children would be qualified in the Skills – Robbie and Con were already powerful Earth-Singers, Katonia was nearing the end of her rock-singing apprenticeship and would soon be assisting me in building the stone cottages typical of our village and those for miles around, and Amarilla was proving herself a more than able Herbalist.

Considering what I knew of Amarilla, I should have known that the stability of those two years couldn't last. I should have been prepared for her to resist the flow again, intentionally or otherwise. I wasn't. When she failed to return from a herb collecting foray into the woods one day, I thought to begin with that she had become overly absorbed in her work, as she was wont to do, and had lost track of time.

'She was looking for herbs she hasn't worked with before, Mail,' I told my wife. 'You know what she's like, she'll have found a new one – more than one, probably – and then she'll have been so focused on working through the energy patterns of all the ailments she knows until she finds one she can cure with it, she won't have noticed the afternoon wearing on.'

'But it's dark,' Mailen wailed. 'She knows I hate her going to the woods on her own, and she's always promised to be home before dark. Of all the rules she's ignored, she's never done it with that one. Something's happened to her, Frank, I know it has.'

'She knows her way home from the woods like the back of her hand, and it's a clear night. She'll be home soon, I'm sure of it, but if it'll make you feel better, Robbie, Con and I will take lanterns and walk to meet her. Okay?'

'Oh, Dad,' moaned Robbie. 'Con and I have been out shifting earth all day, and there's a roast dinner singing to us from the stove. What you're suggesting is tantamount to torture.'

'We'll be back in plenty of time to eat,' I said firmly.

'I'll go,' Katonia said. 'I've been to the woods to help Amarilla before, so I know roughly where she'll be if she's not already on the path home.'

Mailen took hold of Katonia's arms. 'Why wouldn't she already be on the path home? Katonia, tell me, what do you think has happened?'

'I'm sure nothing has happened, but you know what she's like. Dad's right, if she's found a new herb, she won't let up until she knows what she can cure with it. She'll be sitting down with her eyes shut while she's tuned into it, trying to match it to the energy patterns of a hundred and one ailments. She'll have no idea that the sun's gone down.'

My wife looked from Katonia to me with tears in her eyes. 'Maybe we should all go. The more of us there are, the quicker we'll find her.'

'And the greater the chance that more of us will get lost in the woods,' I said quickly. 'You and the lads make a start on dishing up dinner, and Kat and I will be back with Amarilla before you know it.'

'We'll do no such thing. None of us could possibly eat while Am is missing, could we, boys?'

Robbie opened his mouth but was nudged to silence by Con, who said, 'Am will be hungry after a day's foraging in the woods, won't she? Nearly as hungry as me and Rob. We should get dinner ready for when she gets back.'

'Set to it then, you two, help your mum.' I hugged my wife and whispered, 'Back soon, love.'

Before she could argue further, I was out of the kitchen, down the hallway and through the front door, having lifted both my cloak and lantern from their hooks on the way out.

Katonia shut the door behind us both, handing me her own lantern as she swirled her cloak around her shoulders. 'We don't have long before Mum's panic will run away with her,' she said. 'We'd better hurry.'

We waited until we were clear of the cobbled streets of Rockwood before we began calling Amarilla's name. The autumn night was clear, still and cold, and our voices carried easily – but to no avail. The woodland was silent in front of us and as it loomed ever larger out of the dark, I began to feel uneasy. Amarilla may not have noticed the dark falling, but she would have noticed the cold. Where was she?

'This way, Dad.' Katonia pulled on my sleeve as we entered the trees, and walked quickly ahead of me along a narrow game trail that I would never have noticed had I been on my own. I thanked the stars that it was my elder daughter who was with me; she was bright, level-headed and knew her sister better than all of us. She would find her. I hurried after Katonia, calling Amarilla's name. We would find her.

An hour later, I wasn't so sure. Katonia was calling her sister's name with increasing frequency and urgency, her concern rapidly growing in concert with my own.

'We've almost come full circle, we'll be back where we started soon,' she said breathlessly, and tripped on the undergrowth. 'By the wind of autumn, WHERE IS SHE?'

We heard a shout from ahead of us, and hurried towards it, holding our lanterns up as we battered our way through the forest. We saw lights flickering ahead, and more moving towards it. So, Mailen had alerted the villagers of Rockwood.

'Jodral?' I shouted, my brother-in-law's face lit up by his lantern as he looked at the ground in consternation.

'Frank, Katonia.'

'What is it, what have you found?' Katonia said.

Jodral pointed to the ground at his feet, lowering his lantern so that we could see a basket containing a herb dictionary, a pile of fruit and a packet of what appeared to be sandwiches. Next to it, spread on the ground was a cloak. My daughter's cloak.

I spun around, my lantern held high, looking frantically in all directions. 'AMARILLA,' I shouted so loudly that my voice cracked. More searchers, including Robbie and Con, gathered around us in silence.

Katonia dropped to her knees. She reached out with a shaking hand and touched her sister's cloak. 'There are t...two indentations in it. She was kneeling d...down. She must have found a new herb to work with.' She peered into the basket. 'There are no herb samples in here and she hasn't eaten her lunch. Whatever took her away from here, whatever happened, it was this morning.'

I felt as if ice were forming, cold and hard, in my stomach. 'Move back, everyone, move back,' I said, and everyone except Katonia did so. It was too late. Villagers had fought their way to where we stood from all sides in response to Jodral's shout, trampling and tearing at the undergrowth on their way and destroying any signs of anything or anyone who might have approached Amarilla as she knelt, or of which direction she might have taken had she left of her own accord. Unwittingly, I looked up into the trees.

'A Woeful wouldn't have taken her, Dad,' Katonia said in a strangled voice. 'If one had come this way, Amarilla's lunch would be gone and she would have either run home or be around here, injured.'

The cold in my stomach spread to the rest of my body at the thought that one of the huge, fanged beasts created by our ancestors might have hurt my child.

'What if she got injured and tried to run, but only made it so far, or got lost?' Con said in a voice that reminded me of when he was a little boy trying to talk himself out of trouble, rather than the twenty-one-year-old Earth-Singer he was now.

A new sense of urgency swept over me. 'We need to spread out. Katonia and I have already searched the tracks over that way.' I swept my arm in an arc. 'But Con's right. Amarilla could have been injured and forced to run or crawl into the undergrowth. She could have become trapped, or she could have... she could have passed out, or she could be too weak to shout, or... or...'

A loud wailing cut me off. Mailen must have stayed behind to rouse the rest of the village to come and search while Robbie and Con came ahead with the first to have been alerted. But she was here now, and she knew what had been found.

Jodral, one arm around Katonia's shoulders as she stood silently weeping, put a hand on my shoulder. 'We'll find her, Frank. Why don't you take Katonia and Mailen home? Robbie, Con and I can organise everyone and search until we find Amarilla?'

I shook my head. 'I'm not going home without her, Jod. I can't go home without my little girl.'

'I'll take Mum home, Dad,' Katonia said 'She'll listen to me. Just f…find Am, p…please?'

I hugged her and kissed the top of her head. 'I promise.'

I shouldn't have made that promise. I had no idea whether I could fulfil it; as usual when it came to fathering my younger daughter, I was full of doubt. How had I allowed this to happen? What had I missed, to think it was safe for her to come to the woods on her own, when clearly it wasn't?

As I followed my sons further into the darkness of the forest, all three of us bellowing for my daughter, I felt as if I were watching it all happen to someone else. I had to be, because it couldn't be possible that Amarilla was alone out here in the woods at night, possibly injured, possibly even… no. Deep down, beneath my ice-cold panic, I knew she was alive. That knowledge took up the tiniest part of me, but it was there. It didn't prevent my fear that she may be unconscious, trapped or in too much pain to move, from driving me on throughout the night, keeping pace with my sons as we searched and hollered, but it kept me from losing my sanity. She was alive, I just… knew it.

The whole situation was consistent with who Amarilla was. She constantly followed a trail that stretched away in front of her, that she alone had the ability to recognise, to feel, to see, regardless of the disruption to normality it caused around her. But I couldn't see the trail. I was her father. I should have been able to help her, to guide her, but she never allowed me to. She never needed me to. All she needed were her dreams of the black and white, blue-eyed horse who was the subject of the multitude of drawings that covered her bedroom walls. When I thought back to those eyes, my daughter seemed to be looking out of them too, willing me to know what had happened to her.

As the darkness gave way to light, I kicked a tree stump and howled. The feeling that told me Amarilla was alive was the same feeling that had made me sure she would be Horse-Bonded one day. So why couldn't I know where she was and what she was doing? If I could know as much as I did, why couldn't I know that?

'Dad, I think we need to go home.' Con looked directly into my eyes with his blue ones, so like those of both of his sisters. 'You need to eat and get some rest.'

I shook my head. 'I can't go home without knowing what's happened to her. I can't, Con.'

'We need to tell Mum she hasn't been found. She shouldn't hear it from anyone else,' said Robbie. He was ashen. His dark eyes, so full of mischief for the majority of his twenty-three years, were red-rimmed and sad. He put an arm around my shoulders and one around his brother's. 'Everyone's exhausted, but they won't leave until we do. We all need to go home for a bit.'

'Robbie's right, Dad,' said Con. 'Come home? Just for a little while? Then we'll come straight back and carry on searching.'

I allowed Robbie to guide me back along the track we'd been following, towards Rockwood.

The next week passed in a haze of stumbling around in the forest calling for my daughter, eating and drinking because everyone told me I should, listening to my wife wailing, and watching my sons age in front of me. For the first time, they behaved and carried themselves as the young men they were, and I supposed I should have been glad, whilst knowing that I would never have wished for the change to come about because of something like this.

As always, I was grateful for Katonia. Where Mailen took to her bed and I retreated into myself, Katonia took over the running of the household. She organised and cooked meals, looked after me and her brothers when we returned from searching, comforted her mother when I knew she would rather have been out searching alongside us, and all with a consideration for others that far overshadowed her concern for herself.

I found myself angry with Amarilla at times, and wondering why she couldn't be more like her sister. But then I would remember the sense I'd had on and off as I tried to fathom my younger daughter, that there was a good reason for her to be the way she was. A reason I wasn't permitted to know though, even when she disappeared without trace, leaving her family in despair.

As the days went by with no sign of Amarilla, I found that however worried I was, however angry, however sad to see the rest of my family in so much pain, I still couldn't bring myself to grieve alongside them. I still didn't believe that Amarilla was dead. And Katonia, being Katonia, noticed. She sat me down with a bowl of soup on my return from the woods one morning.

'What is that you know, Dad?' she asked.

'How do you mean, love?' I said wearily.

'You're exhausted and you're scared like the rest of us, but where we're all slowly losing hope, you aren't. It's as if you know she's coming home, you just don't know when.'

I glanced around.

'Mum's having a sleep, and I've sent the lads up to wash before they eat,' Katonia said. She took both of my hands in hers. 'Please, if there's anything you know that I don't, anything that I can hang on to, tell me?'

I sighed. 'I can't explain it, Kat, but I know she's alive.'

'How do you know?'

I shook my head. 'I know in the same way that when you and I are rock-singing, we know when there's a rock that's just that bit too big for either of us to sing into the air individually, and in the same way that we know that with our combined strength, we'll manage it between us.'

'You feel it,' breathed Katonia. 'Why didn't you say before?'

'Because although I feel it, where Amarilla's concerned, I always… hesitate.'

Katonia nodded. 'I can see why you would.'

'How is it that you understand her? The two of you are so different.'

'I think it's probably a lot harder being her parent than it is her sister.'

I sighed. 'Maybe.'

'Do you think she's in the woods somewhere, even now? I mean, it's been a week,' Katonia almost whispered, as if trying to say the words in a way that didn't make the situation real.

'I think we'd have found her by now if she were there. I don't know what else to do to find her, though. As usual when it comes to Amarilla, I just don't know what to do.'

Katonia squeezed my hands. 'Maybe we just trust your feeling and wait to see what happens?'

I squeezed her hands in return. 'Maybe we do. I think we keep this to ourselves though, okay?'

Katonia smiled wearily. 'The boys will dismiss it as wishful thinking and Mum will get hysterical again. Yes, I think we keep this to ourselves. Thanks for trusting me, Dad.' She looked up suddenly to the kitchen window, her young ears picking up the sound of a horse's hooves outside just before mine did. 'One of the Horse-Bonded is here.' She looked back at me, her eyes brightening. 'Maybe they can help!'

She stood up so quickly that her chair fell to the grey flagstone floor with a crash, and rushed towards the front door. I was right behind her as she flung open the door and rushed down the path. Robbie and Con came thundering down the stairs and almost landed on me as I stopped behind my daughter at the gate, where a tall, black-haired young woman was dismounting from an even taller, black horse. He turned and nuzzled her shoulder as she landed on the ground beside him, and she grinned and rubbed his nose. 'Thanks, mate,' she said and then called out to the villagers who had apparently accompanied her. 'Thanks for your help, maybe give us a little space for now?'

Our friends obediently dispersed, a few of them looking sympathetically in my direction first. My heart froze.

'You must be the Nixons,' the woman said cheerfully, her dark, almost black eyes shining in her startlingly pale face. 'I'm Rowena, and this is Oak. I won't keep you in suspense, I know what you need to hear. Amarilla's fine. Single-minded and impulsive, as I'm sure you know, but absolutely fine.' She blinked as Katonia flung herself at her, sobbing, and then slowly put her arms around my daughter and hugged her back.

I thought my legs were going to give way, and reached a hand back to steady myself against Robbie.

'Where is she? What happened?' Robbie said.

'She was tugged while she was collecting herbs in the woods. The pull of the mare's mind on hers overwhelmed her to the point that everything went out of her head except finding her horse. She just left everything and ran, and kept on running until I found her in a heap.' Rowena held her hands up quickly. 'Don't worry, I took her to a friend's house where she ate, slept and bathed before continuing on to meet her horse. She's absolutely fine, in fact probably even better than fine now, as she'll be with her mare. I came to let you know what happened and that she's very sorry for all the worry she knows she will have caused.'

Katonia was still clinging to her, crying softly as she listened.

Rowena gently stroked her hair, as if it were perfectly normal to comfort a stranger that way, and Oak rested his chin gently on the top of Katonia's head. I glanced behind me at my sons, to find them standing with their arms around one another's shoulders, both frowning uncomprehendingly at Rowena.

It all made perfect sense to me; everything Rowena had told us slotted into place with how I felt and what I knew of Amarilla. She was alive and well, and with the horse she had known would be her Bond-Partner ever since she was a little girl. I smiled a tired smile. I was so proud of her. She had followed her dreams, her feelings and her heart, just as the Ancients – our ancestors who left the known for the unknown, giving us, their descendants the chance for a better life – had done. Where before I had seen Amarilla as strong-willed and difficult to understand, now I saw her for who she was – a child of The New who did everything we were encouraged to do, albeit to a whole new level. She had caused me to doubt myself as a father, yet she had taught me to trust the intuition of my forefathers, for everything I had felt about her had proven true.

'Is there space in your paddock for Oak to graze and have a roll? We came as fast as we could and he's a little tired,' Rowena said.

I snapped out of my reverie just as Katonia leapt out of Rowena's arms, wiped her face and said, 'I'm so sorry, where are my manners? Of course, come this way. Will Oak be okay sharing with our donkeys? Okay, good. When he's settled, you must come and eat with us. I have soup ready, but I can cook you anything you like if you're in need of something more substantial.' Katonia stopped suddenly and looked up at Rowena. 'Thank you, Rowena, for coming to tell us about Amarilla, you have no idea...'

'I think I do,' Rowena interrupted, grinning.

I found my own voice at last. 'Rowena, thank you. You and Oak are more welcome than you will ever know.'

'Yeah, uh, what Dad said,' Robbie said and Con nodded silently in agreement.

'Cheers, I'll see that Oak has what he needs and then I'll be right with you,' Rowena said, then with a wave, turned to follow Katonia with Oak at her side.

Robbie shook his head. 'All this time, Am was telling the truth,' he murmured. 'My little sister is Horse-Bonded. How is that possible? She's only, what, fourteen, fifteen? No one gets tugged that young. And no one knows they're going to be tugged before it happens, but she's known for years. Or was she making it all up after all, and this is just a coincidence?'

'She's sixteen, Rob,' I said, 'and she wasn't making it up. Come on, let's go inside, we need to tell your mother.'

Mailen refused to believe that Amarilla was safe and well until she heard it directly from Rowena. Still in her dressing gown, she paced the length of the kitchen until voices sounded at the back door.

'Mailen,' I said sternly but to no effect, as my wife flung herself past Katonia and at Rowena, taking hold of both her hands.

'Tell me it's true,' she begged a surprised Rowena. 'Tell me?'

Rowena smiled. 'It's true. Your daughter is safe, well, and Oak has just confirmed that she is with her Bond-Partner, so she's now officially one of the Horse-Bonded.' Her smile faltered and she stepped forward quickly to catch Mailen as she fainted. Katonia and I rushed to help her while Robbie and Con stood watching, apparently unable to snap out of the daze in which they found themselves at all of Rowena's news.

'Lower her to the floor, that's the way,' said Rowena. 'I'll kneel and support her head while she's out, which I doubt she'll be for long, it's just the shock and relief.'

Katonia and I found ourselves obeying Rowena as if it were the natural thing to do. For the second time since she had arrived, I felt grateful to her. She was young – not much older than Katonia by the look of her – yet she had an air of calm competence about her that reassured me as much as her words did that everything was alright, and allowed my exhausted mind to relax. She was Horse-Bonded, I remembered and grinned to myself. She was Horse-Bonded and so was my Amarilla.

'There you are. It's good to have you back with us,' Rowena said as Mailen's brown eyes flickered open. 'Oooof,' she said as Mailen sat up very suddenly, turned and hugged the very breath out of her.

'Mailen, let her go,' I said gently. 'Come on, let her go, then you can get up and have a nice cup of tea and calm down. Rowena's not going anywhere just yet, are you, Rowena?'

Rowena grinned at me and shook her head. 'No way. I expect you all have questions which I'll try to answer, and while I'm here, if you have any for Oak, feel free to ask those too.'

'I have a question,' Con said suddenly.

'Go ahead,' said Rowena as she helped me to lift Mailen to her feet.

'This horse of Amarilla's. Does Oak know what she looks like?'

'She's black and white and she has blue eyes,' Rowena said. 'I can't wait to meet her.'

Con sat down in one of the kitchen chairs with a thump, shaking his head. Robbie just stared at Rowena, who chuckled. 'You didn't believe her then, huh? Well I have to say, I don't blame you, I mean, nothing about this whole situation is conventional, is it? Amarilla even took her horse by surprise, throwing her mind after her the way she did, and that's not an easy thing to do. The mare was beside herself when she asked Oak and

me to help. You seem like such a normal family, I imagine
Amarilla caused a fair few problems growing up? Without ever
meaning to, of course.' She winked.

I laughed, feeling as if a weight had lifted from my shoulders.
Amarilla was Horse-Bonded. She was who she was always meant
to be and now that she was with her horse of a thousand dreams, I
knew she would be happy.

'Everything alright, Dad?' Katonia grinned at me, her
eyebrows lifted in question.

I blinked and grinned back. 'Yes thanks, Kat, I really think it
will be.'

Justin

$\mathcal{I}$ had always struggled to concentrate. When I started school, the problem became very apparent. I was told I had too much energy, no focus and little interest in doing anything about either. Not all of that was true.

'Justin, you need to help me understand,' my mother said gently. 'You're bright, eager to learn and you were so looking forward to starting school, but it's only been a few weeks and your teacher is tearing her hair out trying to get you to stay in one place and stop disrupting your classmates. What's the matter? Are you finding the work too difficult?' She reached across the kitchen table at which she had sat me down with a glass of milk, and lifted my chin with her forefinger so that I looked up into her eyes.

'I have too many thoughts,' I said and a tear ran down my cheek. 'Everything the teacher says makes me think of lots of things I didn't know I knew and it all fills my head until I feel like there's too much of me in my body and I'm all squashed and I need to get out. If I sit still like all the other children, my arms and legs just start moving on their own and then everyone laughs at me.'

'But you're sitting still now.'

I looked down at my legs swinging furiously in turn between the legs of my chair. 'I'm not.'

'Well, you've always been a bit of a fidget, but that won't get you into trouble. If it helps you to stay in your seat, you fidget as much as you like.'

'I told you, the others just make fun of me. They copy me and they laugh,' I said, my shoulders heaving as I began to sob.

My mother reached forward again and cupped my face in her hands. 'Then we'll find a way for you to fidget that they can't see, shall we?'

But they still saw it. When I couldn't think straight because my mind had become jumbled again, when I was feeling the need to leap out of my chair and run around to release all of the energy that had built up inside me, making me want to explode, I would jig my legs up and down; my right one for a bit so that whoever was sitting on that side was only annoyed for a little while, and then I would swap legs and annoy the child on my left. Then I would move the fidgeting to my hands, tapping my thumb and forefinger of my writing hand together when the teacher was talking, and of my other hand when I needed to write. The other children in my class ranged from those who couldn't bear to be around me to those who tolerated me for short periods at a time, but I was too strange to have any real friends.

My older brother, Jase, looked out for me at my mother's behest, checking up on me at break times as I jogged around the playground whilst trying to release the energy that tortured me, and sometimes sitting with me at lunchtime so I didn't have to eat on my own. On the whole, though, school was a lonely and frustrating place for me.

I don't think anyone was surprised when at fourteen, I showed no aptitude for any of the Skills at testing, or that I chose carpentry as my Trade, since my father was a Master Carpenter and more than happy for me to serve my apprenticeship with him. I got along okay, but I still found it difficult to be still for too long at a time. Since a steady hand was necessary, my father frequently sent me off for a run to calm my body and mind so that I was a help rather than a liability. It was a practice I continued once I qualified as a Carpenter in my own right, and during the years that followed as I matured from a lad into a man.

It was during one such run that I became aware of a presence. I stopped in my tracks, pouring with sweat in the autumn sunshine, and looked all around me at the grassy hills that had been challenging my body to such an extent that my mind was relatively clear of thought. There was no sign of anyone.

The presence increased and I sensed a mass of raw, barely contained energy so like mine that I wondered for a moment whether it was my mind convoluting in on itself – but no. This energy, this presence, was comfortable with itself. It knew who it was and what it was doing in a way that I'd never been able to figure out about myself. It had a sense of knowing for which I yearned and instantly knew was possible. And it began to pull at me, drawing me towards itself in a way that brooked no argument, for there was a feeling of rightness about it, as if I had been waiting my whole life for it to happen.

A grin, tentative at first, slowly widened until my face ached. 'YESSSSSSSSSS!' I yelled to the hills. I was being tugged by a horse.

I sprinted home, barely noticing how strange it was when my legs began to protest; always, I had run as a way of keeping them still for a time afterward, yet now I pushed them to their limit because I actually needed them to take me somewhere – for the first time in my life, I had a sense of purpose.

I burst into my father's workshop and bent over, my hands on my knees, gasping for breath. 'Dad, I'm being... I'm being...'

'Keen? You certainly are, that was a shorter run than it normally takes to get your head together, son,' my father teased.

'Tugged. I'm being tugged.'

My father rushed over, took hold of my arms and pulled me upright. We shared the same brown, curly hair, dark brown eyes and slim build but I was taller than he was, so he peered up at me. 'Tugged? By a horse? Are you sure?'

I nodded and smiled, still heaving. 'I'm sure.'

A smile spread across his face, reaching his eyes so that they crinkled at the corners. 'You're going to be one of the Horse-Bonded? Justin, this is absolutely fantastic, your mother will be thrilled! And I'm thrilled. Much as I love you working with me, this is the best thing that could have happened to you, you know that, don't you?'

'Look at my face, Dad. What do you think?'

He laughed and pulled me into a hug, oblivious to the sweat that now soaked him as well as me. 'Come on, let's find your mum and Jase, we have a Quest Ceremony to plan for the morning.'

I would have preferred to have left quietly that evening to find my horse, rather than wait for the Quest Ceremony that my family insisted on organising for me and for which I was convinced nobody would show up. But when Jase took me to one side and pointed out that the ceremony was as much for my parents to show their pride in their son as it was for me, I gave in with good grace and stayed the night.

I was amazed and overwhelmed when the whole village turned out for my ceremony, yet more eager than ever to leave it all behind me and be on my way to find the horse whose pull on my mind had steadily increased during the previous day and night.

I accepted a back-sack from my family that was packed to the brim with everything I would need during my quest to find my horse, hugged them goodbye and then walked quickly between the two opposing rows of villagers, who all wished me luck as they threw flower petals over me, hung tiny horseshoes made of metal, glass, fabric or grass from my clothes and my pack, and, in the case of the village Healers who took up places walking behind me, sang my body to perfect health.

When I reached the last of the well-wishers, I turned and waved to my parents and brother, and blew a kiss to my tearful mother. Then, deciding that it would be rude to run, I turned and walked quickly out of the village.

I loved my family and I knew I would miss them, but I was so different from them. From everyone. I was being tugged by one who was more like me than any of my own kind, I knew it. I could feel it. And for the first time in my life, I didn't feel alone.

It took me two weeks to find my horse. I spent all of that time either running, eating or sleeping – but mostly running. I had never felt so well. Being on the move kept my head straight, and when the time came to sleep, I was tired enough that it came easily and deeply until I woke feeling refreshed and eager to run again. I ran across moorland, into hills which became mountains and then hills again, finally dropping down into flat, grassy plains.

When I jogged around a stand of trees to find a leggy chestnut stallion grazing exactly where I knew he would be, the horse lifted a refined head with a white diamond just above and between his eyes, and stood tall, his ears pricked in my direction.

The part of him that had reached out and pulled me to him continued to do so. As I carried on running towards where he stood watching me, my mind was pulled into his body with his own... and I knew him.

He was limitless energy that could be whatever it chose. A portion of it had funnelled itself into the body that stood before me, just as my energy was crammed into mine. But where I thrashed around in my body, my desperation to expand beyond it, to reconnect with everything I could sense was there, conflicting with my need to live a normal life as a human being, he embraced the choice he had made. He knew he could be everything and anything, and he accepted that he could do that and be a horse simultaneously. I didn't understand how that was possible, yet he was living proof that it was.

We both wanted to run. Needed to run. I could feel from Gas – for that was the name that had attached itself to him in my mind as soon as I felt him barely contained within his magnificent body – that there was somewhere we needed to be. It had to be The Gathering, home of the Horse-Bonded. We would run there together.

Gas turned and fell in beside me, his long legs, bright orange where the sun's rays bounced off them, falling into the two-time rhythm of trot in order to match my pace, when I could feel from him that he would have been more than happy to gallop. When he changed direction, I stayed at his side.

I had never known what it was to feel content, and the feeling surprised me and made me wonder how on earth I had battled my way through my twenty-two years without the beautiful, majestic stallion who ran beside me. He was the other half of me, the half I had missed desperately without even knowing he existed. Now that we were together, the life of loneliness and ridicule to which I had resigned myself had suddenly changed into one full of promise and meaning. I couldn't stop smiling as we ran on.

It was days before we began communicating via thought. Gas was content that we were together and moving towards The Gathering as our bond settled into place, while I was happy just to be included in the bond. Neither of us needed to announce when we wanted to stop to drink, graze or rest – we just knew – so it was a while before the need for conversation arose. When it did, it happened unexpectedly, at least for me.

I feel so different, I thought to myself as I realised that I was struggling to remember how it had felt to be anything other than fulfilled and… peaceful. I only realised that I had also announced it to Gas as we ran side by side through the never-ending grasslands, when he answered me.

That is to be expected.

I glanced sideways at him. *Err, oh. It is? But all we've done is run, eat and sleep.*

That is far from all we have achieved.

Well, yes I get that, I mean we've found one another, we've bonded and we've covered a lot of ground on our journey to The Gathering – and don't get me wrong, I've never been happier – but I feel very different, deep down. More than can be accounted for by what we've been doing.

Your human mind equates learning with toil and discomfort.

Um, yes, I suppose it does.

Yet you have learnt much by doing what you enjoy. By being whom you enjoy.

I'm not entirely sure what I've learnt, I just know that I feel different.

Gas trotted alongside me without reply.

Gas? What have I learnt?

If you need to ask then you have not completed the lesson.

Lesson? You're teaching me stuff already? I thought that would start at The Gathering, when there'll be other Horse-Bonded around to help me.

I sensed his amusement and felt unsure of myself. The momentary flashback to how I had felt my whole life until a few days ago, brought with it understanding.

I've learnt that it's okay to not be normal – it's okay to be me. To be who we are, you and I. I stopped suddenly, yet he needed no warning to halt in step beside me. He lowered his muzzle to my shoulder where he gently rested it, blowing warm air rapidly yet softly against my cheek.

It will be difficult for you to remember once you are back amongst your kind but we have made a beginning.

True to ourselves, Gas and I approached The Gathering at a run. We had been dodging rocks that jutted out of the hills up, down and across which we had been running, when we found ourselves alongside a fast-flowing river. Spurred on by its ferocity as it tore past us, we upped our pace even as the ground in front of us began to drop sharply away.

Gas darted off to the left, closer to the river to avoid yet another rock, but was immediately back at my side once we had passed it. A smaller rock appeared in front of me but my legs were running away with me down the hillside, too fast for me to be able to divert my course through the tussocks of grass without falling. I reached a hand up to Gas's back as he trotted next to me, and supported myself against him as I leapt onto the rock and then off the other side, the weight of my back-sack disappearing during my descent, then punishing my shoulders as it landed back down on them again. I didn't care. I whooped and hollered with the pure joy of running with my Bond-Partner, only quietening down when Gas whinnied loudly, causing me to look down to where the slope levelled out to a wide, grassy river bank.

A man of similar age to me, with brown, shoulder-length hair and a lopsided grin sat astride a slender, dark bay horse. The pair watched us career down the hill towards them and the man leant forward to rub his horse's neck as the stallion let out a shrill whinny and lifted his front feet from the ground in a small rear. I sensed Gas's need to respond to the stallion's protest at our rapid approach, and slowed to a walk and then a stop beside him. He lowered his head and then raised it, appraising the horse before us.

The man, still grinning, slid from his horse's back. 'Go on then, Spider, do your thing,' he said and the stallion leapt off to one side of Gas and me, into a powerful, snorting trot. Gas trotted around him in an arc, also snorting, so that they approached one another from the side. They stretched their necks out and touched nostrils briefly, then they were off, darting between the rocks. They cantered in the same direction, testing one another for speed. They moved closer alongside one another before veering off and away again, bucking and squealing. Gradually, they moved in closer again, then came to a stop, touched noses, squealed and began the process all over again.

'Well, that's my ride cut short, I don't think my Bond-Partner will have a lot left in him after this,' the man said, walking towards me with his hand out. 'I'm Shann, and that lunatic over there is Spider.'

I shook his hand. 'I'm Justin, and that's Gas. I'm sorry we wrecked your ride.'

'Don't be. To be honest, I was glad of the excuse to get off, my legs are killing me.' He nodded back towards where I could see fenced paddocks with horses, crops and livestock, stretching away into the distance behind him. 'Everyone else there makes riding look so easy but believe me, it's not.'

'You're learning to ride? So you've not been bonded long either?'

'I got here a few weeks ago and Feryl – he's the Master of Riding – has been making me suffer ever since. Come on, we may as well start walking back, Spider and Gas can follow on when they're ready. Cool name, by the way. I get it. Most here won't, though.'

I stopped in my tracks. 'You do? And they won't?'

He laughed easily and pointed to where Spider was rearing opposite Gas, who stood watching, unimpressed. 'A spider sits at the middle of its web, its connection to everything around it only limited by how big it decides to spin its web.'

'You saw the same in him that I saw in Gas,' I said.

'Looks like it, and what we see in them is what we have the potential to be. You know that, right? You're the only one I've explained Spider's name to, by the way. Don't repeat it, I can't have anyone thinking there's more to me than they currently think there is.'

'Why not?'

'Because if people start seeing me in a certain way, I might end up becoming that person if I'm not careful, whether I want to or not. Better to be who I want, when I want. Spider told me that and I've noticed he abides by it. I mean, you wouldn't believe there's an ageless sage locked in that body, would you?' Spider had resorted to fly-bucking on the spot in front of Gas, who was still unmoved.

I laughed. 'I guess not.'

We turned and walked alongside the river, a thunder of hooves warning us that Spider and Gas had grown bored of their stand-off and were now in hot pursuit. They galloped past us, manes and tails flying, and I hollered, encouraging Gas on as they pushed themselves to full stretch. His tall, lanky frame easily pulled away from Spider's slighter, less powerful one but the smaller horse didn't give up the race, and tore after him. I felt my horse's joy at having equine company again, and grinned, happy for him.

By the time the horses had run themselves out and were on their way back towards us, we had turned off the river bank and up a path that bisected the paddocks of The Gathering.

'Spider's in one of the paddocks closest to the buildings. I imagine you'll want Gas in one of them too, so you're not far from him when you're about the multitude of chores that you'll be weighed down by the moment the Overseer gets his claws into you?'

I hadn't thought about the fact that I would no longer be with Gas all of the time, and my stomach lurched suddenly. 'Err, I guess. Who do I need to ask, to find out which ones are free?'

Shann chuckled. 'Gas will know. Oh, look out, there they go.'

Gas and Spider flew past us, this time with Spider in the lead, and by the time some enormous grey buildings loomed over us, severing us from the sun's rays, I could just about make out my Bond-Partner grazing in a paddock near their base.

'I had a feeling that might happen – he's gone in with Spider, look,' Shann said. 'We'll shut the gate behind them so that no livestock wander in, but if he wants out, he can let you know. Are you alright, mate?'

I tried to alter my expression from the crestfallen one I

suddenly realised I wore, but failed. 'To be honest, I'm not sure. The last few weeks, when it's just been me and Gas, I've never been happier. And now I won't be with him all the time and I'll be around people again. I'm not very good at that.'

Shann clapped me on the shoulder. 'You're doing pretty well so far. And just so you know, there's no way I'm letting you go anywhere now that I have a fellow newly bonded. I need you to take the heat off me in Feryl's riding lessons, so don't even think of trying to make a bolt for it.'

It was impossible not to return his grin. 'Okay, well, thanks, I guess.'

He chuckled. 'You won't be thanking me once Feryl starts on you, believe me. Come on, we'll go and beg some food from the kitchen and then find you a room.'

'Is it lunchtime already?'

'Nope, it's brunchtime. That doesn't exist here officially, but Turi – she's in charge of the kitchens – has a soft spot for me. Something about a mischievous sparkle in my eye that, now she's mentioned it, I'm trying to cultivate. Do you think this is it?' He looked sideways at me and squinted as he began to walk.

I laughed. 'I'm no expert, but no, I'm pretty sure that's not it.' I followed him towards the buildings with one final, longing glance over my shoulder at Gas.

Remember what you have learnt. Practise remembering it even when it is difficult. I am always with you.

It's okay to be me. Got it, thanks, Gas.

To my surprise, I settled in quickly at The Gathering. I had a lot to occupy me with my share of the chores that kept the place running smoothly, taking care of Gas's needs and learning to ride him alongside Shann's attempts to ride Spider. Gas found being ridden difficult and while I was on his back, so much of my energy was taken up by trying to stay there that my mind was calm and free to try to work out what his problems were, since he was too agitated to tell me.

When I wasn't with him, and back in the world of people, my old habits returned, but Gas's constant presence in my mind reminded me that I could be happy being who I was. I also had Shann. He was always ready with a quip to lift me out of my self-consciousness at the fidgeting I employed to harness my energy and focus my thoughts, until I couldn't help laughing along with him. Then I would relax and be able to think a little straighter without needing to fidget.

The other Horse-Bonded were far more accepting of me than the people of my home village had been, partly due to our shared standing but largely because their horses counselled them to be; often, when I would see one of them glance down at my jigging legs as I ate my dinner, or when their eyes would flick to my fingers tapping together while I stood talking to them, they would pause in the way that we all did when listening to counsel from our Bond-Partners, and then they would look beyond my habits and at me. But it was an effort for them, I could see it, and I imposed my presence on them no longer than was necessary; I learnt to recognise the early signs that I was annoying them and remove myself so that I wasn't subsequently avoided.

Four years passed. Gas and I figured out how to get our bodies working together in a way that meant he could cope with me riding him, and we were a force to be reckoned with during the jumping and speed competitions – Friendlies, as they were known – that were held every now and then.

We went on trips visiting villages so that anyone wanting Gas's counsel could access it through me, which I loved. The attention was always on Gas, and having ridden to the villages, my body rarely needed to fidget while I relayed his answers to those asking questions of him, so I was able to relax and enjoy the company of strangers. Then, when we were done, Gas would indicate his keenness to move on by shifting around on his feet until everyone moved out of his way. The second I was on his back, he would leap into a canter and we would leave in a flurry of dust and hooves, knowing that we were leaving happy villagers behind us and could run to our hearts' content.

I developed confidence in myself because of our bond, our work, and also in no small part due to my friendship with the ever cheerful, ever loyal Shann. My horse and my friend, between them, were a constant reminder that it was okay for me to be myself. Then Amarilla Nixon walked into my life.

I heard about her before I saw her; everyone was talking about her, not just because at sixteen she was the youngest ever Horse-Bonded to arrive at The Gathering, and not just because of the series of calamities that had befallen her on her way there – but because she had named her horse Infinity.

Each Horse-Bonded chose their horse's name based on what they saw when their horses revealed their inner selves during the initial bonding, and all learnt at some point that what they saw in their horses was actually just their own potential. While most wondered what it could possibly mean that Amarilla had named her horse for something that had no limit, I knew exactly what it meant. I had chosen a more obscure word for what I saw in Gas and so had Shann when he chose Spider's name, but I knew Amarilla had to have seen the same thing in her horse that we had in ours. She saw what we saw because whether she realised it or not, she knew what we knew.

I was curious to meet her, but had no expectations as to the type of person she would be. So, when I saw a slim, brown-haired girl walking alongside a black and white, blue-eyed mare who could only be Infinity, I certainly didn't expect my world to suddenly slow down and come into focus as if it had always been that way. A portion of my world suddenly made sense as Amarilla stood blinking frantically at me as if I had completely the opposite effect on her. When she shook my hand, her effect on me only increased and I was able to speak to her as if being normal and friendly came naturally to me, even as my mind tried to work out – calmly and in an ordered fashion for once – what on earth was happening.

'I'm Justin and this is Gas. Do you want to sit down?' I asked her as she continued to blink furiously.

'No thanks, I think I just have something in my eye. Gas?'

I laughed. 'I have a warped mind, but yes, Gas is his name.'

Amarilla held her hand out and as Gas sniffed it, I found myself wishing I could hold it again. Infinity watched me knowingly and I almost blushed. Almost. I lost myself in my horse's unflustered appraisal of our new acquaintances and then made my excuses to leave before I could embarrass myself further.

'Come on, Gas,' I said, and walked away with a hand raised in farewell to the horse and girl who stared after us. She was a sixteen-year-old girl and I was a twenty-six-year-old man, feeling as if I had just met the one person I had never thought to meet – and not just because Shann was alone in finding me easy company for any length of time, but because I, like she, was one of the Horse-Bonded. Our horses were our lives. We rarely married and we never had children, we just didn't have the space to give that much of ourselves to another human. So why did Amarilla Nixon, a mere child, for goodness' sake, leave me feeling as if my life would be incomplete without her?

Your instinct merits trust, was all that Gas had to say on the matter.

As the distance between us and Amarilla and Infinity increased, I began to feel more myself. My thoughts reverted to being scattered bits of thoughts, all bouncing around in my head and vying for attention – Gas had a gash on his knee and we were going to see Adam, the Master Herbalist; it was nearly lunchtime; I needed to persuade Gas to stop playing with Spider so his knee could heal; I was down on the rota to chop wood all afternoon, so I would need a hearty lunch – and for the first time in my life, it was a relief not to be able to concentrate on anything for long.

'Are you alright, mate?' Shann said to me at dinner that evening, clicking his fingers in front of my face so that I blinked and looked at him.

'Err, yes, I think so.'

'You don't know so? Anything I can help with?'

I jigged my leg up and down and tapped my fingers together under the table where I didn't think he could see them, but he knew me too well. He glanced at my arms and legs. 'Jigging and tapping at the same time.' He whistled. 'This is big. What's happened?'

I glanced around at the full dining hall. 'Fancy a walk?'

'What, now?' He looked down at his plate, which he had piled high with sausages and mashed potato.

I shook my head. 'No, you're hungry. It's okay, you eat, this can wait.'

Shann glanced down at the table, which had begun to judder. 'I'll bring it with me. If I don't get you out of here soon, you'll bring the roof down on us all. Come on.' He stood up, holding his plate and a fork, and then turned to walk towards the door.

'Shann!' screeched Turi from the far end of the dining hall.

'I swear she has some sort of magic eye trained on me,' Shann said with a wink, and then lifted the hand holding his fork to wave at Turi. 'Bit of an emergency, Tu, I promise I'll bring the plate and fork back later,' he said and blew her a kiss.

She scowled and mimed tearing her almost completely white hair out, but as Shann walked backwards, grinning and winking at her, her scowl softened until she was smiling and shaking her head.

'I'm the grandson she never had,' Shann said. 'You, however, need to abide by the rules. Don't ever remove crockery and cutlery from the dining hall.'

I chuckled as I held the dining room door open for him while he attempted to spear a sausage with his fork. 'You could get away with burning the place down and everyone would just smile along with you,' I said with a grin. 'Everyone except Rowena that is, I've noticed she's become pretty good at keeping you in line lately.'

'Too much for my liking. She's taken the newbie under her wing though, so I'm expecting a bit more latitude.'

'The newbie? Amarilla?' A blast of wind hit us as we stepped out onto the cobbled square around which the buildings of The Gathering had been built, and I rubbed my arms.

'Huh?' Shann said through an enormous mouthful of sausage and potato.

'Rowena has taken Amarilla under her wing?'

Shann swallowed. 'Yep. Now there's one to watch, far more to her than meets the eye. Where are we going for this walk of ours that's going to leave me with indigestion and probably hypothermia?'

'We'll go and check on the horses. What do you mean, more to her than meets the eye?'

Shann stopped in his tracks, holding a forkful of mash in front of his mouth, and looked at me. He put the forkful back down on his plate. 'You're jigging while you're walking, mate, that hasn't happened before. Whatever's bothering you is going to eat you alive if you don't tell me.'

I rubbed my arms and jogged on the spot trying to appear to anyone else as if I were merely trying to stave off the cold. 'What did you mean about there being more to Amarilla?'

'Come on, Jus, don't say you haven't clocked it – she's called her horse Infinity, so she's one of us. Not only has she seen her potential as being one with the universe, but she's done it at sixteen years of age. Why did that mare of hers tug her so young? There has to be a reason. And judging by your face, I'm getting closer to whatever it is that's causing you to be on the verge of exploding.'

I began to walk again, and he hurried to keep up. We passed the paddock that Spider and Gas had shared when Shann and I were newly bonded to them, and that was now being shared by Infinity and Oak, Rowena's horse. I was glad that they appeared to have taken to their field shelter, as I didn't think I could handle Infinity's all-knowing stare at that moment.

'I met Amarilla earlier today, and she... had an effect on me.'

'What sort of effect? Oh, wait, you don't mean...'

'I'm not sure. That's the problem, Shann, I mean I should be sure. She's a child.'

'She's not though, is she? How many children do you know who are practically qualified Herbalists, have Bond-Partners called Infinity, and not only that, but have known what said Bond-Partner would look like since they were seven years old?'

'How do you know all of that? Oh, wait, Rowena.'

'And that's just the little she's told me. There's definitely a whole lot more.'

'When I met Amarilla earlier, I could think straight. It was like everything that spins around in me all the time just... stopped. Not even Gas has that effect on me. I felt as if I should know her. As if I do know her and that she and I...' I stopped and shook my head. 'I can't even say it, Shann. She may well be everything you say, but she's still sixteen and I'm still twenty-six.'

'So don't sweat it, she won't be sixteen forever. She's going to need friends, so be a friend to her. If she helps you to think straight, you should find it easier than you do with everyone else – me being the exception of course. Just think, Jus, you'll have two friends... two! Maybe even three if Rowena gets on board. Cheer up, mate, your life just looked up.' I grinned, feeling a whole lot better as I always did when Shann was around.

We reached our horses' paddock to find them waiting for us at the gate. Gas was watching me solemnly. *Your instincts merit trust,* he repeated his earlier counsel but then added with more force than usual, *Trust them.* He stared at me in a very un-Gas like way until he knew I had registered the gravitas of his advice, and then, as if it had never happened, swung his head towards Spider, nipped him playfully on the side of the face, squealed and careered off with Spider in tow.

'Gas, your knee...' I threw my hands up in the air. 'It's never going to heal if he and Spider won't stop messing around,' I told Shann.

'Have you ever been able to keep still because someone told you to?' he asked, his grin turning to a grimace as he took a mouthful of cold potato.

'Fair point, well made,' I grinned, then clapped a hand to his back. 'Seriously though, thanks for pointing everything else out too.'

He swallowed and grimaced again. 'No problem. Everything will work out fine, it always does.'

I nodded. I would do as Gas had told me and trust my instincts, and also as Shann had advised. Be a friend. I could do that.

I did manage it too, for the most part. The grounding effect of Amarilla's presence pretty much negated my need to fidget unless I was particularly agitated, but even then, it was much less marked, so I found a new level of confidence when she was around. When Infinity found it difficult to carry Amarilla, Rowena and I helped them to find a way to move better together, in the process finding that our new discoveries also benefitted our own Bond-Partners. When Feryl and his followers bullied Amarilla because she was having help with her riding from Rowena and me instead of from him, I was able to support her without "interfering in another's process" as Gas repeatedly counselled me when I wanted to intervene on her behalf. When Amarilla's difficulties escalated with the emergence of a heart problem, I kept quiet as she requested, helped Rowena to do Amarilla's chores when she needed to go to Infinity for help, and defended her actions in leaving her friends to do her chores while she went off riding whenever – as it seemed to everyone else – she felt like it. I knew she was suffering and it didn't feel like I was doing nearly enough to help her, but it was what she asked me to do.

And in the process of being a friend to Amarilla, I found myself changing. She was like a whirlwind, always driving onwards, looking to change and improve in line with Infinity's continuous counsel. Rowena, Shann and I found ourselves pulled along in her wake, challenging the way things had always been done and trusting both her and our horses that it was for the better.

Where before I had always tried to be as small a presence as possible when in the company of other humans, I surprised myself by being comfortable in the limelight, even when my friends and I were at our least popular.

My bond with Gas allowed me to know who I really was. My friendship with Shann gave me the confidence that it was okay to be that person. Amarilla's friendship drove me to be that person come what may. I felt happy and so, so fortunate.

But then, just as the worst winter we had experienced for years was finally loosening its grip on us all, "that day" happened.

Amarilla had made a big leap forward in her riding, and Shann, Rowena and I had all revelled in her and Infinity's success with them before returning to the buildings to wash before dinner. I had just left my room, looking forward to discussing the latest advancement further as we sat down to eat, when I felt a sudden surge of panic. *Gas? What's happening, what's wrong?*

I could sense him galloping around in the snow and ice, too panicked to frame a thought and answer me. I hurtled down the stairs, cursing Shann for persuading me that the rooms on the top floor of the accommodation block were the warmest, and out into the square. People were flooding out of the dining room in front of me. I ran, my long legs quickly taking me past the bulk of the crowd and out of the far side of the square towards the paddocks, where I found Shann hanging upside down over a fence, grasping for a shovel resting against the dung box.

'Shann, what's happening?'

He grabbed hold of the shovel and dropped back down to his feet, his face ashen. 'Woeful are attacking the horses in the far paddocks. Our horses,' he said and began to run. I stood, rooted to the spot in terror for my horse. 'Get a shovel and follow me,' he yelled over his shoulder, galvanising me into action.

I grabbed a shovel from the next paddock down and took off after him. All of a sudden, Gas filled my vision as he galloped flat out towards me down the icy path. He was lathered in sweat, as were Spider and Oak behind him, and Oak was bleeding. Relief flooded me to the point that my knees buckled. I grasped hold of the fence as Gas and the others passed me, none of them seeing anything except the fastest route to safety. Where was Infinity? She had been sharing a paddock with Gas and the other two.

My eyes widened in horror. She must be either down, or still in the paddock, trying to escape the Woeful that had so terrified Gas and the others. And Amarilla would know. She would be on her way to save her beloved Bond-Partner.

My legs found a new strength as panic took over again. When someone – I didn't even register who – dropped to her knees, screaming as she felt her horse taken from her, I found even more speed. I saw Shann just ahead of me, slipping between the fence rails into Infinity's paddock. And then it was Amarilla who was screaming. I reached the fence just as Shann was overtaking her on the way to where an enormous, black-pelted Woeful crouched on top of what had to be Infinity lying prone on the ground, his talons raised for the blow that would kill her.

For a split-second, I felt relief. Shann was there. He would keep Amarilla from harm and save Infinity. He raised his shovel above his head and brought it down on the Woeful's back, but the Woeful, his face so human and yet so wrong, seemed barely affected. He leapt back from Infinity and stared at Amarilla and Shann.

It was as if time slowed down whilst I registered that the Woeful, a descendant of humans genetically engineered to be killing machines, now stood glowering at the two people I loved most, his fangs dripping with saliva. I was through the fence in an instant and running again, but I was too late. As Shann took another swing, this time at the Woeful's head, the Woeful lashed out with his talons and then fled. I thought my heart would stop as Shann and Amarilla both collapsed to the ground beside Infinity. Had he killed them both? Terror tightened my throat, preventing me from calling out to them even as Rowena screamed from just behind me.

When I reached them, I found Amarilla covered in blood, but alive. I put my hands on her shoulders. 'Am, are you hurt? Amarilla?'

She didn't answer. It was as she reached a shaking hand out to touch her unconscious, bleeding horse that I registered that the blood that spattered her was neither hers nor Infinity's, but that of my best friend, who lay unmoving beside her. Hands pulled his body away and Rowena sank to the ground beside him, holding his hand and stroking his cheek. Then she began shaking him, trying to wake him up even though her tears ran with the truth that neither she nor I wanted to accept.

With my hands still on Amarilla's shoulders, my world spun slowly enough that I could frame one thought at a time. There were lots of people now crowding around Shann but Amarilla was alone with her bleeding, unconscious horse. I was her friend and she needed me. I would focus on that. I couldn't allow myself to even contemplate what had just happened to Shann.

I bent forward to look around at her face. She had her eyes tight shut and appeared to be trying to slow her breathing; she was concentrating, tuning into Infinity's body to see where the damage was. I wanted so desperately to help her, but I was a Carpenter, not a Healer; there was nothing I could do other than keep my hands on her shoulders and hope that she would register she wasn't alone.

When Amarilla began to hum, the bloody patch that had been spreading from Infinity's neck stopped increasing in size. She was tissue-singing, despite having only been trained in herbalism! Pride in her filled my heart and almost blocked out the pain that threatened to overwhelm me as Shann's lifeless body was rolled onto a stretcher and carried away. Almost.

My hands began to shake on her shoulders as tears streamed down my face. Shann couldn't be dead. Shann, who was so full of life, so full of fun. Shann, who was the first to brighten up the dullest of days, who never had a bad word to say about anybody. Shann, who was my best friend. But Amarilla was here. Her horse was dying in front of her, and she was, as always, giving everything of herself to do what her horse needed. If all I could do was keep myself together so that my hands on her shoulders might, just might, give her the strength to do what she needed to do, then I needed to pull myself together and do it. I was her friend.

When more Healers arrived to help her, I gave my place up to them, knowing that they were whom she needed now. I got a roaring fire going nearby and then sat tending it. If I could keep Amarilla warm as she worked into the night, healing her Infinity with no training, just her total belief in herself and her Bond-Partner that she could do it, then I would. And when the Healers came down on her like a hailstorm afterwards for doing it, I'd be there for her then too.

It wasn't long after Amarilla eventually stood up to thank the other Healers for their help, their jobs done, that she fell back down. I stayed up all night, continuing to tend the fire as an exhausted Amarilla slept next to it, protective over her in a way I had no right to be.

When dawn broke and she joined Rowena and me in a grieving, sobbing hug, I didn't want to let her go. She was so young and had so much to deal with, being bullied by Feryl on top of her heart condition, and now Shann having died beside her and her horse having almost followed suit.

So it was that nothing could have shocked me more than to find, in the days that followed, that I began to hate her.

Before Shann's death, I could never have comprehended how

much his loss might affect me. He knew more of me than anyone except for Gas and perhaps my parents. He was an open, uncomplicated, beautiful person, and he had died in front of me in the most brutal fashion. Time and again, when I was both awake and asleep, I saw him protecting Amarilla and Infinity at such enormous cost to himself. I saw the Woeful towering over him, looking him in the eyes while taking out his throat. I heard Rowena's screams and felt, over and over, the pain that had overwhelmed me when I finally accepted that he was gone.

Rowena was locked in her own world of pain, Amarilla was intent on caring for her slowly recovering Bond-Partner, and Shann was dead. I felt lonely, vulnerable and afraid, and I wasn't alone.

When there was talk of organising a hunt for the Woeful who took our own from us, a part of me wanted to join it, however much the thoughts that hammered around in my head, bouncing off the physical limits it imposed as they fought for attention, all agreed that it wasn't the answer.

Where before The Gathering had been a place of companionship, learning and happiness, now a cloud of anger and fear hung over us all – and yet Amarilla seemed oblivious to it all. Her horse had nearly been killed in front of her and it had taken everything out of her to not only heal Infinity, but to stay with her in the freezing weather, tending to her until she was strong enough to make it to a field shelter nearer the buildings – yet she not only seemed immune to the fear and anger that should have taken hold of her more strongly than any of us, she even began to speak of her opinion that we should be helping the Woeful! Helping the murderers who had caused a place of joy and fellowship to become a place of fear and misery. Helping those who had taken my best friend from me.

A part of me still wanted to trust my instinct as Gas had told me to, and be near her. When I was, everything slowed down in my head and her arguments made a little more sense, but the thoughts and memories they provoked in me were too painful to bear, and I would quickly spiral back into fear and increasingly hate. Shann was dead and the Woeful were monsters.

As Amarilla continued to try to persuade me to agree with her that we should help them, I found I could barely stand to be near her. Then, when Infinity was back on her feet and Amarilla began to smile and laugh again, it was too much. I told her I hated her and what did she do? She told me off for having allowed my fear and grief to block Gas out of my mind, and convinced me to calm down and let him back in so that he could help me. I felt ashamed that the youngest, least experienced Horse-Bonded had seen that which I had not.

Gas?

Instantly, he was at my side as I leant against the wall of the field shelter he had just begun sharing with Infinity. He filled my mind with his, replacing everything I had felt since the loss of my friend, with love. I cried. I grieved for my friend without fear or hate for the circumstances, just with love for someone I missed. Immediately, I felt better, yet I still didn't understand how I could have found myself in that position.

You do.

I don't. Shann's potential was the same as mine is, the same as Amarilla's is – to "be at one with the universe", as he put it. But he's gone. The Woeful wiped him out before he got the chance to fulfil his potential.

Your grief yet prompts you to attach blame where there is none.

The Woeful killed him, Gas, I was there.

The Sorrowful helped him to know himself in his entirety and gave him the opportunity to leave.

It WHAT?

He allowed your friend to feel the connection they shared with one another and with all else. He Who Is Spider no longer felt the need to be here once he knew that in reality there is no here.

He Who Is Spider. I remembered Shann telling me that he had seen Spider as being connected to everything else. And Shann had become that, Gas wouldn't lie to me. Shann's learning was complete, his potential, his life purpose, fulfilled. Through my tears, I smiled, happy for him whilst still devastated for myself.

Movement caught my eye and I looked up to find Shann standing in front of me, grinning – an impression of him, anyway. He was there and he wasn't, like a rainbow just before it fades to nothing. He nodded, winked and then disappeared.

'Shann?' I stared for what seemed an eternity at where I'd seen him, willing him to come back. Eventually, I gave up. *Gas, how did I see Shann? I mean, I did just see Shann, didn't I?*

Souls who incarnate into human form use their bodies as shields from the truth so that they can learn experientially what they know energetically. Your shield is thinner than most so you feel and see what few others can. It is a condition that has overwhelmed you in the past. You have recognised the one who can help you to achieve the same as your friend. When you do you will be aware of far more.

But Shann is dead. When he experienced his oneness with everything, he left his body. I'm not ready for that, I'm not ready to die, Gas. I'm only just beginning to enjoy this life of mine. You're here with me, and then there's Amarilla... I feel as if there's so much I have to do. I know what's possible, but I don't want to die, I really, really don't.

Gas dropped his head down and began to munch on some hay from a large pile, on the other side of which lay Infinity, snoozing peacefully.

Gas, am I going to die young, as Shann did? I asked him.

You know that death does not exist. He Who Is Spider has just demonstrated that it does not. Yet you fight what you know. It is all that holds you back.

From what?

Gas munched on his hay, his light brown eyes holding my own. *You must decide whether you trust those who would help you.*

Of course I trust you, you know I do, I'm just scared.

Trust is rendered useless by fear. Focus rather on those you love for in them you will find the trust that eludes you.

There was a rustle as Infinity shifted slightly, raised her head and looked at me pointedly, her eyes a paler version of her Bond-Partner's.

Something settled inside me. The thought of what was ahead scared me witless, but I knew I would always have my wise and beautiful Bond-Partner in my mind and by my side; I would always have the image of Shann smiling at me, encouraging me from beyond his body; and, as I felt my love for Gas and Shann, I was able to trust both my instinct and Infinity's gaze that told me I would always have Amarilla and Infinity too. Come what may, I had everything I would ever need.

I was jerked from my musings by the sound of Rowena shouting outside, and from the sound of it, at Amarilla. I sighed and rubbed Gas's forehead. *Thanks, Gas.*

He lowered his head back down to his hay and continued to munch. I pushed myself away from the cold, stone wall and walked towards the shouting. I paused in the doorway of the field shelter and looked back to where I had last seen Shann. 'Thanks, mate,' I said, my voice shaking, and then whispered, 'for everything.' I walked out into the snow.

Elinora

$\mathcal{I}$ used to be rubbish at making decisions, and those that I did manage to make usually ended up being the wrong ones. The last of those was agreeing to marry Reckin. He was twenty-eight and the latest in a long line of talented Earth-Singers. I was twenty-five and my close and extended family were all Farmers. Reckin's and my union would not only benefit both families, but would help me to realise that a settled life was what I wanted. Or so everyone told me.

Growing up, I had always thought about travelling. I had an urge to see different landscapes, speak to people other than those in my village and learn of their own experiences and travels. When the time came to test for the Skills, I showed no aptitude for them and had no interest whatsoever in any of the Trades. I just wanted to travel, but I was too young to go off on my own, so fell into farming with the rest of my family.

I loved them all – my strict, hard-working father who, as he repeatedly told us, only wanted the best for my sister and me; my soft, kind mother, who always wiped away my tears when my father had given me another lecture on family responsibility and unity; my mischievous sister, Peony, who never failed to put a smile on my face; my many aunts, uncles and cousins; and tall, red-haired, blue-eyed Reckin. He had been my best friend for as long as I could remember and I did love him, I just wasn't sure it would ever be enough for either of us. He deserved someone who would commit to him wholeheartedly, and I deserved... what, exactly? I asked myself the same question, over and over, but could never quite arrive at an answer.

It took me weeks to consider his proposal.

'Reckin's a lovely man, hard-working and loves his family,' Peony reminded me as I sat watching her change her baby daughter's nappy. 'You'll be happy once you're wedded and settled, I know you will – just look how married life is suiting me. I'm the same person I was, only...'

'Calmer,' I interrupted. 'More content, less wild.'

She looked at me. 'I'm still funny though? Please tell me I'm still funny?'

I grinned. 'Putting all of your clothes on inside out and back to front and then refusing to acknowledge the fact just to make me smile after my latest run in with Dad – yes, you're still funny. Being married and having children could never change that, and that's why I also don't think it can change the fact that I just feel there's something out there for me.' I swept my arm towards her open kitchen window. 'Something that I need to be doing. And before you say it, it isn't having babies.'

Peony handed me her freshly bathed and dressed baby, who gurgled happily as I nestled her into the crook of my arm. 'See, you're a natural.'

'I love her, I love both your children, you know I do, but...' I looked back wistfully towards the open window.

'None of our family have ever moved further than a village or two away and even then, some of them persuaded their new families to move back here with them. We're the Stensons. We stick together, always have, always will,' she told me. 'I really don't think there's anything more for you out there than you already have here.'

I felt as though something were wrapping itself around me from head to toe and gradually tightening. It was comforting in a way, yet I wanted to fight my way out of it. I wanted to be free.

I was quiet at dinner that evening and when my father demanded to know whether I had come to a decision where Reckin was concerned, all I could do was shake my head miserably.

'You're keeping the poor man hanging for no good reason,' he said sternly. 'If travelling was the right thing for you to do, you'd have been long gone by now. It's time to put it out of your head for good, accept what a good life you have here and put Reckin out of his misery. Put all of us out of our misery, come to that; your behaviour is embarrassing us all, Elinora.'

I looked at my mother, who smiled sympathetically. 'Ellie, you're my daughter and I love you but you've always had your head in the clouds. One minute, you want go travelling, the next you can't stop talking about Reckin. I've kept my thoughts to myself up until now because I want your decisions to be your own and I want you to be happy, but for what it's worth, I think your father is right. You're twenty-five. If travelling was truly for you, you would have been drawn to work as a Herald or a Pedlar and you'd have left years ago. Once you're married, everything will settle into place for you, just see if I'm right.'

But I remained unconvinced, even as I allowed my mother to talk me into accepting Reckin's proposal.

Everyone was delighted, and to begin with, I allowed myself

to be swept away with the excitement of planning the wedding with my mother and prospective mother-in-law. I designed Reckin's wedding bracelet, and stood hand in hand with him every evening at the site on which our new cottage would be built, discussing our future.

'Are you okay, Ellie?' Reckin said one evening as we stood where our kitchen would be. It was a month before the wedding, and we had been debating what size table to ask the Carpenters to make for us, and how many chairs.

I blinked. 'Um, yes, sorry. Six chairs to allow for all of the, um, children you want... I mean I want... I mean we want, yes, that, er...' I scratched my head. 'That sounds fine.'

'You're trembling.' Reckin took my hand. 'Ellie, what's the matter? You do want all this, don't you? I know it's been hard for you to finally put your ideas of travelling to one side, but you said you had done. You said you wanted this. Have you changed your mind?'

I looked up into his blue eyes as they searched mine, and my heart went out to him. He wanted all of this so badly and I had committed to it all. To him. I sighed. 'I haven't changed my mind, it's just, well, you know exactly what you want and you always have, Reckin. This life we're standing here planning in minute detail is something I've only just come around to, and it's all just a bit overwhelming.'

'Come around to? You make it sound like a compromise,' Reckin said softly. I looked away from him, unable to bear the hurt that dulled his eyes. 'You still want to go off to goodness knows where, don't you? You want to, but you can't make the decision to actually pack up and leave, so you've agreed to marry me as your second best option.'

'It's not like that, Reckin, really it isn't.'

'Then what is it like? I gave you all the space you needed to make your decision, despite my brothers teasing me, telling me that it would be my proposal that finally gave you the guts to do what you've always wanted and leave; despite my parents asking me three times a day whether I'd heard from you and how rude and abnormal it was to be left waiting so long; and despite being terrified that my brothers were right and I'd frightened you away. I waited so that you could make your decision free of any pressure. So that your decision would be your own. You agreed to marry me.'

'Yes, I agreed to marry you. But somehow, that agreement seems to have turned into agreeing to have four children, each one two years after the one before, to having my whole life mapped out in front of me so that there's no point in me even living it to find out what happens!'

'But we know that's what we'll do, don't we?'

'Why? Because that's what your parents did? Because that's what everyone in your family does? Is that a reason to do anything, just because everyone else does? Haven't you ever thought about what's possible, Reckin? About what we could do if we thought about what we want instead of just doing what's expected?'

Reckin shook his head. 'This is what I want. I want the life I was born into and I want you in it with me, Ellie.' He turned and walked slowly away.

I hadn't meant to hurt him, I'd just wanted him to understand my point of view, but I had hurt him nevertheless. I was just about to go after him when I felt pulled to walk in the other direction, out of the village. I turned to look across the fields, but could see no reason to walk that way... yet I couldn't ignore the feeling that I should, that all the answers to all of my questions lay in that direction.

A lone orange sycamore leaf drifted to land at my feet, a reminder that autumn was upon us and the nights were rapidly drawing in. I should be getting home, Reckin and I were expected for dinner. Reckin! He had gone clear out of my mind. What was wrong with me? I should go after him.

Suddenly, my whole body lurched. It was as if whatever it was that had drawn my attention across the fields had grabbed hold of me at my belly button, and tugged hard. Tugged. My mouth fell open in shock. I was being tugged. That had to be what it was; a horse had chosen me as a Bond-Partner and was pulling me to them so that we could bond, then we would communicate mind to mind.

Everything fell into place; for the first time, my life made sense. I would become one of the Horse-Bonded. I would learn from my horse as we travelled from village to village, meeting new people, and I would pass on my Bond-Partner's counsel to any who asked for it, just as the Horse-Bonded who had visited Bluesprings had always done for all of us.

I had learnt of the Horse-Bonded when I was a child, as everyone did, but I never dreamt that I would join them, that one day, a horse would choose me. Every muscle, every bone, every nerve in my body wanted me to run to my horse as fast as I could, but that wasn't how things were done. I needed to let my family know so that they could give me a Quest Ceremony to send me on my way to find my Bond-Partner. With a last, longing look across the fields, I turned and ran for home.

My father was cutting a pie into quarters while my mother spooned steaming vegetables onto four plates, when I rushed through the back door into the large, sandstone-walled kitchen with its light oak work surfaces, table and chairs. They both looked up and then past me, expecting to see Reckin.

'Mum, Dad, I'm being tugged! A horse has chosen me, isn't

that fantastic? I know we'll have to cancel the wedding, and believe me, no one feels worse about that than I do, but I'm so excited. I can't believe it! One of the Horse-Bonded! Me! I'll be able to travel and help people as I learn from my horse. I'll miss you all, of course I will, but this is everything I've ever wanted, even though I never realised it, you have to see that? I need to have my Quest Ceremony and be off as soon as possible. Will tomorrow be too soon?' At last, I registered my parents' faces, and stopped talking.

My mother's lips quivered and a lone tear ran down her cheek as she stood holding a forgotten spoonful of peas over the plate for which they had been intended. My father glared at me with fire in his dark brown eyes as he turned the pie knife over and over in his hand.

'Mum? Dad?'

My mother lowered the peas to the plate with a shaking hand and then sat down heavily in one of the chairs and put her head in her hands.

'No, Elinora,' my father said, then clenched his jaws together as if to prevent himself saying anything else.

'No, tomorrow isn't too… too soon for my Quest Ceremony?' I said and licked my suddenly very dry lips only to find that my tongue was equally dry.

My father glared at me with such intensity that I was forced to look away. 'There will be no Quest Ceremony, for you will not be leaving on a quest to search for a horse. You have committed to marrying Reckin. You will be a wife, a mother and a Farmer, as you agreed, and you will be content with your decision.' He slowly, carefully, put the knife on the work surface and then left the kitchen, closing the door firmly behind him.

My mother was now weeping silently. I rushed to sit next to

her, and put an arm around her shoulders. 'Mum, I'm sorry, I'm so sorry, but I couldn't have known this would happen, could I? No one knows whether they'll be tugged by a horse, we're all told not to give it any further thought once we've been taught about it because it will likely never happen to any of us, but it has, Mum, it's happened to me.'

'And finally, you've found the way out you've always wanted, no matter who it hurts,' my mother sobbed. She lifted her head from her hands and looked into my eyes with a sudden fierceness. 'Are you even sure that you're being tugged? That you're not so desperate to get away from us all that you're imagining it?'

I sat back in my chair. Was I imagining it? Had my argument with Reckin, my vision of my whole life mapped out before me without room for choices or the decisions that I was so bad at making, frightened me to the point that I was just imagining a way out of it all? I supposed it was possible. The pull on my mind suddenly increased and I wanted desperately to follow it – but what if it were just my imagination acting up even more because my mother was so upset with me? We never argued. She was reasonable, rational and kind, and she was my friend as well as my mother.

Her eyes softened as she read my indecision. 'Ellie, it will be alright. Your father will calm down and realise that you're just suffering from pre-wedding nerves. It's very common and in your case, it was only to be expected. I'll finish dishing up and put your father's dinner in the oven to keep warm. You and I will eat together and then you can get a good night's sleep. Maybe tomorrow, you and I should have a day off from working and planning the wedding, and spend some time with Peony? She always cheers you up.'

I noticed that she avoided asking where Reckin was and

whether he knew about my state of mind. I didn't think that telling her about my argument with him would ease the situation in any way, so, feeling exhausted, I nodded and managed a weak smile. She patted my hand, wiped her tears away and fetched the pie.

As she spooned it onto the plates and dished up the remaining vegetables, it occurred to me that she had been terribly upset if all she thought was happening was that I was having a pre-wedding panic, and moreover, one that she had expected. But as part of my mind continued to be pulled – or, if it were indeed my imagination, pushed – in the direction of the either real or imaginary horse, while the rest of it became ever more deeply mired in confusion and indecision, my exhaustion only worsened until I was glad to take myself to bed hours before I was normally tired.

I slept fitfully that night. I kept dreaming that I was trying to run towards where I knew my horse was calling for me, but in the way of dreams, my legs were too heavy to move and I couldn't keep my eyes open for long enough to really see where I was going. I would wake drenched in sweat and in ever greater turmoil as I wondered whether I were going mad and my mind was just conjuring up ever more convoluted ways to tell me to run from a marriage that would hold me still forever. Every time I fell back to sleep, I dreamt exactly the same dream.

When, finally, I woke to daylight instead of darkness, the stillness of the house told me that my father and his brothers – one unmarried, the other widowed – who always breakfasted with us, had already left to harvest the fields alongside the Earth-Singers of Reckin's family, who would sing the soil into the air for them, exposing the crops below.

My heart sank. My father would apologise to Reckin for the part of my behaviour about which Reckin knew nothing, and Reckin would think he was apologising for our row, which was between the two of us and nothing to do with my parents. Nothing was ever simple, at least when it involved me. Everyone else seemed to just know what they wanted, and get on with living happy, uncomplicated lives. What was wrong with me? Why couldn't I do that and save us all the hassle and heartache?

As if in response, the pull on my mind increased dramatically and I knew, just as I had the day before, that the answers to my questions lay at its source. So why was I still here? Why was I doubting myself? Because it was what I always did. I was sure of something until I wasn't. And the more I thought about it, the less sure I became until I drove myself and everyone around me mad with my indecision.

I didn't bother to look at myself in the mirror as I washed and dressed in my favourite faded, red leggings and matching pullover, but I must have looked a state, as my mother was unable to hide her shock when I wandered into the kitchen.

She quickly rallied. 'My suspicions were correct, my darling, you need a day off. I told your father and he was fine with it, so he left you to sleep.' She bustled to my side, put an arm around my shoulders and tried to turn me around. 'Why don't you go and have a nice, hot bath while I cook you some breakfast, and then once you've eaten, we'll go over to Peony's?'

'So you can both tell me how great I am with children and that I'll be a wonderful mother?' I said miserably. 'If it's all the same to you, I'd rather have a bit of time to myself.'

Her face fell. 'Right, well, okay, I can see why that might be a good idea. What will you do?' she added, her voice slightly higher pitched than usual.

'I don't know, probably just go for a walk. Thanks for the offer of a cooked breakfast, but I'm not that hungry. I'll just take an apple with me.'

'Well, make sure you're back for lunch, then. You can't wander around on an empty stomach all day.'

'Fine, I'll see you later.' I took an apple from the bowl on the kitchen table and then wandered towards the back door, barely remembering to put on my boots before going out to the paddock at the back of the house. I didn't fancy walking along the street, bumping into everyone who would be wanting to know how the wedding plans were going, how excited I was, what was left to do, and why I looked like a pile of donkey poo. I grinned to myself as I pictured the look that would have crossed my mother's face had I voiced the reason for my choice of exit.

I picked my way between our many chickens, who were all pecking at the grain scattered for them by my mother while the sun rose, as she did every morning. I climbed the fence at the far end of the paddock and found myself knowing unequivocally in which direction I should walk. That was a new sensation. No inner discussion with myself, no pondering of the options and weighing up the pros and cons, just a definite sense that took me in the direction my heart wanted to go. It may have been my imagination that a horse was pulling me that way or it may have been real, but whichever it was, that was the way I was going.

I put my apple in the pocket of my pullover for later, and concentrated on feeling my way. When I reached the site for my and Reckin's cottage and paddock, I passed it without even looking at it. For the first time ever, I knew I was going in the right direction, for the right reasons, and I wasn't about to let thoughts of anything else interrupt the relief of feeling that way.

The longer I walked, the stronger I felt, and the more sure of myself. I smiled and couldn't seem to stop. I began to munch on my apple, feeling hungry now that my stress and worry had lifted.

I walked through pastures I recognised until I found myself walking through those I didn't. I took my boots and socks off and carried them as I waded through a shallow river I had never seen before, glad that the autumn sun was still warm enough to dry my leggings as I continued on my way. I picked fruit from bushes and trees that appeared along my path as if they had all been placed in exactly the right spot to sustain me on my journey. After twenty-five years of feeling out of place, finally, I was feeling as if I were in the right place at the right time, even though I didn't know where I was, or even what time, exactly, it was. I decided that it must have been past lunchtime, not that it mattered.

Lunchtime. Something jogged my mind, distracting me from my path. What was it about lunchtime? My mother was expecting me. My new, perfect world fell away from me. My smile vanished and all of a sudden, I felt tired. My family would be wondering where I was, and even if I turned around to go home now, I would be unlikely to get there before dark, let alone for when I was expected. Then there would be questions, followed by all of the opinions as to what I should do, what I should think, how I should behave. Everything that up until seconds ago had seemed so easy, so perfect, so… me, would just become a muddle again.

I stopped walking and sat down on a boulder. Immediately, the pull on my mind increased, drawing me to where I knew my horse and the life I had always wanted to live, waited for me. But I couldn't go like this, could I? I couldn't just disappear without a word to my family, without food and clothes, without even a coat? What had I been thinking?

I hadn't been thinking, I realised, and cursed myself for an idiot. I should go home. I rose from the boulder and tried to walk home, but I couldn't seem to make my feet move as quickly or as lightly as when I had been walking in the opposite direction. It felt wrong. It was the right thing to do, though, wasn't it? I went and sat back down on the boulder and cried as the confusion and indecision that were so familiar to me, swamped me yet again.

I wanted to go to my horse, but now that I had let my old enemies into my mind, I couldn't be sure there even was one. What if my mother were right after all and I was just imagining it all? Like a lonely child hankering after an imaginary friend? I should go home. I got back to my feet and made them move, one after the other, back the way I had come.

My heart hurt. I massaged my chest, thinking I must have knocked myself, but no, as my heart beat within it, it actually hurt. I remembered back to when my aunt had died. Through his tears, my uncle had described having exactly the same sensation. But how could I be heartbroken to be going home? My loved ones were there.

The sensation only got worse, the closer I got to home, and I realised that it wasn't because I was moving closer to home, but because I was moving further away from that which still pulled at me. My... horse? I stopped, turned around and took a few steps back towards where I knew, all of a sudden, that my horse – MY HORSE, I affirmed to myself – also moved towards me. I wasn't imagining it.

As if to reassure me that I wasn't, the pull on my mind increased further. I smiled. My horse was real. I would go home, tell my family that I was leaving whether they saw fit to give me a Quest Ceremony or not, and then I would pack my bag and walk in the direction that would make my heart whole again. I could argue back and forth about what my mind was experiencing, but my heart would hurt as long as I ignored my horse's call, I just knew it.

'I'll be coming back,' I called out softly, and hoped that somehow, my horse would hear me.

Thankfully, I knew where I was by the time darkness fell. The sky was clear and I found my way home without issue. I had to make myself walk up the front path to Stensonhouse, feeling, strangely, as if it had suddenly ceased to be my home. I left my boots just inside the front door, walked down the hallway to the kitchen and paused at the closed kitchen door, listening to the low murmur of voices within. My parents were there, and from the sound of it, so was Peony. Good.

I opened the kitchen door. My father and Reckin were sitting together at one end of the table, each with a glass of ale. Peony sat nursing her baby at the other end of the table, and my mother appeared to be making her a cup of tea. I could smell the stew that I knew would be bubbling away in the oven.

Peony grinned. 'Been paddling?'

I looked down at my leggings, still wet from my return through the river. I had kept warm by keeping on the move, but now that my attention was drawn to my condition, I began to shiver.

'You've got time for a bath before the stew is ready, and then we can all sit down together and have a nice family meal,' my mother said with a nervous glance towards my father and Reckin, before smiling a little too brightly at me.

Reckin looked at me uncertainly but my father watched me with a steady gaze. My heart began to beat more quickly and as a consequence, the pain of being apart from my horse increased. In any other situation, I would have dithered but my heart left no room for delay. I had to tell them now.

'I love you all, you know that…'

'Ellie, let's pop outside for a quick chat?' Reckin interrupted, a hint of desperation in his voice. He got to his feet and held a hand out to me.

I shook my head very slightly and fought back tears at the look of panic on his face as he lowered his hand.

'Elinora, go up and have a bath please. Your mother has worked hard to cook us all a lovely meal and we WILL all sit down and eat it together,' my father said. He lifted his glass and banged it down on the table.

Peony got to her feet, still nursing her daughter. 'Come on, Ellie, I'll come with you, and you can tell me about your day.' She raised her eyebrows and nodded almost imperceptibly behind me towards the hallway and stairs.

It would have been so easy to do as they all said, but I knew that the pulling at my mind would only get worse and the pain in my heart would only be prolonged if I didn't say what I needed to. I took a deep breath and tried again.

'You know I love you all, please don't ever question that, but you have to let me go. A horse is tugging me and I need to answer the call and become one of the Horse-Bonded. I need to be who I was always meant to be. You have to see that it all makes sense? Reckin, I love you, but you deserve so much more than I can ever give you. Mum, Dad, thank you for your love, your support and your patience. I'm sorry I can't be the daughter you want, but hopefully in time, you might still be proud of me. Peony, help me out here?'

Everyone looked at my sister, who sighed and sat back down. 'Ellie, I can't. I think Mum's right, this is all just pre-wedding nerves. We all know how rare it is for anyone to be tugged by a horse, and no one from this village ever has been. That's why we're all here for you, so that we can have a nice meal together, you can relax and calm down, and then we can all put this little blip behind us.'

My parents looked at me triumphantly, knowing that I would give in and admit to just having one of my ditzy Ellie moments. Reckin didn't look so sure, however.

'Reckin, I'm so sorry,' I said. He sat down, his shoulders slumped. I ground my teeth and clenched my fists in order to keep myself standing firm. If I ran to him and hugged him as I wanted to, my family would take it as a sign that I had realised the error of my ways.

My father stood up, his eyes blazing. 'I think,' he said in a quiet, clipped voice, 'that you had better dine alone in your room. You can use the time to consider all of the hurt you're causing and then, when you've calmed down and realised how ridiculous you're being, we can talk again.'

Reckin looked at my father and shook his head slowly, resignation in his eyes. Then he got to his feet and looked at me. 'Be happy, Ellie,' he said and left through the back door.

'Ellie? Seriously? Are you just going to let him go?' Peony said.

'If I could take him with me, I would, but the Horse-Bonded don't marry, you know that. And anyway, he wouldn't come. He has to be free to live the life he wants and I have to be able to do the same.'

My mother put one hand to her forehead and the other to the back of a chair to stabilise herself. 'Ellie, you're not the first to struggle with the idea of commitment and you won't be the last, but this... this fantasy of yours...'

'It is NOT a fantasy,' I said, shocked by the strength of my voice. 'I am NOT imagining that a horse is tugging me and I WILL be leaving tomorrow, with or without a Quest Ceremony. You know me, Mum, I've never been certain of anything in my life, but I'm certain of this – my horse is out there, calling for me. The idea of committing to Reckin terrified me, you know that. Committing to a life as my horse's Bond-Partner doesn't scare me one bit, in fact I feel as if I've been waiting my whole life to do it.'

'ENOUGH!' My father slammed his hand on the table. The rest of us all jumped and the baby began to cry. Peony put her daughter over her shoulder and gently patted her back while glaring at my father and me in turn.

'I'm going to my room,' I said, my knees shaking. 'Please try to remember that I love you and I'm not doing this to hurt you, it's just what I have to do. I could have left without telling you where I was going, without saying goodbye, but I didn't. I wanted you to understand, and to go with your blessing, but if I have to leave without it, I will.'

I walked quickly from the room, pulling the door shut behind me, and then leant against the wall, trying to slow my breathing. I had done it. I had made a decision – that admittedly wasn't really a decision since it had been spelt out so clearly for me – and I had stuck to it. My stomach rumbled and I hoped that someone would bring some food up to me, but if not, I would eat once everyone was asleep. I had preparations to make for the morning.

I dragged my back-sack from under my bed and began to pile my clothes into it; a spare pair of boots, leggings, warm shirts and pullovers, thick socks, underwear and a thick cloak as well as a coat. If my family wouldn't give me a Quest Ceremony – during which hunting gear, items of food and tokens of good wishes were generally bestowed upon the person departing to find the horse who was tugging them – I would just have to gather food and eat as I went, as I had earlier that day.

When fear nagged at me that I had no idea how far away my horse was, and it was possible that I could find myself in the middle of nowhere with no food or hunting gear when the winter snows came, I found that it was quickly replaced by calm. I knew, without knowing how I knew, that my horse wasn't far away and that once we were together, everything would be okay.

Footsteps sounded on the stairs followed by a shuffling noise outside my bedroom door, and I waited for it to open. When the footsteps retreated, I opened the door to find a tray on the floor, on which was a big bowl of stew, a hunk of bread and a glass of water. So, no one wanted to talk to me, or presumably, to even look at me.

I took the tray into my room, kicked the door closed and sat down on my bed to eat, although I no longer felt hungry. Why did everything always have to be so difficult? My head was so full that it was pounding. A firm, even pull on my mind reminded me that I wasn't alone and gave me a sudden strength and clarity. I would eat, I decided, whether I wanted to or not.

I had a long, hot bath before I retired to bed, not knowing when my next would be. It dawned on me as I lay amongst the soap suds, that for other prospective Horse-Bonded, the evening before leaving to find their horse was probably an exciting time; a time to celebrate with their family at having been tugged, and of anticipation at the prospect of the whole village turning out for their Quest Ceremony the following morning. I felt a flash of anger that my family couldn't be more ashamed and upset that it was happening to me – not that they believed that was what was happening, of course. Then I just felt sad. Sad that they didn't believe me, sad that they weren't behind me, and sad that I would be leaving without their support.

I almost wavered and doubted myself again. Almost. Then the urge to get out of the bath and run to where my horse was pulling me, combined with the ache in my heart from having been that much closer to my destination and having walked away from it, pulled me up short. I sat up in the bath, scrubbed myself clean with an almost manic ferocity, dried myself off and dressed for bed. I was going to get the rest I needed. Tomorrow would be a big day.

I lay in bed, listening to Peony leaving and my parents talking and moving around downstairs. When I thought of my family, I felt turmoil. When I thought of my horse, I felt calm. I focused on how happy I had been during my walk earlier that day, and drifted into a deep, restful sleep.

I woke at sunrise and was immediately aware of the pull being exerted on my mind. I grinned, despite my anxiety over what I would face when I went downstairs. Today I would travel the same path as yesterday, only today I would keep going, leaving everyone's disappointment behind me. There would be no more uncertainty, no more confusion, just excitement for what lay ahead.

I dressed quickly, heaved my back-sack onto my shoulder and went downstairs. I dumped the back-sack by the front door and went into the kitchen to find my mother, father and uncles sitting at the table, eating breakfast. My mother looked up at me apologetically. My uncles, so like my father in appearance if not so stern in demeanour, stood up whilst holding plates piled with buttered toast. One of them moved to the back door, the other to the kitchen door behind me.

'Er, morning, everyone,' I said, looking from one of them to the other.

'Morning, love, there's porridge on the stove. Help yourself,' my mother said. My uncles both nodded at me without comment from their positions by the two kitchen doors. My father didn't look up or acknowledge me as he spread butter on each piece of toast on his own plate.

I moved self-consciously to the stove and spooned some porridge into a bowl. It smelt of the apple that my mother had cooked and stirred through it. My favourite. 'Thanks, Mum,' I said as I sat down next to her. 'Uncle Raz, Uncle Den, why are you standing up?'

Uncle Raz, my father's younger brother, winked at me and then shifted uncomfortably from one foot to the other.

Uncle Den, the eldest of the three brothers, was more forthright. 'Because your father asked us to, Elinora.'

I looked at my father. 'Dad? What's going on?'

He looked up at me as if I'd asked what colour the sky was. 'You really have to ask?'

My mother put a hand on his arm. 'Col, we agreed that I would speak to Ellie,' she said softly.

My father looked up to the ceiling, clamped his jaws together and focused back on his toast. I looked at my mother expectantly.

'We just think you need a few days here at home with us, while you calm down,' she said. 'Then you'll be able to think more rationally.'

I looked back at my uncles, who both refused to meet my eyes. My earlier excitement and good cheer about what the day would bring, deserted me, leaving only the ache in my heart and the constant pull on my mind to keep my thoughts focused. 'I'm perfectly rational, thank you, and, as I told you last night, I'm leaving today. You clearly have no intention of giving me a Quest Ceremony, and that's fine. But I am leaving.'

'NO, YOU ARE NOT!' my father shouted. I noticed for the first time that he looked dreadful. His rapidly greying, thick, wavy hair was tousled, as if he had been running his fingers through it. He had dark rings under eyes that flashed with anger and his skin had a grey tinge to it.

'Are you feeling unwell?' I asked him.

He looked at me whilst shaking his head for what seemed an eternity. Then he threw his head back and laughed the most horrible laugh. 'Did you hear that, Maggie?' he asked my mother. 'Elinora wants to know if I'm feeling unwell! Me, who has worked his finger to the bone to provide a good life for her, but which, apparently, isn't good enough for her. In fact it's a life that's so repellent to her, she's concocted the most ridiculous story to get away from us all!'

My mother looked at me pleadingly. 'Ellie, I have a proposition for you. Please, stay here with us for a couple of days and then if you still think you're being tugged, we won't stop you from leaving.'

I couldn't believe what I was hearing. 'You intend to keep me here, whether I want to stay or not,' I said, my voice trembling.

'You're not well, Ellie, we're worried about you,' my mother said. 'Is it really too much to ask that you compromise with us on this?'

'I'm not well? I'm feeling more sure of myself than I ever have, and you call that being unwell?' Doubt suddenly stabbed through me. What if I were unwell?

My mind was immediately tugged so fiercely that I gasped and came back to myself. Back to my new self. The self who was sure what I was feeling and what I wanted.

I sighed. I couldn't blame my family for thinking I was having some sort of breakdown, not really. Maybe I should agree to stay for two days, to prove to them that I was perfectly sane and well. It would hurt me, I knew it would, but if it would convince them and allow them to be happy for me to leave, then it would be worth it. I ignored the uneasy shifting in my stomach at the truth that I thought I knew but didn't want to admit.

'Okay,' I said, 'I'll stay for two days. Two mornings from now, if I'm still sure I'm being tugged, you'll accept it and let me go?' I couldn't believe I was bargaining with my parents for my release, but I didn't see what else I could do.

My father refused to look at me, confirming what the shifting in my stomach that was rapidly turning to nausea, still told me. Before I could challenge him to admit that he would never let me go, that it was he who was panicking that the life he had chosen wasn't turning out exactly as he had expected, that it was he who wasn't well, my mother said, 'Oh, Ellie, you'll be glad you agreed to this, in two days' time, you'll be glad, believe me.'

I wasn't hungry any longer. It was no longer just my heart that ached; my whole body hurt at defying what my mind wanted it to do – what my very soul wanted it to do.

I pushed my porridge bowl away and got to my feet. 'I'm going to my room, if I'm allowed through the door.'

Uncle Raz looked between my father, who didn't look up, and me. When he saw me looking at him, he flushed and looked quickly away. 'Er, of course,' he said. He looked back at my father and when he still received no guidance, went through the kitchen door ahead of me into the red, sandstone hallway, and stood before the front door so that I had to squeeze past him to go up the stairs. I couldn't look at him.

I undressed and got into bed, covering my head with the purple quilt that matched the rest of my bedding and clashed appallingly with the red walls. I closed my eyes and tried to breathe slowly and calmly. Two days and two nights, that was all I had to get through and then I would leave whether my family tried to stop me or not.

The tugging on my mind became stronger as the morning passed. I breathed slowly and surely, taking strength from the horse who took an increasing amount of my mind away from my troubles, and using it to prevent my body from moving.

A knock on the door was followed by my mother's voice by my bed. 'That's it, love, just rest. I've brought you some sandwiches and juice for lunch, I'll leave them here by your bed for when you get hungry.' I had no spare strength to answer her.

When next she spoke, her voice sounded anxious. 'Ellie, come on, please eat? Look, I've brought your favourite, fried eggs and tomatoes on toast, won't you have some?' My quilt was slowly peeled back so that the smell of the food my mother had cooked wafted up my nose. I barely noticed it. All of my concentration was taken up with staying still when every part of me wanted to run to my horse. I kept my eyes closed, focused on breathing and, when dark eventually fell, resigned myself to a long night of the same.

When my mother brought me some breakfast and found all of the food from the previous day untouched, she quickly departed. There was the sound of raised voices downstairs and then heavy footsteps on the stairs. My father shouted at me for what seemed like forever. I couldn't hear his words for the pounding in my head at what I supposed, with a detached curiosity, was hunger and thirst now as well as the strain of resisting the pull on my mind, now at an unbearable level.

When he finally left me alone, my sister's voice took the place of his, along with one I recognised but couldn't immediately place. That realisation pierced through my concentration and I heard the voice say, 'There's nothing wrong with her body. She's hungry and dehydrated, but apart from that, despite appearances, she's fine.'

Erasmus, the village Herbalist, that was who it was. So, my family thought I was physically ill, as well as insane. I immediately had to revert all of my concentration to staying where I was so that I didn't jump to my feet and out of the first floor window in my desperation to get to my horse, proving them all right.

The next thing I knew, I was being hauled upright and a glass of water was held to my lips. I was very thirsty, a small part of me realised. I opened my mouth and drank. When spoonfuls of food were held in front of me, I opened my mouth and accepted them, chewing and swallowing each mouthful with no idea what the food was. When I was left alone, I fell asleep with the comfort of knowing that as soon as it was light, the torture would be over.

When dawn broke, I snapped back to myself. I could leave. As soon as my intention matched that for which my heart and soul yearned, my world snapped back into focus. The pull on my mind was overwhelming, yet soft, comforting and… reassuring at the same time. I was going to my horse. Everything would be okay.

I rushed to the bathroom, washed quickly but thoroughly and then dressed in fresh leggings, shirt and pullover. I sighed in exasperation as I found my back-sack under my bed, empty, its contents back in my wardrobe. I repacked it and heaved it onto my back, putting both of my arms through its straps; I would take no chances that I might be parted from it. I went down the stairs to find Uncle Den positioned before the front door. I shook my head at him and he had the good grace to look away. I went into the kitchen to find my parents at the table and Uncle Raz in front of the back door.

'It's lovely to see you up and about, love,' my mother said, leaping to her feet and spooning more of my favourite apple porridge into a bowl.

'Thanks, Mum, that smells lovely. It will set me up nicely for the day ahead.'

'So you've finally decided to stop pretending to be ill, well I guess that's a start,' my father said.

'I wasn't pretending to be ill, I was fighting the urge to run to my horse. It's been a nightmarish couple of days, but now I'm all set to go, I'm feeling a lot better. When I find my horse, I'll be complete.'

'When you've spent weeks walking in circles, you'll be even more ridiculous, is what you'll be,' my father said, crossing his arms in front of his chest. 'I won't allow it, Ellie, this nonsense has to stop. I'm exhausted, you're exhausted and your mother's at her wit's end.'

'I've fulfilled my part of the bargain. Two days have passed, and I'm still certain that I'm being tugged. You have to let me go, Dad,' I said firmly.

He shook his head, his eyes bloodshot and his hair even more unkempt.

'Mum?' I said desperately.

She merely shook her head. 'I just don't know what to do for the best, love.'

'Then let me go. You promised you would let me go. If you don't, I'll never forgive you. Never,' I repeated, looking between my parents and then to each of my uncles.

They all watched me in stony silence as I slowly, carefully, forced a whole bowlful of porridge down my throat, and then helped myself to another, knowing that I would need it since my family clearly had no intention of allowing me to leave, let alone take any food with me.

When I stood to go, my parents stood up too. 'I love you both but I'm leaving now,' I said.

'Ellie, you can't go, not like this,' said my mother.

'She's going nowhere,' growled my father.

I opened my mouth to argue but before I could utter a word, a furore erupted outside. There was a thrumming sound on the ground, voices shouted and chickens flapped and squawked in the paddock. Uncle Raz turned, opened the back door and ran outside. I saw my chance and sprinted after him, arriving in the paddock just as a sleek black horse skidded to a stop in front of us. He towered over us both. His body was slender but he had a huge, muscular neck that was arched almost upright with just the top of his neck and his head curving downwards, making him appear even taller than he was. His black forelock, mane and tail were thick and impossibly long, and his lower legs were swathed in yet more long hair. His eyes were such a dark brown that they appeared black. They glistened in the dawn light as he lowered his head and sniffed the top of mine.

I smiled up at his chin. 'I was just coming to find you,' I said.

While your intention was pure your ability to act on it was in doubt.

All of the stress, anxiety and pressure of the last days, weeks, months – in fact years – fell away as his thought became words in my head. Words that I understood. Words that held no judgment but rang with truth, knowledge, experience, wisdom, reassurance and love.

I've never been very decisive, I admitted. *Even when I felt you pulling at my mind to come to you, I doubted myself. Now you're here, everything is so clear and I can't believe I ever felt confused or unsure.*

You did not know that which has now become obvious to you.

Which is?

It will benefit you to assign words to it for yourself. He stepped back and looked down his nose at me.

Tentatively, I reached up to the soft, velvety black skin of his muzzle and stroked it, then rested a hand on his cheek. I felt him settle into the place in my mind where I would always know what he thought and how he felt. The ache in my heart disappeared. It felt light and full of love for the magnificent being in front of me as a feeling of rightness swept over me.

The truth is in my heart, not in my head. My thought formed almost by itself.

You have confused yourself and those around you with your tendency to think your way forward when feeling your way would have eliminated doubt. Had your ancestors not trusted their feelings you would not be here.

So I'm a throwback to the ways of The Old, then? I'm a failure?

Failure is a construction of the human mind. Your experience will allow you to understand and help those with the same tendency to think when feeling would better serve them.

I sighed. *I've given my family and friends such a hard time. They do naturally what I find it so hard to do, and they believed me ill when I suddenly knew what I wanted.*

They will benefit from the realisation that there are ways to live a life other than how they feel is right for them. There is perfection in every situation. It can be difficult to see yet it is there.

I frowned and smiled at the same time, then I began to laugh. My view of myself, of my family, of my world had been turned upside down in a conversation between two minds that had taken place in no more than a few blinks of my eyes, and yet I felt absolutely fine about it, as if nothing would ever be too strange, too difficult or too much to cope with, ever again.

'Ellie?'

I jumped at Uncle Raz's voice beside me, and moved to my horse's side so that I faced him and the rest of my family. My parents stood open-mouthed, clutching hold of one another as if the world were about to end. Uncle Den was just behind them looking equally stunned. Peony was pushing her way past them to stand with Uncle Raz.

'I couldn't believe what I was hearing, so I had to come and see for myself,' she said. 'He's, um, he's big, isn't he? What's his name?'

I put a hand up to my horse's neck. *What is your name?*

You must decide for yourself. He expanded rapidly within my mind until I was aware of nothing but him. He was calm, wise, and so sure of everything – himself, his bond with me, our purpose – in a way that was foreign to me and yet called to me. I felt him welcome his name as I chose it.

'Resolute. His name is Resolute,' I said.

I had a Quest Ceremony after all. When my father asked if I would consider waiting until that afternoon before leaving with Resolute, so that they would have time to organise one for me, I knew the reply I wanted to give, but I wasn't sure I should. Before I could ask Resolute what to do, he wandered away and began to graze the grass of our paddock while the chickens pecked unconcernedly around him. I felt him waiting for something. And I remembered. *The truth is in my heart, not my head.* I could feel his contentment; he and I were together and everything else was incidental.

'May we stay for a few days?' I asked. 'There's enough grass in the paddock for Resolute and I can bring water out to him. Then maybe we can all get used to the fact that I'm absolutely, definitely leaving?'

My parents and Peony all rushed to me at the same time and we hugged, laughed and cried. When they had finished, my uncles hugged and congratulated me, followed by a horde of our neighbours who all glanced longingly in Resolute's direction, but left him to eat in peace.

The days that followed were among the happiest of my life. Resolute was more than content to graze and rest in our paddock after long days of travelling to reach me, and I loved sitting in the grass near his head, either chatting to him in my mind as if he had always been there, or just watching and listening to him tearing at the grass and then munching it in an almost hypnotic rhythm.

Members of my family came and sat with me sometimes, and

at others stayed back and watched from a distance, talking amongst themselves. Their happiness and excitement increased as they accepted what was happening and what it meant, not just for me but for them, having a member of the Horse-Bonded in the family. When the time came for me to leave, it was with their blessings.

My Quest Ceremony was like no other, not least because Resolute was present, so there was no actual need for a quest. I left my family's house through the front door as was usual, though having a large, black horse follow me through the house from the paddock, just about fitting through the doorways by lowering his head to his knees, was anything but. When he appeared at my side, my family presented me with my back-sack, filled with clothes and food, and with cooking and hunting gear hanging on the outside.

There was cheering from the villagers as they stood in two lines facing one another, creating a pathway for my Bond-Partner and me to walk down. Resolute was unflinching as dried flowers were thrown over us both, and little tiny horseshoes made from metal, grasses and in some cases, coloured cloth, were hung not only from my clothes and hair as was customary, but in his mane and tail.

The humming behind us announced that the Tissue-Singers and Bone-Singers had begun work on us both, ensuring we were in optimal health before we left on our travels. I stopped in my tracks, wondering if Resolute would welcome unasked for interference in his well-being, but then immediately felt the answer in his calm enjoyment of his body relaxing where it was a little tense, and tightening where more tone was helpful to him.

When we eventually reached the end of the human corridor, we found a lone figure waiting just beyond it. Reckin's eyes were red-rimmed, but they held wonderment as he watched Resolute's approach. We both stopped in front of him and Resolute slowly reached out his black nose to Reckin's face. Reckin stepped back, his eyes darting to mine in alarm, but when I grinned and nodded, he stood his ground and looked back to the huge, black horse who stretched his neck out in order to blow warm air onto Reckin's cheek and then gently nuzzle him.

Reckin smiled and reached a tentative hand to Resolute's neck. 'You promise me you'll look after her, okay, big fella?'

I threw myself at Reckin and hugged him for all I was worth, trying not to cry. 'You're one in a million, and one day very soon, you'll find a person who's worthy of you,' I whispered.

He hugged me back and then held me away from him. 'You'll come back some day?'

'I'm sure we will.'

He nodded. 'I'm happy for you, Ellie. I may not look it at the moment, but I am. See you around.' He chewed his lip as he turned and walked away.

I nodded at his retreating back and murmured, 'See you around.' Then I looked up at Resolute, his black face stark against the bright blue autumn sky. *So, where are we going?*

The Gathering. Our contribution is needed.

The Gathering? Home of the Horse-Bonded? I don't feel qualified to contribute anything to anyone, let alone to people who've been bonded for years. I mean what could I possibly do to help them?

A time of considerable change is approaching. There will be a need for those who can hold to feeling their way forward when fear would have them do otherwise.

But I've only ever done that once, and it was because of you.

Then there is no need for concern for I yet exist.

I laughed. *Are all horses funny or is that just you?*

I made no jest. The bond that joined us thrummed with his

absolute commitment to me and our lives together as Bond-Partners, his belief – no, it was more than that – his knowledge that I would be someone other than who I was now; someone who could make a difference.

I felt humbled and overcome with gratitude towards him, and more than a little over-awed. Instantly, his confidence in me flowed through our bond, taking up more and more space in my mind until I could think of nothing else. I smiled and couldn't stop.

Aleks

hen I realised that the incessant, intolerable pull on my mind was being exerted by a horse, I was horrified.

I had my life exactly as I wanted it. I rose at the same time each day, ate the cooked breakfast that my mother prepared for me, collected the packed lunch that she put by the front door so I couldn't go without it, then walked the short distance to my workshop for a satisfying day of working through my orders until it was time to tidy up and return home for dinner. I would go for a walk every evening, occasionally varying the route but never the amount of time I was out. On my return, I would write my workplan for the following day, listing each job and the amount of time I intended to spend on it, so that I knew exactly what awaited me when I woke up the following morning, and could be confident that I would finish my working day on time.

I was a Glass-Singer. I found it satisfying beyond measure to sing different sized, randomly placed grains of sand from a pile, into something of smooth, organised beauty. The quality of my work was unsurpassed and I was always in high demand, so when people commented to my parents how strange it was that their thirty-five-year-old son still lived at home, my parents' reply that I was so dedicated to my work, I simply didn't have the time to devote to a family of my own, was readily accepted. It was the truth, but not all of the truth. My parents knew – for I had told them on numerous occasions – that the chaos of marriage and screaming children held absolutely no appeal to me whatsoever, and never would.

I was nearing the end of a very satisfying day's work, and had just finished singing into existence the last of a set of ten jars, each one identical in size, colour and glass thickness, when the pulling on my mind started. To begin with, I thought that a draught had somehow found its way into my workshop; it felt as if the air around my head had merely been displaced slightly. But then I had a very definite sensation just by my right temple. It was as if my skin were being pinched and pulled away from my head, and my mind were being drawn out through the pinch, pulling me towards the door and out of the village in a northerly direction. No, I decided, that was ridiculous. I scowled and brushed at my temple. It had taken a lot of concentration to get the glass precisely the same thickness not only throughout each jar I had just sung, but throughout the set. I had overdone it, that was all.

Knowing that it would tax me, I had put the order of jars at the end of the list for that day, and I smiled in self-congratulation that I had been right to do so. A strange sort of headache was a small price to pay for the satisfaction of a difficult job done to perfection.

I lifted the tray and carried it to the bench by the door, where my completed orders awaited collection. I had learnt to put them there, so that when people came to collect their glassware, they only needed to step just inside the workshop, if at all. Any further than that and they just brought mess and endless chatter, both of which had the potential to throw me off schedule.

I was a step away from the bench when the sensation in my head increased very suddenly. I swayed where I stood and almost dropped the tray. With shaking hands, I lowered it to the bench, gasping in horror as one of the jars toppled over. I picked it up to check it wasn't damaged, but my mind was pulled firmly and without mercy away from my intended inspection. My hands flew to my head and I dropped the glass.

The sound of my creation smashing on the stone floor brought me back to my physical senses immediately. I stared down at the multitude of tiny fragments of glass in shock. Never, in nearly twenty years of being a Glass-Singer, had I broken a result of my efforts. Never had order become chaos.

As if having waited respectfully for me to mourn my loss, the tearing of my mind from its safe haven in my head resumed, combining with my horror of having a self-created mess to clear up and the prospect of finishing work late for the first time ever, to render me almost senseless.

A small part of my mind seemed to step away from the larger part that was suffering so many kinds of trauma, and pondered at the cause of my discomfort and distress. It wasn't until I fitted what was happening to me with something I remembered having been taught as a child, that I arrived at the horrifying answer that I knew had to be the correct one. A horse had chosen me as a Bond-Partner. Said horse had taken hold of my mind and was pulling it so that I would be forced to follow until I found my tormentor and we entered into a lifelong bond. We would communicate mind to mind and I would have to pass on the wisdom of the horses to all those people who were incapable of sorting their own lives out and needed help.

The whole idea was repugnant and intolerable. I absolutely

would not leave the comfortable life I had created for myself for one of upheaval and uncertainty, and certainly not when it was imposed on me by someone else. I was strong-willed and self-disciplined, so I could and would just ignore the tugging, and carry on with my life as normal. I grabbed a broom and began to sweep up the glass. I would soon have it sung into a new jar of equal perfection to the rest.

The pull on my mind began to pulse, as if knowing that would make it more difficult to ignore. I breathed in and out deeply. I could do this. I swept the glass into a pile and fetched the dustpan and brush, annoyed to find that each sweep of glass into the dustpan coincided with a beat of the pulse. Then I grinned. I would use the rhythm of the pulse to my advantage. I would create an even higher level of order in my mind, where everything I did was in time with the regular beat. I continued to sweep in time, now on purpose. Then I stood up on one beat and paced towards the sink in time with the beats that followed. I poured the glass fragments into a sieve on one beat, turned the tap on with the next, and moved the fragments under the water flow by shaking the sieve to each subsequent beat, until they were clean.

I emptied the fragments onto a towel and patted them dry, still keeping to the rhythm. This was easy. A well-ordered, well-disciplined mind could cope with any level of disruption. I would just keep going until the horse gave up. But then the rhythm of the pulse suddenly sped up and the tugs rapidly increased in strength, until I found my legs moving in the direction in which my mind was being pulled. I reached the door but managed to prevent myself from opening it by grabbing hold of the bench covered with my completed works. No, no, no. I would go back to my workbench and finish my day's work and then I would go home. I turned back to the room, but the conflict between my body and mind kept me from moving. A wave of panic swept over me. I was in charge of my life. Me. I would not be pulled from it by a horse, of all things.

Suddenly, the pulling lessened and my mind was flooded with softness and warmth, a sensation that reminded me of when I was a small boy and my mother would lift me out of the warm, scented bath that had soothed me and left me feeling sleepy, and wrap me in a fluffy towel, singing to me as she gently patted me dry. I had felt so comfortable, so loved, so safe.

The pull on me slowly increased again. It would be okay, wouldn't it, to follow it? I turned back to the door, opened it and went to step outside, leaving my worklist uncompleted and broken glass on the draining board. I snapped back to myself. What was I thinking? I couldn't leave! But as I turned back into my workshop again, the tugging on my mind ramped up to an unbearable level, forcing me to turn back towards the cobbled street so that it would recede.

'Aleks, are you alright?' someone called out, I couldn't even begin to try to recognise who.

'Yes, fine thanks, just forgotten something,' I said and turned back into my workshop yet again.

'You don't look alright.'

I was desperate to get back in my workshop and close the door before whoever it was tried to interfere – help was only help when I decided I wanted it and subsequently asked for it – but I couldn't make myself move against the tide that wanted to sweep me out of the workshop and away from it for good. I grabbed hold of the end of the bench and tried to pull myself inside, but still couldn't find the will to move. Panic flared in me again. I didn't have control of myself. I was vulnerable.

Immediately, the soft, soothing feeling was back, but unlike previously, it didn't fill my mind. It wove itself through my terror, as if encouraging me to embrace my vulnerability, as if assuring me that it was a good thing. I was suddenly very desperately and overwhelmingly afraid.

'NOOOOOOOOOOOOOOO!' I shouted and threw the bench away from me. I didn't flinch at the sound of many days' work crashing to the ground, and I couldn't even find it in me to cringe at the fact that there were now glass fragments of all different colours and thicknesses from the different pieces, intermingled on the floor. I sank down onto the top step of the five that led up to my workshop, panting. I was dizzy and my heart thumped so hard and fast that I was terrified it would give out.

'Aleks?' My mother's hands cupped my face as she looked searchingly into my eyes. 'Aleks, whatever is the matter? When you didn't come home at the normal time, I thought something must have happened, but… this?' She looked past me at the devastation I had created.

'I'm being tugged, Mum,' I muttered, 'but I can't go. My life is here. My work is here.'

'You're being tugged? By a horse? Aleks, that's amazing, I'm so proud of you.' My mother sat down on the step beside me and put her arm around my waist. 'Everyone, Aleks is being tugged!' she called out to the crowd of people now gathering on the cobbles at the foot of the steps. 'He's a bit overwhelmed, so give us some space, would you? Tell everyone we have a new Horse-Bonded among us!'

There were shouts of congratulation and then everyone dashed off to share the news.

'I understand why you aren't thrilled about it,' my mother said in a low voice, 'but you'll still be able to do your glass-singing once you're at The Gathering, and you'll find a new routine to settle into with your horse. Everything will be okay. Aleks?' When I didn't look at her, she took hold of my chin and turned my face to hers. 'It will be fine. You won't be going anywhere for a day or so as we'll need to collect everything you'll need for your quest to find your horse. By the time you leave, you'll have come around to the idea, you'll see. Come on, get up, let's get you home before you draw another crowd. I'll come back later and clear up the mess.'

I shook my head. 'No, I can't leave it like that, Mum, you know I can't.'

'What I know, Aleks, is this. Your life is changing and you need to accept it. I know how hard that will be for you but you don't have a choice, so don't resist it any more than the mess in your workshop tells me you already have. Come on, your dinner's on the table.'

I allowed myself to be led home by the hand as if I were a child. I may as well have been, for that was the last time I remembered feeling as powerless. Blessedly, the pulling on my mind had abated to a mild, almost polite reminder of the direction in which I would need to head when it was time for me to leave the village in which I'd been born, grown up and had planned to live out my days.

As my mind became more my own once more, thoughts arose rapidly within it, all vying for attention. My walks had taken me out into the nearby hills and pastures, but I had never been further than that. What was out there? What would I eat? When would I eat? What if I couldn't find my horse and I was lost and alone forever? What if I did find my horse and we bonded – what would my life be like? I knew the Horse-Bonded travelled around a lot, but to where and for how long? What if I met people I didn't understand or who didn't understand me?

My life was unravelling and I was petrified. By the time I got home, my fear had turned to exhaustion.

'I think I'll just go to bed, Mum,' I said.

She nodded. 'Shock is tiring. A good, long sleep will do you good and then when you wake, you, your dad and I can sit down and talk this through. When you can see the way in front of you again, you'll feel better.'

I didn't. The only things of which my parents could assure me as I forced my breakfast down the following morning, were that they would give me a decent amount of food to take with me on my journey to find my horse, and that, being summer, the weather would be kind. They couldn't tell me what was beyond the four valleys within which they had lived their lives, how long my quest would take, what I would do once I'd found my horse, or any of the other unknowns that went hand in hand with being tugged, because they didn't know.

Any thoughts of returning to my workshop during that day, or doing anything other than preparing for my departure, caused the pull on my mind to increase. I felt too brittle to challenge it so I went along with having my hair cut and choosing the new trousers and shirt that I was told were essential for me to look my best for my Quest Ceremony.

I ate the lunch that was put in front of me even though I couldn't taste anything and had to wash every mouthful down with water so that it didn't stick in my throat. I nodded and tried to look appreciative as my mother explained which food packets contained what and how to cook the contents of some of them, using which of the many cooking utensils she was attaching to the outside of the new and rapidly filling back-sack she had acquired for me.

When dinner time came, I forced down as much food as I could and then sat in silence while my parents chattered excitedly about the future that awaited me.

After dinner, I rose, feeling even more exhausted than the evening before, and intending to go to bed. My father, mistaking my intention, held a hand up. 'You've gone for your evening walk alone for as long as I can remember. May I accompany you on your final one?'

I smiled weakly. 'I guess so. I don't feel like going far though.'

'No problem. You choose the way and set the pace. After you.' He motioned for me to go ahead of him towards the front door.

I left him to smile and wave to all of those who passed us and congratulated me. I looked down at my feet until we had left the stone cottages of the village behind us.

'That's exactly how you're going to need to handle the next few days, weeks – however long it takes you to find your horse, son,' my father said.

'Sorry?' Where before my voice had been confident and strong, I barely managed a whisper.

'Your mind will dictate where you go and you won't find that comfortable, so you'll need to focus on just putting one foot down after the other. Count your steps, like you used to when you didn't want to go to school. Before you know it, you'll be with your horse and everything will feel easier.'

I laughed huskily. 'My life has been reduced to counting my own footsteps. Somehow, I can't find it in me to be happy about that, no matter how much everyone tells me what an honour it is to be chosen by a horse and be one of the Horse-Bonded.'

'For most people, it is. You've met the Horse-Bonded who've passed through the village. They have a presence, a bearing, that demands respect. They love their horses and have so much pride in them and the counsel they give us all. Have you ever met one who seemed anything other than happy with their lot?'

'No, but they aren't me. I was happy before.'

'And you can be again. You will be again. Your mother and I are prouder of you than you'll ever know, Aleks. Hopefully, you'll make it back here in the next year or two, so we can meet your Bond-Partner.'

I wondered whether I would live that long. When I was in charge of what I did and how I lived, I was safe. Now I wasn't in control of anything and as a result, anything could happen to me. I wanted to hate my future Bond-Partner yet when I tried to feel that way, I remembered the softness, the warmth that had tried to soothe me and I found I couldn't. So, all I was left with was my fear. Focus on putting one foot in front of the other. My father was right, it was all I could do.

I endured my Quest Ceremony through a haze of fear and misery. When my parents handed me the back-sack they had filled with clothes and food, and adorned with cooking equipment, it felt as if they were handing me the end of my life. As I walked between the two opposing rows of villagers all congratulating and cheering me, I wanted to grab hold of each in turn and beg them to take my place. With each tiny ornamental horseshoe that they hooked into my clothes and back-sack as a way of sending their love and good wishes with me on my quest to find my horse, my terror increased.

When I reached the end of the human corridor, I wanted desperately to run back to where my parents stood proudly waving on our, no, on their front doorstep, but I knew I wouldn't be able to; my mind would be yanked back towards the horse I was being forced to leave my home to find, and I would be no more able to resist it than I had been on my previous attempts.

My father closed his hand into a fist. Then he raised his forefinger and mouthed, 'One,' followed by his middle finger, 'Two,' his third finger, 'Three,' and his little finger, 'Four.' Then he closed his fist and shook it slightly. 'You can do this.'

I nodded, gritted my teeth and turned to walk out of the village. One. Two. Three. Four...

By the time I had reached forty thousand steps, it dawned on me that I should probably stop and eat something. I had spent the best part of the day walking up and down hills, some grassy, others covered in boulders and scrub, while the summer sun beat down on the top of my head whenever the bulbous, white clouds that shaded me the rest of the time, allowed it to. Terrified that I would run out of water, I had drunk only sparingly from one of my many water flasks, and I felt dizzy and faint.

I looked around myself. All I could see were boulders and bushes, but just because I couldn't see anything that might threaten me, it didn't mean it wasn't there. The relative calm that counting my footsteps while following my mind had afforded me, shattered. I needed to hide. My eyes darted from boulder to bush as I tried to decide which would provide the best shield from the unknown. That was the worst thing about the hideous situation in which I saw myself – I didn't even know of what I should be terrified, so I was terrified of everything.

The pulling on my mind increased and I almost cried, but as soon as I paid attention to my horse, the pulling decreased again and was replaced by that same soft, gentle presence that had soothed me before. I felt as if there was nothing that should concern me, as if it would be perfectly safe for me to just sit down where I was, or by a nearby boulder against which I could lean and be in the shade of the tall, prickly bush behind it. Yes, that looked inviting – but exposed. If I had come across the spot in which I was standing, then so could anyone or anything else.

My fear ramped up again, telling me to move on, but the soothing presence increased in direct proportion with it, allowing me to remember that I needed to rest and eat. I swayed a little and managed to muster the wherewithal to decide on a compromise. I would rest and eat, but I would do it between the boulder and the bush. Just let something try to get to me through solid rock or past all of those prickles.

I lowered my back-sack to the ground by the bush, dropped to my knees and crawled slowly, painfully, between the bush and the boulder until I judged I was completely out of sight. Ignoring the blood that oozed through the rips in my new shirt and trousers, I reached for my back-sack and dragged it in after me. I found a green food packet – green was a meal that could be eaten raw, red needed cooking, yellow was breakfast cereal, blue was fruit and white contained herbal preparations – as soon as I opened the drawstring. My mother knew me well. I ripped it open and, with the soothing presence more dominant than my fear now that I was hidden from sight, I found I was ravenous, and tore into the round of cheese and bacon sandwiches within.

I picked all of the ornamental horseshoes from my clothes and pack while I ate, depositing them in a pocket, then drained my water flask and put it on top of my back-sack to make sure that filling it would be uppermost in my mind when I moved on. I had five others, but I wanted them all full, all of the time. A slight pang of fear stabbed at my full stomach at the thought that my food store was no longer at a hundred percent. I was no hunter so I had no means of replenishing my food stores unless I came across villages, and what were the chances of that? Horses didn't live in villages, they lived in the wild and that was where I was being dragged. To the middle of nowhere, where I could run out of food and water, where I could fall down a hole and die, and no one would know.

The soothing presence increased again and kept on increasing but this time, as had happened once before, it wove its way around and between my fears rather than attempting to obliterate them, as if trying to make them into something else; as if trying again to tell me that being vulnerable was a perfectly acceptable situation in which to find myself. Well it wasn't.

The presence continued to increase until I found my eyes fluttering shut. When I opened them, it was dark – well, almost. There was a tiny amount of light filtering its way between the leaves and prickles of the bush that both sheltered and hid me, and the questioning tone of the few birdcalls I could hear confirmed that it must be dawn. I had slept the evening and night through, out in the wild, with only a few twigs to keep me from harm.

I winced as I moved; I was still sitting up with my back against the boulder. The presence that had sat so peacefully, so reassuringly in my mind with me yesterday now pulled again quietly but insistently. I sighed and persuaded my stiff, aching body to crawl out of my hiding place, pushing my back-sack in front of me. I stayed still, listening and looking all around, then stood and stretched, my fear rising again. I was out in the open and I didn't feel safe standing still. I would eat on the move.

I found another green food packet, hung my empty water flask on the outside of my back-sack where it would knock me, reminding me to look for water, and shouldered my gear.

As soon as I was moving in the direction of the tugging, it decreased again, leaving my mind to panic afresh at the lack of control I had over my life. One. Two. Three...

I managed fifty-four thousand steps that day before scrambling into the lower branches of an enormous oak tree for the night. The following day saw me achieving nearer thirty thousand, on account of the fact that the clouds had cleared overnight, allowing the sun to pound relentlessly down on the top of my head. I stuck to rationing my water despite frequently coming across streams from which I could replenish my flasks, and found myself giddy with dehydration by mid-afternoon, to the point where I could no longer count my footsteps, and my panic was free to flare yet again.

I responded to the presence more quickly this time as it intertwined itself through my terror of passing out in open countryside where I was easy prey, of dying alone, and of everything else that was even more frightening for being unknown. I managed to stand still for a moment, slow my breathing, and allow myself to accept that I needed to forget my rationing and just drink.

When I had emptied a whole flask and felt better, I realised that I needed a hat. Tiredly, I unpacked all of the food packets until I reached the clothing stores that I had so far left untouched. A white sunhat gave me instant relief when I put it on my head. I straightened and looked down at myself. My shirt and trousers hung off of me in shreds as a result of my forays into the bush and tree that had sheltered me for the last two nights, and were covered in dried blood. I was a mess. What did it matter, though? Being clean and well dressed was no guarantee of survival. The horse tugged at my mind again. I sighed, picked up my back-sack and trudged on.

It took me three weeks to find the horse who had become both my tormentor and my pacifier. Three weeks and almost a million steps. I was on my third shirt and my fourth pair of trousers, only having donned new ones when the previous ones fell off. I had crawled into bushes and under tree roots, climbed countless trees and even layered sticks over myself on two occasions in my desperation to hide, whenever I wasn't moving.

My boots were in remarkably good condition, but my scratched and torn skin was not. The only weight remaining in my back-sack was that of my water flasks – all but two empty – and the red food parcels, the contents of which I was convinced I would poison myself with if I attempted to cook them. My cooking utensils had all been torn from my back-sack during my crawling and climbing efforts anyway, yet I couldn't bring myself to dump the food. It represented my last hope of coming across civilisation and someone who might cook it for me, and I clung to that hope almost as much as I had slowly become accustomed to clinging to the sense of my horse in my mind. Any time I panicked at my situation and my lack of control over it, the sense increased, soothing and reassuring me, making sure I knew that I wasn't alone. As the days and then the weeks passed, I began to accept that I probably never would be and much as I hated it to begin with, I began to trust the horse; to trust that maybe, just maybe, I would survive my ordeal.

I knew she was a mare as soon as I first set eyes on her grazing the lush, green grass of the valley below the hill I had just topped. Her pull on my mind ceased instantly but, still too scared to be still when out in the open, I kept moving towards her.

As I got closer, the grey blob in the distance became a slender, grey body atop long yet strong-looking legs. Her white tail flicked constantly to keep the biters away as she pulled at the grass, and her jaws moved from side to side in her large head with its generous features; longer ears than seemed proportional, a nose that barely tapered to a black, velvety muzzle and huge, dark eyes with long, white eyelashes. She oozed with the gentleness, softness and kindness that I had sensed from her whilst on my way to find her, and I had trouble reconciling the beauty I could see and feel with the sense of fury I had felt towards her.

I stopped a few paces from her. 'Well, I'm here. You forced me to leave my home and my family, and I'm finally here.'

She raised her head and I felt my chest soften as her dark eyes found mine. *Had your soul not been expecting my call then you would not have heard it.*

The words that appeared in my head were mine and yet not mine. The fact that they were accompanied by the same sense of soothing calm that I knew was her, confirmed exactly where the thoughts behind them had originated.

Believe me, there was no part of me that was expecting your call. Right back at her, or so I thought.

You attempt to convince me so that the noise of doing so will delay you from accepting that which you know to be true. The words that my mind attached to her thoughts were so unexpected, so repugnant, yet I could feel, somehow, that she was telling the truth for it was impossible for her to do otherwise. There was a sense of patient knowledge and wisdom about her and her thoughts that left me feeling like a helpless child who knew nothing.

I panicked. 'I ATTEMPT NO SUCH THING!'

She merely blinked and stared at me, her jaws still moving from side to side as she chewed her mouthful of grass.

'I was happy before you tugged me. I had a life I loved. I was comfortable and safe, exactly the opposite of how I am now.'

You have never been safer nor more in danger than you are in this instant for neither truly exist.

I couldn't reply, for truth to tell I didn't understand what she had just told me. But, as with her last statement, there was a sense of truth about her thoughts, and the calm assurance that accompanied them told me that she was letting me know I was okay. I found that I believed her. Immediately, something fell into place between us, something invisible to my eyes yet tangible, as if I should have been able to see it.

Our bond existed before either of us were born. What began as an agreement between our souls became a bridge between our minds. It bodes well that you are aware of the possibility of its visible manifestation for it is that for which we will aim.

I sank to my knees in the grass beside her. *I feel as if I'm suddenly someone else. I can't seem to be angry with you for turning my life upside down. I'm not hidden and anything could come for me out in the open like this, yet I feel as if here is where I need to be. I don't understand anything you've told me and yet I feel as if I must be understanding, somehow, for your thoughts to be having this effect on me. What's happening to me?*

She stretched her neck towards me and gently nuzzled the top of my head, breathing her warm reassurance into me with long, slow breaths. *Our bond has awakened you to the existence of your soul. You cannot yet hear it well but you can hear me. For now that is all that is necessary.*

I accepted her thoughts instantly, relieved to be able to understand them. *So I just need to be able to hear you, and I'll keep feeling okay? I'll be safe?*

I sensed her gentle patience as she framed her reply. *It is not possible to be otherwise regardless of any illusion to the contrary. Our bond will not protect you from the illusions you create nor will it dictate how you feel. It will however provide choices of which you were previously unaware.*

It doesn't feel like I've had many of those so far.

She returned to her grazing. *That is because you yet resist the part of yourself that came here voluntarily. Do not concern yourself. Understanding will come with time.*

I could find neither the strength nor the will to argue with her. *So, what now? The only food I have left needs cooking and I have nothing to cook it with. It's probably gone off, anyway, I've been travelling so long.*

We will be at The Gathering by the time the light fades.

My heart lifted. *The Gathering? The home of the Horse-*

Bonded? We're that close to it? It's lucky you got here before I stumbled on it on my way to find you, isn't it? I'd have looked a right idiot arriving there without a Bond-Partner.

You would not have reached it without me. I have been waiting in your path for some time.

For some time? You mean you got here and then just stopped? You could have come to meet me but you left me to struggle on alone?

Did you at any time feel that you were alone?

Well, of course I did... my thought stopped in mid flow for the untruth of it jarred with the consistent feeling of truth that had accompanied all of hers. She may not have been with me in body, but she had been with me every step of the way in my mind. *I still would have found it easier if you had come to me earlier. I'm much more comfortable now I'm here with you than when I was by myself,* I protested.

You would not have tolerated my physical presence before now. Your soul knew me immediately. Your mind required time to trust me before it was ready to accept our bond.

Everything seems so straightforward the way you put it, yet it feels anything but. I've never been so frightened, so exhausted, so powerless.

Yet you survived it all. You have proven to yourself that you can endure extreme discomfort and emerge unscathed.

I got to my feet and looked down at myself. *Hardly. My clothes are ruined and I'm covered in cuts, scratches and bruises.*

It was not your physical condition to which I was referring. She lifted her head and began to walk.

I stared after her. *Oh, I see, you're meaning the whole "what doesn't kill you makes you stronger" thing?*

That would imply that you previously lacked strength. I merely draw your attention to the fact that the part of you that is never separate from me has remained unaltered throughout the experience despite the part that is aware only of yourself having found it difficult. She continued to walk away from me, her long, fine tail flicking from side to side. I hurried to catch up with her and then walked by her head.

It's not that part of me I'm bothered about.

You value your personality more than your soul. That is a usual tendency in humans yet it is more pronounced in you than in most.

And that's a bad thing?

Good and bad do not exist. It is more a matter of what serves you and what does not. It is difficult to release patterns that are no longer helpful but you have courage and determination. And you have me.

I didn't understand what it was that was meant to be difficult, but the gentle sense of confidence that accompanied her words pervaded my mind and then my body. It was as if all of my muscles that were tired and slack suddenly found strength and I walked with a new sense of purpose.

I have you, I confirmed. *I do. I can feel that. Thank you. What do I call you?*

You must choose my name according to what you see and feel next. Steady yourself against me for you may become unsure on your feet.

Why? What are you going to... oh. It was as if she were everywhere at once. She was in the grass under my feet and the warm air that parted before me. She was the birds that swooped above us as well as the insects they plucked from the sky. Tendrils burst out of her in all directions and connected to everything I could see, everything I could hear, everything I could feel and everything else beyond.

I stumbled and she stopped walking. I put one hand on her

shoulder and one on her neck as I fought to stay upright. 'Nexus,' I breathed. 'You're Nexus. How can you concentrate with all of that going on all the time? It's like being surrounded by millions and millions of people all screaming at once.'

How do you make sense of all the feedback your body gives you in any given instant?

I considered for some time while my dizziness subsided. 'I suppose I give priority to the bit that's the most uncomfortable,' I said eventually.

Nexus began to walk again. *It is the same. My attention is drawn to that which needs help to rebalance.*

I walked beside her, so deep in thought that for the first time in three weeks, I paid no attention whatsoever to my surroundings. *Are you telling me that you're here with me because out of everything that exists, I'm the most unbalanced?*

I merely advise that the two of us chose to share our lives because we can improve our balance together. We are a partnership.

A partnership. I had never had one of those, nor wanted one, and yet the feeling she attached to the word made me want this one. It had pulled me from everything I held dear and pushed me so far beyond my limits that I had lost all my reference points for what constituted a normal, civilised way of life. I wanted those reference points back, yet I was shocked to realise that I wanted my partnership with Nexus more.

Try to remember that when you experience difficulty. We are here.

I tripped over a tussock of grass in surprise as I looked up to find that we had left the hills behind us and were walking beside and against the rapid flow of a wide river. Off to our left were paddocks of horses, crops, meadow grass, and what looked like goats and sheep, that stretched for as far as I could see. I stopped walking and after a few moments, Nexus stopped too and looked back at me, her huge, dark eyes soft and knowing.

I couldn't go there. My clothes were in tatters, what if they all laughed at me? What if there was no room for me and I was told to leave? What would I do? Where would I go? What if there was a room for me but I didn't like it? What if I didn't like the food? What if I had to eat when they told me and not when I wanted? What if they had enough Glass-Singers there and I had to do manual labour to earn my keep? It would be better for Nexus and me to just go to my home village and enjoy our partnership there.

Lack of certainty allows opportunity, Nexus told me, her thoughts so kind, so gentle that I almost believed she was telling me something I was glad to know. Almost.

Lack of certainty is terrifying, I corrected her.

Certainty stifles your soul.

But I need it.

Then be certain of this. I will be with you constantly. We will find a way forward together. A sense of calm confidence accompanied her words and I found my feet beginning to move despite my fear.

'You promise? You promise you'll be with me, all the time?' I whispered.

I could be nowhere else.

The ground began to vibrate beneath my feet and a thrumming noise made me turn to see a tall, black horse swamped by a mass of long, flowing hair, approaching at speed. His neck was huge and arched so high above his shoulders that I could only just see the head of the dark-haired woman sitting astride him. Nexus whickered to him and he slowed to walk just behind us. I could feel Nexus's desire to go and greet the handsome stallion, yet she stayed with me.

'Hi, I haven't seen you before, are you newly bonded?' the woman called out.

'Well, obviously. I mean, I don't go around looking like I've fallen out of a tree ordinarily.' I flushed, unused to having to make excuses for myself.

The woman laughed, her deep green eyes sparkling. 'Don't worry, other newly bonded have arrived here in a far worse state. I'm Ellie, this is Resolute, and that,' she pointed in the direction of the paddocks, 'as I'm sure your Bond-Partner will have told you, is The Gathering. You're both very welcome here.'

'She has. Her name is Nexus, by the way and I'm, er, I'm Aleks.'

'You don't seem very sure?' Ellie chuckled and held a hand up. 'I'm sorry, I shouldn't laugh. I know exactly how you're feeling. When Res and I arrived here, I was reeling with everything he'd told me on our way here – most of which I didn't understand, by the way, and a lot of which I still don't – and so nervous about actually being here, I almost forgot my own name too. It's nice to meet you, Aleks, and you, Nexus.' She nodded to Nexus, who lifted her head and peered down her nose at both Ellie and Resolute, her nostrils flaring as she drew in long breaths, as if trying to decide whether they were worthy of her attention when I knew she had decided immediately that they were.

I smiled. 'She's glad to meet you both too.' My stomach rumbled loudly and I flushed again.

'Come on, I'll see Res to his paddock, we'll help Nexus to choose hers and then I'll show you around, starting with the dining hall.' Ellie winked and Resolute walked a respectfully wide circle around Nexus until they were in front of us.

We followed them to a path that turned away from the river and wound between the paddocks. When we reached the gate of the first paddock, Ellie slid from Resolute's back. His body almost appeared too slender for his neck and legs, although I decided it was the huge amount of mane, tail and leg hair that gave that impression.

Ellie removed his saddle, dunked a sponge into a bucket of water by the gate and washed her horse down. 'It's tough on him, being black when it's this hot,' she said over her shoulder. 'Nexus has the right idea, don't you, beautiful?' She looked directly at my mare as she spoke to her and I felt Nexus warm towards her.

Ellie picked up each of the black stallion's feet in turn and peered into them, flicking a stone out of one. Then she opened the gate to his paddock and he trotted in. Several horses whinnied and cantered over to him. 'The grey mare is Integrity, and the small, dainty chap is Noble. They're Resolute's preferred field companions. As soon as one decides to change paddocks, the other two are never far behind.'

Fear stabbed at my stomach. 'The horses change paddocks by themselves? How do you know where to find them? How will I know where Nexus is?'

Ellie smiled. 'She's part of you, you'll always know where she is. You really are newly bonded, aren't you?'

I rubbed my face. 'I only found her this morning. I'm a little...'

'Overwhelmed?'

I nodded and rubbed Nexus's nose as it rested gently on my shoulder.

'You need to eat, have a bath and then spend some time back with Nexus and you'll feel a bit better.' She put a hand on my arm. 'I promise you, you will, Aleks. You're among friends. We've all been where you are now, we all know how you feel and we'll all give you the space you need until you feel a bit less disorientated.'

I wasn't comfortable with her touching me, but I managed a weak smile. 'Thank you.'

'You're welcome. Come on let's get Nexus to a paddock so she can get out of this heat.'

Once I had tested the theory that I could always know where Nexus was, been assigned a workroom from which I could do my glass-singing, settled into a bedroom, collected new clothes from the Tailors, and received my first set of chores to contribute to the running of The Gathering, I formed a routine in my head that immediately allowed me to feel better.

I found that I liked the food, of which there was a decent choice at all three mealtimes, and although I abhorred the shared bathroom situation, I learnt that if I rose early, I could bathe at the same time each day and before other people's dirt had a chance to accumulate.

My initial terror at sitting on Nexus was rapidly replaced by a love for riding as she soothed and calmed me enough that I could follow the instructions I was given. Feryl, the Master of Riding, was a patient teacher and by the end of the first week, I not only felt safe on Nexus's back, but as if I belonged there. I began to believe that my mother had been right and I could learn to enjoy being at The Gathering after all.

But then the rota of chores changed. Not only was I assigned some I didn't want to do, but they didn't fit into the routine I had established for myself. I went to the Overseer – a huge man called Mason who had a head and beard of black hair, and was in charge of setting the rota – and protested, demanding to be returned to my chores of the week before. He told me that he wasn't thrilled at having to take his turn at his current role either, but, like everyone else, he was fulfilling his duty to the best of his ability, and I should do the same.

I shouted, I pleaded, I even stamped my foot at one point, but to no avail. It was only Nexus weaving her way through my panic at yet again having no control over my circumstances, that finally calmed me down.

I went back to my room and worked out a new, less satisfactory routine. It was days before I settled into it and then of course there were only a few more days until the weekly rota change occurred again.

Ellie took to coming to my room on sunday evenings, when the new rota was pinned to the board in the dining hall, and walking down to dinner with me. On the way, she would encourage me to keep my focus on the part of my mind I shared with my Bond-Partner when I read the rota, and I did try. Nexus would weave her soothing calm through my panic and discomfort, assuring me that any change inflicted on me was a positive challenge and something to be welcomed, despite all of my instincts screaming otherwise. Her influence helped to varying extents, depending on how big the change to my routine was.

I coped better with the change of chores if they were at least at the same time as the ones of the previous week. When the chores and times both changed, however, it was too much. I would shout, rail and sulk. Often, I would storm back to my room, pack my gear and march down to Nexus, demanding that she leave with me. She would politely refuse and ease me through my temper with her usual gentle, comforting presence. Once I had exhausted myself, she would remind me how far I had come; that despite my difficulties, I had survived all of the changes to my physical circumstances each week and was learning and changing as a result. It didn't feel like it.

Where most of the Horse-Bonded avoided my company as much as possible, Ellie continued to hang around me. Something to do with "following a feeling" – Ellie was all about doing that – though she would never say what that feeling was.

As weeks became months and months became years, I very slowly, very gradually became used to the weekly changes. I moaned every time, but I finally reached a point, five years after arriving at The Gathering, where the changes felt like part of the routine itself.

My confidence in life restored, I took Nexus's advice and began to visit villages to offer her counsel to anyone who wanted it. Our first trips were short, just day long visits to nearby villages with a packed lunch, and back in time for dinner. When we not only survived those trips but returned with me feeling glad we had made them, I accepted Ellie's invitations for us to accompany her and Resolute on longer trips, sometimes lasting several weeks.

Ellie would write down for me exactly which villages we would be visiting, with whom we would be staying and for how long, what food we needed to take with us, where the horses would be able to graze and drink while we were travelling, and when we would be back.

I would feel Nexus's pride in me as I rode her away from The Gathering despite my fear at – even with Ellie's itinerary in my pocket – the number of unknowns that could cause our trip to spiral out of control. On our return, Nexus would weave her delight at the number of people we had helped and my personal achievements as she saw them, through my extreme happiness at having survived, giving me even more cause to celebrate.

It took more out of me than I ever suspected was in me to begin with, but with my Bond-Partner's help and Ellie's support, I fought my way to being a functioning member of the Horse-Bonded.

But then Amarilla Nixon arrived at The Gathering with her

Bond-Partner, Infinity, and my new world – the world that I had spent so many years making safe for myself – shattered.

Not only had Amarilla and Infinity been hunted by a Woeful on their way to The Gathering, putting an end to any further trips to villages by Nexus and me, but Amarilla seemed intent from the outset on causing constant upheaval, bringing chaos to where there had been calm.

It began with her rejecting Feryl's teaching methods and her subsequent formation of a group of rebels who taught themselves to ride their horses differently from the way the rest of us rode ours. I refused to even consider the fact that the way Feryl had taught me may not have been quite right and, despite Nexus's quiet suggestions that I may like to watch what Amarilla and her friends were attempting to achieve with their horses, I was furious with them for their suggestion that we may all need to change the way we rode. I was even more furious with Ellie when she told me one day that she had one of her feelings that they may be right.

Then some Woeful attacked The Gathering. I was so terrified that I couldn't leave my seat in the dining room, even when everyone else rushed out to defend their horses. Nexus was with me instantly, weaving her love and reassurance amongst my fears and calling for me to focus on her instead. When I finally did, I was able to rush outside to where she waited for me in the cobbled square around which the huge, grey stone buildings of The Gathering were arranged, having jumped out of her paddock. She was always in one of those nearest the buildings as she knew I found it difficult when she was further away.

I thanked the stars above that my fears had kept her safe, as it was those in the furthest paddocks who were killed or injured – among them, Infinity, Amarilla's Bond-Partner, who was grievously wounded.

I almost felt sorry for Amarilla, but then I was furious with her all over again. Infinity and the others had only been in the far paddocks so that the rebels could continue their ridiculous attempts to improve on Feryl's teaching without interference. And two horses and two people were dead because of it. I thought that at least they would realise their efforts had brought them nothing but trouble, but as it happened, once Infinity was recovered and their riding sessions resumed, more rebels joined them, including Ellie!

'You should come and watch them ride, Aleks,' she said one lunchtime. Nexus made her presence in my mind ever so slightly stronger and then nudged me. She actually pushed my mind towards Ellie's suggestion!

Nexus, why? You like the way I ride you, don't you? You've never complained.

They attempt that which is difficult for good reason.

Which is?

But Nexus pointedly turned her attention back to grooming her field mate. I argued with Ellie instead. 'You could have lost Res because of their foolishness. Integrity and Noble moved to the furthest paddocks so their Bond-Partners could join the rebels' riding sessions. They died as a result of the Woeful attack, and had it been a day later, no doubt Res would have moved by then too and been with them. It could have been him, Ellie.'

Ellie reached across the table, took hold of my hand and squeezed it. 'Aleks, Resolute is okay with everything that happened, and he says that those who died are all fine where they are now too. He's adamant that I don't give in to the fear that's taking hold of everyone. It's not easy and I'm scared at times, but right back when Res and I bonded, he told me that feeling my way forward when fear would have me do otherwise would be the way I could help people – and I'm trying to help you. Just come with me, sit on the fence and watch them ride, that's all I'm asking. Check with Nexus, I'm sure she'll agree with me.'

'She does,' I said sullenly and pulled my hand back. 'And I still don't like being touched.'

Ellie lifted both of her hands. 'Okay, okay, I'm sorry, I just find it hard watching you struggle so much. It's a hug you really need, but I suppose that's out of the question?'

I glared at her and she laughed. 'So, we'll settle for you coming with me to watch "the rebels", as you insist on calling them?'

I sighed. 'Fine.'

'Great, come on then, they'll have already started.'

I was completely unprepared for the scene that awaited us. One minute, Amarilla was riding Infinity. The next, they were moving around as one being – that was the only way I could think of to describe it. I couldn't see them as being separate from one another, and they almost seemed to glow with the state they had achieved, until they parted company.

Amarilla lay on the ground and Infinity went mad, bucking and throwing herself around. Just along from me, Feryl laughed, and for the first time, I felt uneasy about him. What I had just seen had transported me from my place on the fence beside Ellie, to somewhere else entirely, somewhere familiar that called to me, that felt safe, though the route there felt anything but. And Feryl didn't seem able to see it.

Infinity came to a stop near him. Amarilla walked up to her calmly and remounted, despite Feryl's taunts. She was so young and yet she wasn't; she moved and spoke in a way that seemed far beyond her years. Infinity had thrown her to the ground and could very well do so again, yet all I could see in Amarilla's eyes as she looked at her horse, was love. I knew what my response in such a situation would have been and I felt ashamed.

Amarilla and Infinity spared me from hating myself for too long by quickly recovering their state of oneness, the sight of which had exactly the same effect on me as before. My jaw dropped at the sheer beauty of them moving as a single entity; their power and strength were far greater than either of them would have been able to generate alone, and again, I thought I could almost see a glow about them. I had that same feeling of familiarity about the other-worldliness of it all, as if I had seen it many times before, though I knew I couldn't possibly have.

I never missed any of the rebels' riding sessions after that. More people began to ride with them, hoping for help to improve the way they rode their own horses. Ellie kept badgering me to join in with Nexus, but as more joined their riding sessions every day, I became increasingly uneasy about the number of people and horses all sharing the same riding paddock. I couldn't see enough space for Nexus and me, or how the rebels could possibly help so many people at once. Nexus kept quiet on the subject, but I could feel that she was waiting for something.

When Amarilla and the rest of the original rebels announced that they would split all of the horses and riders into groups and teach from the ground so that they could be of more help, Nexus contained herself no longer. *Their assistance will benefit us both. We will join them,* she told me gently and simply.

I found myself unable to argue when Ellie put me down to ride in the group that would be taught by Amarilla and Justin, despite the hammering of my heart, my shortness of breath and my urge to run and hide in my room.

'Don't look so terrified, Aleks, Amarilla and Justin are both really nice. And Res and I won't be far away, we'll keep an eye on you.'

'But you'll be in the same group as Nexus and me, won't you?'

'No. I know you won't like it, but while I have a feeling that they're who you need, I'm drawn to Quinta's group. I don't know why, I just am.'

She Who Is Resolute perceives with accuracy, Nexus noted.

I sighed. 'Okay, fine, but if I don't like them, I'm swapping to the same group as you.'

There was no need. There was something about Amarilla's lack of confidence in herself – which transformed into something else entirely when she was either relating her experiences with Infinity or teaching – that resonated with me. She was a very kind, patient and articulate instructor and I could feel how much Nexus enjoyed our sessions with her. Nexus wanted us to achieve that which Amarilla and Infinity had, and I knew I owed it to her to try.

When my resolve wavered, I only had to feel Nexus's determination – so unlike anything I had felt from her up until that time – and I would remember seeing Amarilla and Infinity merging into one being. Nexus wanted that for us and I wanted it too, for then I would never feel scared again. I didn't know how I knew that, but I did. It was as if the image Amarilla and Infinity had presented called us to a place I knew but had forgotten. A place of ultimate safety.

And so it was that when Amarilla announced she was off on a mission to help the Woeful – and not just the group of genetically enhanced humans that had hunted and killed horses and people at The Gathering, but ALL of them – I found myself being talked into going.

'You can't change instructors now,' Ellie told me whilst chewing a mouthful of sandwich. 'If Amarilla's going, then you need to go with her so you can carry on learning from her.'

I grimaced at the sight of half-chewed bread churning around in her mouth as she spoke. 'I'm absolutely not going looking for any Woeful. No way. I mean, seriously? It's a suicide mission.'

'I don't think it is, and neither does Res. What does Nexus think?'

'She won't want me to put myself in danger.'

'So you haven't asked her.'

I scowled. 'No, I haven't asked her.'

Ellie just sat staring at me, her green eyes devoid of their usual sparkle, and filled with an intensity that reminded me of the blue-eyed, ever superior Infinity. I rolled my eyes. 'Fine, I'll ask her if you stop talking with your mouth full.'

Ellie grinned. 'Deal.'

We must remain with They Who Are Infinity. You know why, Nexus instantly chimed in.

What? But it's a preposterous idea! The Woeful are dangerous, I'm not going actively seeking them just because Amarilla is, and neither are you.

Our place on the trip is already assured. Her thought was accompanied by a sense of anticipation, excitement even.

How?

It was never in doubt. You need only adhere to the human formalities in order to confirm our attendance.

But I don't want to go. There's no knowing what we would be letting ourselves in for. I can't do it, Nexus, I can't.

She expanded her presence in my mind. *You have become well accustomed to doing that which is difficult. You are prepared for the challenge. I am with you. That will never change.*

You're changing, though. You want more for yourself.

I will always be the Bond-Partner you need.

I sighed. *And I should be the Bond-Partner you need. I'll do it, Nexus, I'll ask to join the group leaving to find the Woeful, but I'm scared. As always, I'm scared.*

And as always you will make the choices that will allow you to triumph. I felt her pride in me. Her love for me. I loved her back with all of my heart that I'd never thought had room for anyone else.

I put my head in my hands and sighed. 'I can't believe this is happening.'

'What?' Ellie asked.

'Apparently, Nexus and I are already going. I just have to cement my place in the group that has assembled around Amarilla by making a formal request to join it, and that won't be easy; Rowena's going, and she hates me. Are you coming to confirm your place alongside me?'

Ellie shook her head. 'I'm not going, Aleks, my place…'

'WHAT? You told me to go when you haven't got the guts to go yourself?'

'It's not about courage, it's about knowing where I'm needed, and that's here. Res and I have nearly achieved the balance and harmony that Amarilla, Justin and Quinta all have with their horses. When we do, Justin will be free to go on after Amarilla as he wants to do, and Quinta will need me here, teaching alongside her in his place. Res and I are so close, Aleks. With Quinta's help, we'll get there and then I'll be able to repay all the effort she's put into helping me. My place is here. Yours is with Amarilla and Infinity, I know it.'

It was days before I summoned up the courage to ask Amarilla if Nexus and I could join her on her mission. I waited until she was alone with Infinity, whom she was grooming in the paddock shared by all of her friends' horses. Infinity watched me as I climbed between the fence rails, her blue eyes softer than usual as she watched me approach her Bond-Partner.

'Um, Amarilla?'

'Aleks, hi! Sorry, I didn't hear you coming,' Amarilla said, straightening up from where she had been brushing the underside of Infinity's belly. 'How are you?'

'I'm, err, I'm okay thanks. Listen, I just wanted to ask you whether Nexus and I can come with you when you leave on your search for the Woeful? Only it's just that we… well, we appreciate the help you've been giving us and we really don't want to change instructors. And besides, Nexus is adamant that our place in the group is, um, well, assured.'

Amarilla's momentary stillness told me that she was listening to Infinity. Then she smiled. 'It is. Of course you and Nexus should come with us.'

I nodded. 'Thank you. So, when are we leaving?' I swallowed hard at the thought.

'In four days' time. Will that give you enough time to prepare?'

I swallowed again. 'To be honest, I can't even begin to imagine.'

Amarilla peered up into my eyes. 'I don't think any of us think this will be an easy trip, but we'll be okay,' she said, putting an arm under Infinity's neck and hugging her. 'We'll have our horses and each other, so everything will be alright. It will, Aleks.'

Her love for Infinity, the trust they shared, was palpable. It hung in the air around them, joining them as one just as their perfect balance did when they were horse and rider. It made my fears seem irrational and the way in front of me suddenly very obvious.

They Who Are Infinity call to you without words yet you hear them. You have come far, Nexus told me, her pride so fierce that it shocked me. *Where once you allowed fear to define you now it is love and trust to which you turn.*

It feels easy while they're standing in front of me and you're in my mind, but when I leave them and you turn your attention to something else, I'll start panicking again. You know that as well as I do.

And you know I will help you to cope. Once the four of us are together constantly the way forward will again be clear.

I nodded slowly and Amarilla smiled at me.

'You're definitely okay with me coming?' I asked her. 'By all accounts, I'm not very easy to be around.'

'By all accounts, neither am I,' she said and chuckled. 'Vickery and Jack aren't exactly popular at the moment, either, and come to that, we're not going for four days and that's plenty of time for Rowena to get on the wrong side of someone.' I found myself laughing along with her, which felt strange. 'So yes, I'm definitely okay with you coming and so will everyone else be. See you in four days?'

I stopped laughing and swallowed again. 'Yes. See you in four days.' I turned and left her to continue grooming Infinity.

'Four days,' I said to myself as I climbed through the paddock fence. Four days until I left the known for the unknown. I thought back to the last time that had happened. Then, I had been dragged away, leaving a workroom full of smashed glass behind me. This time, I would walk away freely, my only leavings at The Gathering being the elegant works of perfection that were all the more beautiful for the fact that Nexus was in my mind when I sang them from sand into glass.

Nexus. I could see her head over her paddock gate in the distance, and picked up my pace. When I reached her, she pricked her ears and whickered. Her long, white eyelashes swept down against the black of her lower eyelids as she blinked slowly and then stared at me as she often did when she wanted me to pay particular attention to something she was about to tell me. One word appeared in my mind. *Together.*

I rubbed her cheek. *Together.*

Other Books by Lynn Mann

The Horses Know Trilogy

The Horses Know

The Horses Rejoice (The Horses Know Book 2)

The Horses Return (The Horses Know Book 3)

Horses Forever (A Sequel to The Horses Know Trilogy)

In Search of Peace (A Prequel to The Horses Know Trilogy)

The Strength Of Oak (A Prequel to The Horses Know Trilogy)

A Reason To Be Noble (A Prequel to The Horses Know Trilogy)

Did you enjoy Tales Of The Horse-Bonded?

I'd be extremely grateful if you could spare a few minutes to leave a review where you purchased your copy. Reviews really do help my books to reach a wider audience, which means that I can keep on writing!

Thank you very much.

I love to hear from you!

Get in touch and receive news of future releases at the following:

www.lynnmann.co.uk

www.facebook.com/lynnmann.author

Acknowledgments

Thank you so much for reading my books – in doing so, you have allowed me to write more of them, as well as these tales. I've so enjoyed getting to know some of my characters better, and hope you have too!

Thanks as always to my editorial team: Fern Sherry, Leonard Palmer, Rebecca Walters and Caroline Macintosh, and cover designer Amanda Horan, who all make the process so enjoyable for me.

Printed in Great Britain
by Amazon